Diploma in
Pre-school Practice

Penny Tassoni

www.heinemann.co.uk
✓ Free online support
✓ Useful weblinks
✓ 24 hour online ordering

01865 888058

Heinemann Educational Publishers
Halley Court, Jordan Hill, Oxford OX2 8EJ
Part of Harcourt Education

Heinemann is the registered trademark of
Harcourt Education Limited

Text © Penny Tassoni, 2004

First published 2004

08 07 06 05 04
10 9 8 7 6 5 4 3 2 1

British Library Cataloguing in Publication Data is available
from the British Library on request.

ISBN 0 435 45209 6

Designed by Carolyn Gibson
Typeset by ⊼ Tek-Art, Croydon, Surrey
Original illustrations © Harcourt Education Limited, 2004
Printed in the UK by Bath Press Ltd

Contents

Acknowledgements

My thanks on this project go to Camilla Thomas for her forgiving attitude towards my author queries and, of course, to Mary James. I would also like to recognise the work and time of Barbara Thompson, Claire Power, Sally Thorpe and Sue Bayliss who provided me with their own valuable insights. Finally, I need to thank the Tassoni Team once again for giving me a wonderful emotional backdrop for my writing.

Penny Tassoni

The author and publisher would like to thank the following individuals and organisations for permission to reproduce photographs:

Almay pages 147 and 183;
John Birdsall pages 56 and 88;
Corbis page 15;
Getty Images/photodisc page 24;
Getty Images/Taxi/Ron Thomas page 104;
Sally & Richard Greenhill page 207;
Harcourt Education/Gareth Boden pages 71, 80, 102, 136, 163, 171, 189, 263, 264, 267 and 287;
Harcourt Education/Gerald Sunderland pages 2, 5, 8, 47, 55, 120, 141, 248-9 and 274;
Harcourt Education/Haddon Davis pages 115, 117, 160, 218, 221, 224 and 240;
Mother & Baby Picture Library page 259;
John Walmsley/Education Photos page 129.

Crown copyright material on pages 85 and 198 is reproduced under Class Licence Number CO1W0000141 with the permission of the controller of HMSO and the Queen's Printer for Scotland.

Every effort has been made to contact copyright holders of material reproduced in this book. Any omissions will be rectified in subsequent printings if notice is given to the publishers.

Introduction

Welcome to your Diploma in Pre-school Practice course. Working with young children has always been a demanding, but rewarding career and today, the early years sector is experiencing major changes. Firstly, more and more children are coming into pre-school care which presents us with both opportunities and, of course, challenges. Secondly, views about how best to promote young children's learning are changing and developing. These changes are reflected in the introduction of the *Foundation Stage* and more recently *Birth to Three Matters*. For those of us working in the pre-school sector, it is a good time to be embarking on a course of study. The Diploma in Pre-school Practice is a respected level 3 qualification and will give you the underpinning skills, knowledge and confidence to steer you through these exciting times.

Course structure

The Diploma in Pre-school Practice consists of three core units and a choice of three optional units. In order to gain the complete qualification, you will need to study each of the core units and choose one of the optional units. All of which are covered in this book.

Core Units
Core Unit 1   Promoting Children's Development
Core Unit 2   Early Learning
Core Unit 3   Best Practice in Pre-school Settings

Optional Units
Option Unit 1   Working with Children with Special Educational Needs
Option Unit 2   The First Year of Life
Option Unit 3   Community Development

Assessment

In order to gain certification, you will need to complete an assignment for each of the units that you study. These assignments are set by the awarding body (CACHE) and can be found in your candidate handbook. Core Unit 1: Promoting Children's Development is currently assessed externally – this means that it is marked by an external examiner. The remaining assignments will be marked and moderated within your centre.

About this book

This book has been written specifically to help you with your Diploma in Pre-school Practice. It provides information in a clear and accessible way and will support the teaching that is being provided by your tutors. The book has been written to match the Diploma in Pre-school Practice syllabus and so is a good tool to aid your study of the units and the completion of the assignments.

Features of this book
The units in the book follow the headings of the syllabus closely. Specific features of the book will not only help you develop your understanding of the

relevant issues within pre-school settings, but also adds interesting topical information to give you a holistic understanding of child care.

Good Practice	Practical suggestions for promoting good practice in a pre-school setting.
Key points	A list summarising the key topics covered in that section.
Applying theory to your practice	Activities and theoretical learning tasks which help you relate the theory to your own experience.
Point of interest	Provides key definitions and key features of important theorists and their theories.
A quick think!	Short topics or questions encouraging you to think about the current issues raised in the text.
Case studies	Case studies of real (or simulated) childcare related issues. These are aimed at enabling you to explore key issues, broaden your understanding and see the theory in practice.
Thinking and research	Activities giving you topics to think about, check out and research.
Test your knowledge and **Practice assignment task**	Questions at the end of each unit which help test the knowledge you have gained as you worked through the unit.
Glossary	Throughout the text you will meet words which are highlighted in **bold**. These are key words that you will be expected to know and understand through your course. The meaning of these words can be found in the glossary on pages 311–12.

Good luck with your course!

Penny Tassoni

Promoting Children's Development

Professionals working with children need to have a working knowledge of child development and the way in which adults can support children's overall development. This knowledge will allow you both to plan more effectively for groups of children and to meet individual children's needs. A good understanding of child development is also vital when supporting children's behaviour and providing information for parents. This chapter particularly concentrates on children's development in the age range 1 to 5 years. Development in children under 12 months is covered in detail in Optional Unit 2: The First Year of Life (pages 247–85).

This unit is divided into four sections:

▶ Understanding the development process

▶ Influences on development

▶ Observation and assessment of development

▶ The role of adults

Understanding the development process

Watching the ways in which children grow and develop is a rewarding experience for professionals and parents alike. This section looks at the usual patterns of development that most children go through, and considers some of the theories that explain this process.

> *Nothing beats the satisfaction I get from watching children constantly growing and changing. It feels like one minute they are struggling to put on their coats and the next they are helping younger ones with theirs.*
>
> *Pat, pre-school supervisor, Bucks.*

Development between 1 and 5 years: the crucial years

The first five years of a child's life are considered the most crucial in terms of development. In these five years, a huge amount of learning takes place. Children develop physical skills, language and socialisation skills, attitudes towards learning, and feelings of independence and confidence. In this way, each child begins to develop his or her own unique personality.

Many studies show that children who have been deprived of stimulating and caring environments in these early years are left with a permanent delay in some aspects of their development. In areas of development such as language and emotional development, some psychologists therefore talk about a 'critical' or 'sensitive' period in which development needs to take place.

Development is measured in different areas

Whilst every child is very much an individual, it is also helpful to understand that development usually follows a set sequence or pattern. Babies, for example, babble before they produce actual words, and walk before they run. These sequences of development have been well documented over the years, and this information can help us to work out the stage of development that a child has reached. The overall development of children is usually divided and measured in five different areas, as the spider diagram below shows.

Young children learn to walk before they run

Physical development
This area of development encompasses the range of movements that children make. It includes balance and walking, as well as smaller movements made by the hands.

Cognitive development
This area of development is also referred to as intellectual development. It is the 'thinking' part of the child. It covers the development of memory, concepts such as time and measurement, and problem solving.

Social development
This area of development looks at the way in which children relate and play with other children and adults.

The five areas of development

Emotional development
This area of development considers the child's feelings of security, as well as the ability to express and control emotions.

Language development
This area of development includes listening and comprehension as well as speech and non-verbal communication. In older children, it also includes literacy.

How development is measured: norms, expectations and milestones

To measure children's development, professionals look at the skills that children have acquired in different areas, including language, physical development and social development. These skills are sometimes referred to as **milestones** and are usually linked very broadly to children's ages. The age band given is always an 'average' age. You should note here that 'average' is a balance, thus some children will inevitably show some skills earlier, while others develop later. An example of a milestone for a baby is smiling. Most babies are smiling at six weeks, but some will do so earlier than this, and others start smiling later.

The charts on pages 8, 13 and 20 state the development that children are expected to show by different ages. These charts show '**normative**' or 'expected' development. While these charts can be helpful, they should be seen as a guide only. They give a picture of *most* children's development rather than the individual child's.

KEY POINTS
- ▶ Development usually follows a set pattern or sequence.
- ▶ 'Normative development' and 'expected development' are terms used to suggest what the majority of children are doing at any given age.
- ▶ Charts showing 'normative' or 'expected' development should be seen as approximate guides only.
- ▶ It is best to avoid labelling children as 'ahead' or 'behind' – there are wide variations in the rate at which children acquire skills.

Measuring development

Q. What is the difference between growth and development?
A. The term 'growth' refers to the way in which cells subdivide to, for example, allow bones to lengthen. 'Development' refers to the skills that the child masters. Many aspects of children's development are firmly intertwined with growth; for example, babies cannot walk until their bones are long and strong enough to take their weight.

Q. What should I do if a child I work with is not showing 'expected' development?
A. Firstly, remember that charts of expected and normative development are only guides. Observe the child a little more closely and consider how far he or she is from the expected milestones. If the child appears to be showing significant delay, you should then talk to the child's parents. It may be that the child is different at home, or that the child's parents are also concerned. The next step is usually for the parents to talk to their health visitor or GP. In the meantime, you should continue to observe the child, remembering to focus not only on the areas of difficulty but also on the child's strengths.

Q. What should I say if a parent wants to know what is 'normal' development?
A. There is no 'average' or 'normal' in child development. Every child is an individual, so there is always some variation in the speed at which children show certain skills. Comparing and labelling children is potentially very damaging. Find out if the parent has any particular concerns and talk to them about these.

APPLYING THEORY TO YOUR PRACTICE

Walking is a key milestone in a baby's development. Ask five parents at what age their child began to walk.

1 Compare the ages to the milestone for walking on page 8. What differences are there?

2 Why is it important to use normative development charts as a guide only?

THINKING AND RESEARCH

The Foundation Stage was introduced in England in September 2000. Most pre-schools, nurseries and childminders are expected to follow this curriculum, which is linked to children's development.

In pairs, see if you can research the answers to these questions.

1 What age of children is the Foundation Stage aimed at?

2 What is the idea behind the Foundation Stage?

3 Give an example of a Stepping Stone and show how it links to normative development.

Expected physical development, 1 to 5 years

Physical development concerns the way in which children control their bodies and make movements. Bearing in mind that babies are not mobile at first and are born with a bundle of reflexes (see page 248), it is incredible to think that by the age of six or seven years most children have acquired all the physical movements needed for adulthood. Afterwards, children simply become more skilled and stronger at these movements.

Types of physical movements

The movements that children make are often divided into groups.

Fine motor

This broad term covers small movements that are generally made using the hands.

▶ Fine manipulative skills
These movements require the fingers and thumbs to carry out co-ordinated small tasks, for example, threading beads onto a string. Quite often, these movements also require hand–eye co-ordination.

▶ **Fine motor** skills
These movements involve the wrist and hand, for example, unscrewing a lid from a jar.

Gross motor

This is another broad term, which covers children's large movements.

▶ Gross motor skills
These are movements that are made using the whole limb, for example,

kicking a ball or moving the arm to throw a beanbag.

▶ Locomotive skills
These are movements that enable mobility. For babies, this may mean rolling, crawling or bottom shuffling; for older children, it is walking, running and skipping.

Co-ordination

In order to achieve many physical skills, a blend of movements are required in the right order. The maturation of the central nervous system plays a key role in helping children to become co-ordinated (see below). Children gradually become more co-ordinated as they practise particular movements and skills, and learn to use their hands, feet and eyes together.

▶ **Hand–eye co-ordination**
Many activities require hands and eyes to work together. This is what is meant by hand–eye co-ordination. To pour a drink, for example, the brain needs to take information from the eyes and use it to inform the movements to be made with the hands.

▶ Foot–eye co-ordination
In addition to hand–eye co-ordination, children also have to learn to guide their feet. Climbing stairs and kicking a ball requires this type of co-ordination.

▶ Balance
Balance is a complicated skill, although one that most of us take for granted. Most children rely on visual input for balance, and the ability to balance develops with age. Balance is required for children to carry out any task in which their weight shifts from one foot to another, e.g. walking, hopping and climbing.

> **A QUICK THINK!**
> *Think of three skills that you have used today which require hand–eye co-ordination.*

Physical development is essential to children's overall development

Physical development is an essential ingredient in children's overall development as it allows them to explore and thus learn about the world around them. The development of physical skills also helps children to become increasingly independent, for example, as they learn to feed and dress themselves. This independence helps children to become confident.

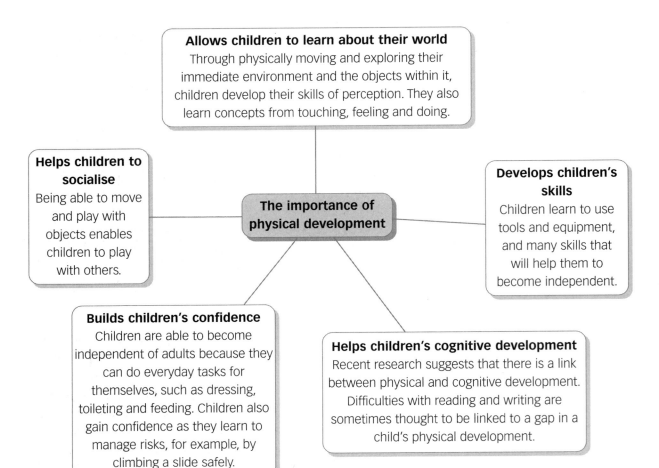

Allows children to learn about their world
Through physically moving and exploring their immediate environment and the objects within it, children develop their skills of perception. They also learn concepts from touching, feeling and doing.

Helps children to socialise
Being able to move and play with objects enables children to play with others.

The importance of physical development

Develops children's skills
Children learn to use tools and equipment, and many skills that will help them to become independent.

Builds children's confidence
Children are able to become independent of adults because they can do everyday tasks for themselves, such as dressing, toileting and feeding. Children also gain confidence as they learn to manage risks, for example, by climbing a slide safely.

Helps children's cognitive development
Recent research suggests that there is a link between physical and cognitive development. Difficulties with reading and writing are sometimes thought to be linked to a gap in a child's physical development.

Key principles of physical development

The three key principles of physical development were first outlined by Arnold Gessell, an American paediatrician (see below).

1 Development follows a definite sequence

As we watch children growing and developing, we can observe a pattern emerging by which certain movements have to be in place before others can develop. For example, children have to be able to walk before they can skip (see also page 8).

2 Development begins with the control of head movements and proceeds downwards

Babies gain control of the head and top of the spine before other parts of the body. This is thought to be a survival mechanism, as it is important for babies to turn their heads to feed.

3 Development begins with uncontrolled gross motor movements before becoming precise and refined

At first, the young baby's arm and leg movements are uncontrolled. However, some control is quickly gained, first of the arms and then of the wrist and hands. By six months, most babies are able to take an offered toy with reasonable ease.

As an adult, you may have had a similar learning experience if you have learnt to use a computer with a mouse. Most people struggle at first to keep the mouse visible on the screen; gradually, more refined movements are learned, which allow the mouse to be positioned more accurately.

Arnold Gessell – a key theorist

Arnold Gessell (1880–1961) is known for his work on children's physical development. Through his observations of babies and young children, he developed a theory of physical development that has served as the basis for subsequent research. Gessell suggested that the maturation of the central nervous system underpinned development (see below), with stimulation not necessarily having a significant role. However, this view did lead to some paediatricians adopting a 'laissez-faire' attitude towards children with disabilities, which has been subsequently challenged.

The links between the central nervous system and physical development

Children's physical development is underpinned by the central nervous system, which comprises the brain and the spinal cord. The central nervous system is responsible for collecting, interpreting and sending out information to all parts of the body. This information is continually collected through the body's senses of taste, touch, smell, sight and sound. It is then transformed into electrical pulses that are carried by the nerves up through the spinal cord and into the brain. From the information that is received, the brain then responds and sends out instructions to muscles, glands and organs, again using the network of nerves. The whole process is surprisingly quick, which means that the body can quickly take action against possible danger, for example, withdrawing from something that is very hot. The speed at which information flows through the body means that many of our movements feel 'automatic'.

The brain takes in information through the senses and then makes sense of it. This allows us to recognise someone very quickly

In babies and young children, the central nervous system has to mature. Babies are initially reliant on the many survival reflexes with which they are born; the central nervous system has to learn how to interpret and control these responses. This is a gradual process, which is why a baby's movements are at first so unco-ordinated. The need for the central nervous system to mature is one reason why different children walk, talk and move out of nappies at different rates.

Children learn to walk at different rates

Stages and sequences of physical development

Understanding the sequence of children's physical development is useful. It will allow you to match activities to the age groups of the different children with which you work. Below is a chart of normative development that shows the milestones or skills that most children have developed by different ages. It is, however, essential to remember that such charts can act only as a guide, and that when planning it is also important to remember the needs of individual children.

Age	Fine motor development	Gross motor development	The carer's role	Toys and equipment
12 months	▶ Picks up objects with thumb and forefinger ▶ Picks up and holds toys such as rattles ▶ Points to objects ▶ Holds cup with help ▶ Puts small objects in a container	▶ Mobile – either crawling, rolling or shuffling (some children may be walking) ▶ Sits up unsupported for long periods ▶ Walks with assistance ▶ Tries to crawl up stairs	To support this stage of development, carers need to supervise carefully and give plenty of praise and encouragement. We need to spend time playing alongside the child – e.g. making a tower of bricks for them to knock down or putting a cuddly toy in their truck to push along.	▶ stacking beakers ▶ large balls ▶ push-and-pull toys ▶ bricks
15 months	▶ Holds and drinks from cup using two hands ▶ Builds tower of two blocks ▶ Makes marks with crayons ▶ Tries to turn pages in books	▶ Crawls down stairs feet first ▶ Walks independently ▶ Seats self in small chair	Carers need to supervise children of this age very carefully, as they are keen to explore and may start to climb. Children enjoy discovering new toys especially if they make sounds. We can help children by showing them	▶ picture books ▶ bricks ▶ shape sorters ▶ toys that make music ▶ large crayons

Age	Fine motor development	Gross motor development	The carer's role	Toys and equipment
			how to use toys and by playing alongside them. Children of this age can often follow simple instructions – e.g. they may collect their hat and put it on. These early self-help skills need to be encouraged and praised so that children gain in confidence.	
18 months	▶ Strings four large beads ▶ Turns door knobs and handles ▶ Pulls off shoes	▶ Bends down from waist to pick up toys ▶ Squats down to look at toys ▶ Rolls and throws a ball ▶ Walks down stairs with adult help ▶ Pushes and pulls toys while walking	The main role of the adult is to allow children the time and space to play. Children are likely to spend more time playing alone and may play quite repetitively – e.g. putting objects into and out of boxes. As children gain in self-help skills – e.g. taking off shoes and coats – they need to be praised and allowed time to complete the task.	▶ prams ▶ rocking horses or chairs ▶ threading toys ▶ bricks ▶ toys to ride on
2 years	▶ Uses a spoon to feed him or herself ▶ Zips and unzips large zippers ▶ Places five rings on a stick ▶ Draws circles and dots ▶ Builds a tower of five to six bricks ▶ Begins to use a preferred hand	▶ Kicks a ball that is not moving ▶ Climbs on furniture ▶ Puts together and pulls apart snap-together toys ▶ Walks up and down stairs confidently	Children of this age are enjoying exploring their environment and are beginning to have favourite toys and activities. Going to play parks and using swings and rocking equipment are a particular treat. Children's self-help skills are developing, although there may be times when the child becomes frustrated – e.g. an arm of a coat may be twisted and they cannot get their hand through. Praise and encouragement needs to be offered and we need to look at ways of making children feel independent.	▶ rides and sits on toys ▶ push-and-pull toys ▶ shape sorters ▶ bricks, crayons ▶ dough ▶ picture books

Age	Fine motor development	Gross motor development	The carer's role	Toys and equipment
3 years	<li> Turns pages in a book one by one <li> Holds crayon and can draw a face <li> Uses a spoon without spilling <li> Washes and dries hands without help <li> Puts on and takes off coat	<li> Walks and runs forwards <li> Walks on tiptoes <li> Throws large ball <li> Kicks ball forward <li> Jumps from low steps <li> Pedals and steers a tricycle	Children of this age are starting to enjoy playing together and enjoy new challenges. Adults need to provide stimulating activities that allow children to develop their fine motor movements – e.g. painting, cooking – as well as opportunities to engage in pretend play.	<li> large outdoor apparatus <li> puzzles <li> paints and crayons <li> dough <li> sand and water <li> tricycles <li> prams <li> dressing-up clothes
4 years	<li> Buttons and unbuttons own clothing <li> Cuts out simple shapes <li> Draws a person with head, trunk and legs <li> Puts together 12-piece jigsaw puzzle	<li> Walks on a line <li> Aims and throws ball <li> Bounces and catches large ball <li> Runs, changing direction <li> Hops on one foot <li> Pedals and steers a tricycle confidently	Children at this age are gaining in confidence and are able to become more independent. We can encourage them to wipe up spills, pour drinks and tidy away. This will help prepare them for school. Most children of this age enjoy being busy and playing co-operatively.	<li> balls <li> climbing frames <li> slides <li> materials for creative activities <li> crayons <li> glue <li> scissors <li> puzzles <li> construction toys <li> books
5 years	<li> Forms letters, writes own name <li> Draws recognisable pictures of trees, houses, people and animals <li> Colours in pictures neatly <li> Dresses and undresses easily <li> Completes 20-piece jigsaw puzzle <li> Cuts out shapes using scissors quite accurately <li> Draws around a template	<li> Skips with a rope <li> Runs quickly and is able to avoid obstacles <li> Is able to use a variety of large equipment – e.g. swings, slides <li> Throws large ball to partner and catches it <li> Hits ball with bat or stick	Children are starting to enjoy playing games with rules – e.g. snakes and ladders, chase, etc. Adults can help by introducing new games into their play – e.g. hide-and-seek – as well as encouraging children to make up their own games. Adult support and encouragement is needed as there may be times when arguments break out! We should also be encouraging children to be as independent as possible – e.g. folding their clothes when changing, hanging up their coats.	<li> hoops <li> balls <li> roller skates <li> bicycles with stabilisers <li> large equipment <li> creative materials – e.g. paints, crayons, card and paper <li> construction toys <li> board games

Age	Fine motor development	Gross motor development	The carer's role	Toys and equipment
6–7 years	▶ Is able to sew simple stitches ▶ Cuts out shapes accurately and neatly ▶ Handwriting is evenly spaced and may be joined ▶ Drawings are detailed and representative ▶ Makes a simple sandwich ▶ Ties and unties laces	▶ Rides a bicycle without stabilisers ▶ Runs ▶ Chases and dodges others ▶ Hops, skips and jumps confidently ▶ Kicks a ball with direction ▶ Balances on a beam or wall	Children of this age are independent and able to do many day-to-day tasks – e.g. tidying away, laying the table. They are gaining in confidence and enjoy trying out new activities – e.g. making models, origami, cooking. They are starting to have preferences and their own hobbies – e.g. some children will be learning to swim whilst others may go to karate or dance lessons. By 8 years, some children may need to be encouraged to join in some types of physical activities. This is often due to self-consciousness – e.g. they feel that they are not as good as other children.	▶ bicycles ▶ skateboards ▶ roller skates ▶ balls ▶ bats and rackets ▶ kits – e.g. modelling kits, origami ▶ jigsaw puzzles ▶ board games

Stages and sequences of physical development

Frequently asked questions

Q. There is a child in our group who doesn't enjoy physical activities. Should we make him join in?

A. Some children lack confidence in their physical movements. However, putting these children under pressure can actually result in them feeling less confident. A good starting point is to carry out an observation to see how well co-ordinated the child appears and whether he or she has any particular difficulties in everyday movements. Sometimes a child who is not interested in physical play might not see properly, or may be finding it difficult to balance.

It is also worth thinking about the types of equipment and play that the child does enjoy and encouraging physical movements accordingly. For example, a child who enjoys playing quietly with cars may be encouraged to roll cars down a slide or along a fence outdoors.

Expected social and emotional development, 1 to 5 years

These two areas of development are often written about together because a child's social development is linked to their emotional development. A good example of this is friendship: a child who is very aggressive and cannot control his or her anger may find it hard to sustain friendships. As with all areas of development, children gradually develop the skills and understanding required. In addition, these areas of development are thought to be linked especially to children's direct experiences.

What is social development?

Human beings are understood to have an underlying need to be with others. Indeed, most people have a lot of social contact – we generally live, socialise and work with other people. Children have to learn how to be with others. Social development is thus particularly about the ability to form and sustain relationships, which includes the ability to adapt our behaviour in ways that are acceptable to others. (Note that behaviour is covered separately on page 77.)

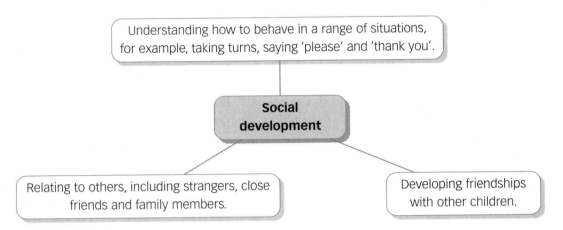

Understanding how to behave in a range of situations, for example, taking turns, saying 'please' and 'thank you'.

Social development

Relating to others, including strangers, close friends and family members.

Developing friendships with other children.

What is emotional development?

Emotional development is a very complex area. It includes the development of our personality and values, as well as the feelings we have about ourselves. Children's emotional development affects their underlying ability to build relationships and to socialise.

Emotional development includes:

- the development of self-awareness and confidence
- being self-reliant and independent
- being able to leave a main carer
- controlling emotions such as anger
- expressing emotions such as joy, anger and sadness
- understanding and empathising with others
- moral development.

From birth to 1 year

Important social skills are learnt in the baby's first year. Babies learn some of the skills of socialisation. They learn that making eye contact, smiling and laughing can keep their carer's attention.

The first year is also critical in terms of emotional development. Babies need to develop a strong bond – or attachment – with their carers. In some ways, developing this bond may be instinctive as, at birth, babies are able to recognise the smell of their mother and are quickly soothed when they hear her voice. Babies who have a strong bond or attachment with their primary carer at the end of their first year will be more comfortable when they socialise with others.

From birth to 1 year (contd.)	1 month	Watches primary carer's face.
	3 months	Smiles and coos.
		Enjoys being handled and cuddled.
	6 months	Laughs and enjoys being played with.
	8 months	Fears strangers.
	9 months	Plays peek-a-boo.
		Discriminates between strangers and familiar adults.
	12 months	Is affectionate towards family and primary carers.
		Plays simple games such as pat-a-cake.

1–2 years

During this year, children learn more social skills. They are able to play with their primary carers and are comfortable with other familiar adults. They start to explore their environment but need the reassurance that their primary carer is nearby. At the end of this year, children often start to notice other children and become able to play alongside them.

In terms of emotional development, children are very dependent on their primary carer. They will protest and cry if their primary carer leaves them and it is important that they are left with someone who is familiar to them. Although they are still dependent on their primary carer, they are starting to realise that they are individuals. They recognise and begin to use their own names.

The end of this year also makes a change in many children as they become increasingly aware of what they want. They begin to show anger and frustration if they cannot have their needs met individually.

15 months	Begins to explore environment if familiar adult is close by.
	Begins to use words to communicate with.
	Has a stronger feeling of being an individual.
18 months	Language is increasing.
	Points to objects to show familiar adults.
	Explores environment and shows some independence but still needs familiar adults.
	Strong emotions – e.g. anger, fear and joy – are shown.
2 years	Plays near other children – parallel play.
	Begins to talk when playing – pretend play.
	Imitates adults' emotions.
	Strong emotions – e.g. anger, fear and joy – are shown.

2–3 years

This is an important year in a child's life although it is often not an easy one for carers – hence the expression 'the terrible twos'!

Children in the first part of this stage are keenly aware of what they want to do, although they become easily frustrated because their own physical and language skills are not developed enough to meet these desires. They also find it difficult to understand why they cannot have what they see because they lack the concept of ownership or objects being unsafe. Frustration is often vented through temper tantrums or inconsolable crying. These tantrums and strong feelings lessen as children gradually develop more language and physical skills.

2–3 years (contd.)	Carers working with this age group need to be very sensitive and organised so that children are not in a position where they can become frustrated.
	Children often need their comforters with them during this year to help them feel more secure, especially as many children will also be having their first experience of being separated from their primary carers on entering pre-school settings. This is an important step as children learn to socialise without the back-up of their primary carers. The first experiences of separation need to be carefully handled and children entering pre-school settings will need a lot of reassurance from early years workers.
	There is also a wide variation in the way that children progress over the year, so it is hard to put times to these steps.
	During this year most children will:
	▶ move out of nappies
	▶ have a strong sense of their identity, including their gender and age
	▶ be happy to leave their primary carer for short periods
	▶ start taking an interest in other children and playing with them
	▶ show concern for other children – e.g. telling primary carer if baby is crying
	▶ start to wait for their needs to be met.
3–4 years	This is a more settled year for children. Most of them are happy to leave their primary carers and socialise with other adults and children. The first real friendships start to develop, with children seeking out particular friends. Social skills – e.g. turn-taking, sharing and concern for others – are shown. Emotionally, children still need reassurance from their immediate carers, but are more independent and may play by themselves for longer periods. They still feel strong emotions, and quarrels and temper tantrums are still apparent at times.
	Many children will still be reliant on their comforters, especially when they are unwell or unsure of a situation.
	▶ affectionate towards family, friends and carers
	▶ wants to help and please primary carer and other familiar adults
	▶ imitates – in play – actions seen – e.g. putting teddy to bed, feeding dolls
	▶ shares playthings
	▶ plays with other children – mostly pretend play
	▶ shows concern for other people – e.g. rubs back of crying baby.

Stages and sequences of emotional and social development

Socialisation – a process beginning with the main carer

Babies first learn about other people by being with a main carer. For most children, the main carer will be the child's mother or father; for other children, it will be another family member, a foster parent or an adoptive parent.

The role of the main carer in the child's life appears to be quite critical. The main carer and baby often form a close tie or bond. The process by which this happens is referred to as '**attachment**'. It was initially thought that a baby forms only one close attachment: to the person providing him or her with the most time and care. However, it is now recognised that a baby can form equally strong attachments to other people who play a significant role in his or her life.

Developing relationships outside of the family

A strong attachment to at least one key person remains essential to the child's early life and social development. From this secure base, babies and toddlers are ready to explore and learn about other people. They do this at first by watching the reactions of the main carer to other people. A toddler, for example, will often peep out from behind the main carer's legs to watch the dialogue between the 'stranger' and the main carer. Learning in this way is called '**social referencing**'. By about three years of age, children begin to feel more comfortable with people who are

This child is learning about the world from his secure base

not family or familiar to them, but for short periods only. They gradually understand that they can leave their 'secure base' and come back to it.

Qualities of different relationships

Recent work by Willard Hartup (1989) suggests that children's relationships can be defined as either vertical or horizontal:

Vertical and horizontal relationships

- Children's relationships with parents, teachers and adults are vertical because they are not equal – adults have greater experience, skills and knowledge than children do.
- Children's relationships with each other are horizontal because they are at a roughly equal stage of development.

Both types of relationship are essential to a child's overall emotional and social development. In vertical relationships, children gain skills and learn about social behaviour; in horizontal relationships, children have the opportunity to practise their social skills.

Social stages of play

As part of the socialisation process, children learn to play with other children of a similar age. Playing with other children is an important part of a child's social development – it appears that it allows the child to practise his or her social skills.

The socialisation process begins with the baby learning to play and respond to adults and carers. Gradually, he or she begins to take an interest in other children, although the child will watch them initially rather than engage in play.

The sequence by which children are able to engage in play with others was first noted by Mildred Parten in the 1930s. Her social stages of play are widely recognised, although it is now thought that babies are generally more aware of

Age	Stage	Features	Examples
0–2 years	Solitary activity	The child engages in play and is uninterested in children of a similar age.	Millie and George are just over one year old. They rarely make eye contact and play by themselves. They each attract their carer's attention when they want company.
2–4 years	Parallel activity Associative play	The child is happy to play with the same materials as another child. Little communication and eye contact takes place between them.	Josh and Niamh are both playing with cars. They are two and a half years old. They each have their own game and move out of each other's way. Aran sees that Gracie has a ball. He gets a ball from the basket too. Aran sees that Gracie is kicking the ball. He kicks his too and laughs. The child begins to be more aware of other children and may copy their play.
4–7 years	Co-operative activity	The child plays and engages with other children. He or she is able to take turns and, when older, negotiate roles and ideas.	Joe is four years old. He is waiting for his friend, Tom, to return from washing his hands so that they can start a game. They talk about what they are doing and take turns.

The social stages of play

others, and that many three-year-olds engage in a type of co-operative activity (called associative play). In addition, it is worth noting that older children who are capable of playing co-operatively may sometimes choose to play by themselves.

The development of friendships

As children get older, friendships play an increasingly important role in their lives. By the time they reach their teenage years, children's relationships with their friends are as important as those with their families. Learning about friendships and having particular preferences begins quite early in childhood, as the table below shows.

Age	Features	Examples
0–2 years	Children notice other people, including adults and older children, and are fascinated by other babies. By the age of two years, toddlers play side by side.	Ritchie is 12 months old. He crawls over to look at a baby who is in a carrycot. He peers in and wants to touch the baby's eyes.
2–4 years	By the age of three years, most children show a friendship preference for particular children with whom they play regularly. They play with children of the same or a different gender, and the activity appears to be more important than who is there.	Jasmine is four years old. She looks round the room to see if she can find her friend, Ross. She likes playing in the home corner with him.
4–7 years	From this age, many children show stable friendships, although they will play with other children. Friendships tend to be with those of the same gender.	Charlene, Helen and Jodie skip together during play time.
8–11 years	Friendships are generally based on what the children enjoy doing together. They are usually with children of the same gender. There is some evidence to suggest that boys' friendships are group-based and more relaxed, with girls having closer but fewer friendships.	Tom goes out to play with some of his friends. They all enjoy sport and often get together with a couple of boys from a neighbouring school. Katherine has two close friends. They all go to drama and netball clubs after schools.

Stages of social interaction

The importance of self-reliance and self-help skills

Most of us take for granted the ways in which we are able to do many different things for ourselves and take the initiative. For children, the development of self-reliance is essential to their budding self-confidence and ability to take responsibility for their actions. Skills such as being able to dress and pour a drink, or learning to cope with choice, encourage the child to become more self-reliant. For adults working with children, this means thinking about the ways in which children can be helped to do things for themselves – for example, asking a young child to fetch his coat, rather than getting it for him.

Self-help skills include:

- getting dressed
- choosing activities
- tidying away toys
- pouring drinks
- laying out tables ready for snack time
- carrying trays
- preparing simple foods, for example, peeling a banana or cutting a kiwi fruit.

Expected language development, 1 to 5 years

Being able to communicate is an important skill that most of us take for granted. Language has many purposes: it helps us to communicate with other people, and is understood to play an important role in processing information and organising thought. While most of us think of language as just speech, it is important to remember that language is also about listening, reading and writing, and includes sign languages such as British Sign language.

> **A QUICK THINK!**
>
> *What have you used language for today?*

What is language?

Linguists who study language development and the nature of language have concluded that all languages, regardless of where they are used, share certain features. It is particularly interesting that all languages have 'rules', which linguists refer to as grammar. Children have to learn these rules, which include the actual sounds that are used in speech.

The number of sounds that are needed in any language varies. In English, children need to master forty *phones*, or sounds, in order to pronounce words. It is thought that the babbling stage that all babies go through reflects their need to sort and rehearse these sounds while the toddler and pre-school child learn how to put sentences together. Amazingly, babies and children appear to go through this process without needing to be 'taught'.

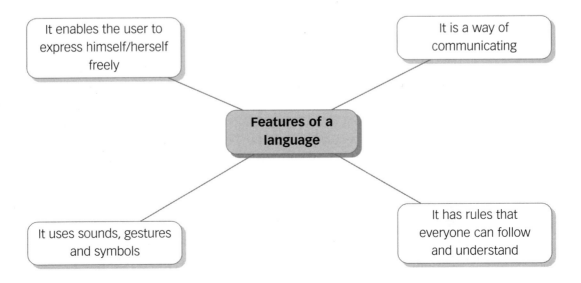

It enables the user to express himself/herself freely

It is a way of communicating

Features of a language

It uses sounds, gestures and symbols

It has rules that everyone can follow and understand

The development of language in children

As with many areas of development, children appear to follow a set pattern when learning language. In addition, there seems to be a critical period in which children need to be 'switched on' to language. This begins from birth, with babies in their first year tuning into their home language and learning how to gain attention and read other people's expressions. This first year of language development is very important and is known as the **pre-linguistic phase**.

Comprehension, or receptive language, appears before expressive language, and at the end of their first year, babies are likely to understand as many as 20 words. The baby will speak his or her first words later, with many parents recognising their child's first words at around 13 or 14 months.

The chart on page 20 shows the 'linguistic' phase of language development from around 12 months of age onwards. As with other areas of development, it is essential to remember that the speed at which children learn and pass through milestones can vary enormously – this chart can be a general guide only. It is, however, useful to note that most children can be understood by people who are not their parents or carers by the time they are three years old. Children whose speech is still very unclear or not developed at this age may need additional support.

The emergence of first words

At around 13 or 14 months, many parents report that their toddler is beginning to use his or her first words, although he or she will continue to babble. These words may not be pronounced correctly but they have meaning for the child and the adult. Many of children's first words are usually linked nouns, for example, 'cat', 'drink', 'mummy', although words such as 'come', 'go', and 'no' are often also present. Furthermore, children generally use the same word for several meanings, for example, 'dink' may stand for all foods and drinks as well as spoons and items used for feeding. To vary the meaning of the word, children also use gestures, such as pointing, and change the tone of their voice. These one-word meanings are referred to as '**holophrases**'.

Telegraphese

Once toddlers have begun to use single words, the next step is to begin combining words. Mini sentences are created by combining two words, for example, 'daddy–gone' or 'cat–more'. This stage of speech is referred to as 'telegraphese' because the non-essential words have been missed out (in a manner similar to old-style telegrams). It is thought that the child is able to choose the key words that will have meaning in a sentence because these are the ones that have been stressed by adults in their speech to the child.

Language explosion

From around two years of age, children suddenly begin to learn and use more and more words. Where previously words had emerged relatively slowly, children now acquire several new words each week. After a few months, it becomes hard to track how many words a child has acquired because he or she

Stage	Age	Linguistic stage	Examples
First words	12 months	First words are often present at 12 months alongside babbling, although parents and carers may not realise them. Babies use gestures such as pointing to attract their parents'/carers' attention. Receptive language is strong – most babies understand about 20 words and can interpret facial gestures.	Harry points his finger to a cat that he sees. Sari waves when she hears the words 'bye bye'.
Holophrases	12–18 months	Receptive language is developing very quickly. At 13 months, most toddlers understand about 50 words. Toddlers use single words or 'holophrases'. By 15 months, most toddlers will speak about ten words.	Anya goes to fetch her coat when her mum says that they are going to the park. Mark says 'dink' when he sees his beaker.
Two-word utterances – telegraphese	18–24 months	Once toddlers can speak several words, they begin to combine them to make mini sentences. Vocabulary increases as children learn around ten to 30 words a month. By two years, many children can speak about 200 words.	Simon says 'bye cat' when a cat gets up and leaves the room.
Language explosion	2–3 years	Vocabulary increases dramatically. Sentence length begins to increase. Plurals, negatives and questions are used.	Kate says, 'Park to see fishes. No cats in park. Fishes in park.'
Virtuous errors	3–4 years	Speech is intelligible to adults who are unfamiliar with the child. The child is beginning to use longer and more complex sentences. Children begin to use grammar, for example, plurals and past tenses, but may make virtuous errors. Speech patterns and expressions are copied from adults.	Damien says, 'We wented to my grans and we saw lots of sheeps.'
Fluency	4–8 years	Language is fairly fluent by four years of age. Children enjoy talking and using language to entertain, explain and argue. From five years onwards, children begin to enjoy jokes and be interested in print. By six to seven years, children have mastered very basic reading and writing skills.	Rayan asks George if he knows what time it is when an elephant sits on a fence. George says he doesn't know. Rayan replies, 'Time to get a new fence.' They both laugh.

Stages of linguistic development

has learnt so many. It would appear that once a child has 'clicked' about words, he or she steadily acquires and uses them in increasing numbers.

Virtuous errors

When learning language, all children make grammatical mistakes. One example is that they may add 'ed' onto the end of every verb, saying things such as 'I swimmed'. These mistakes are actually logical ones that arise from the child's attempt to apply the rules of grammar. Roger Brown, a linguist, refers to such mistakes as 'virtuous errors': they show that the child has developed some understanding of grammar. Grammatical mistakes gradually decrease, although they will be found in most children's speech until they are six or seven years old.

Can all children develop language?

While it is generally accepted that humans have an in-built ability to learn language (see also page 51), not all children are able to learn spoken language. For some children, their cognitive development means that they cannot process and think in symbols. As spoken language is based on symbols, this prevents them from mastering it. For example, when the word 'cat' is said, a cat does not necessarily appear – the word stands for the actual animal. Children who find it hard to process symbols are therefore often taught Makaton signs or a picture-based system of communicating. These help children because visual symbols or pictures are closely related to the action or object.

Makaton and other visual-based systems of communicating are useful because children can understand the link between the words that are being used and their meaning. The decision to use visual systems of communication with children is normally taken on the advice of speech therapists and in conjunction with parents. For some children, this is a short-term measure as, once they learn how language works, they are able to use and increasingly understand speech. Note that Makaton is not a complete language and is used as an aid to communication.

Scissors (to cut)   Drink (cup)   Ball

Some common Makaton signs

Children who learn more than one language

While most people speak one language only, many children speak a different language at home from the language they use in the setting. Where a child speaks two languages, he or she is referred to as **bi-lingual**. A child who can speak more than one language is referred to as **multi-lingual**. The development of the second, and in some cases third, language depends on two key factors:

◗ the age at which the child is exposed to the language
◗ the length of time that the child is exposed to the language.

Children who learn another language as a baby

Children who are exposed to more than one language as babies or toddlers usually make similar progress to other children, although they may be slightly later in saying their first few words. The slight delay in producing first words is thought to be caused by the baby needing more time to 'tune in' to two different sound systems. The advice given to parents and carers who are hoping that their child will learn more than one language is that the child should learn to associate a language with a person, for example, the mother always speaks in Greek, the father speaks in English. This helps the baby to 'tune in' and learn the grammatical rules of each language. Speakers jumping from one language to another can be a primary cause of delayed or confused speech in bi-lingual children.

Children who learn another language in a pre-school setting

Some children enter the pre-school setting with little or no English. For these children, extra support is required to help them acquire the new language. The process of learning a new language as a young child remains similar to that of a baby learning its first language, although the process is faster. Children begin by 'tuning in' to the sounds being used. Receptive language quickly develops, with children developing an understanding of certain key words. Once they have some receptive language, single words emerge, followed by short sentences. The speed at which children learn the new language depends on the quality of the adult support and the emotional environment of the setting.

GOOD PRACTICE ✔

Helping children who are learning the language of the setting

◗ Find out about how much language the child has already learned.
◗ Make sure that the child is allocated a key person to help him or her settle in.
◗ Provide plenty of one-to-one support for the child with the key person, to help him or her 'tune in' to the sounds of the language and learn some key words.
◗ Do not force a child to speak – words will appear only when the child is ready.
◗ Repeat key words and use gestures so that the child knows what you are referring to.
◗ Simplify sentences as you would with a baby or toddler.
◗ To help the child learn some first words, use books with simple pictures of objects and activities.

Rayan speaks Turkish at home and has very little English. He goes to the Busy Bee pre-school three times a week. Rayan's key person, Becky, has built up a good relationship with him and his parents. Together they have agreed that Rayan will need to settle in gradually. When Becky works with Rayan, she makes sure that he can understand her by using facial gestures and repetition, and by pointing to objects. She tries to stress the key words in any sentence and repeats them. She has also made Rayan a simple picture book. Together they look at the book when the other children are having their story. Rayan points to the pictures of the sand pit, water tray and other objects that he recognises. Becky repeats the names of the objects. Becky also organises games of picture lotto that Rayan and other children play together. In the first few weeks, Rayan needed to stay close to Becky, but he is now keen to play with the other children. He is beginning to point to things and say single words.

1 Why do young children need to be offered emotional support when joining a setting?

2 Give two reasons why Rayan needs to spend time with his key person.

3 Why are facial expressions and gestures important in helping a child to learn a language?

Expected cognitive development, 1 to 5 years

Cognitive development is a complex area that is the source of much scientific interest. It generally concerns the way in which we organise our thinking, and our ability to make sense of the world and what is happening to us. Problem solving, prediction and noticing patterns are examples of skills related to cognitive development. While children are learning to organise their thoughts and are discovering about the world, their thinking and logic appear quite different from that of adults. This section focuses on the expected cognitive development in children between one and five years of age, and considers some of the components involved in processing information.

Brain function

The brain remains a source of mystery, although scientists are discovering more and more about how it works. We do know that thought is about making connections: scientists see areas of the brain literally light up while thinking occurs. These connections are made via neural pathways, which can be thought of as similar to the branches of a tree. What is particularly interesting is that babies and young children are still developing these branches – their brains are literally growing. This may be a key reason why most young children think in different ways from adults. The knowledge that babies' and young children's brains are still developing also places considerable responsibility on adults who work with them: babies and children need to be stimulated through play, activities and language so that their brain function can develop.

The brain creates a perception using information from our senses – such as smell and sight

Taking in information – perception

A good starting point when looking at cognitive development is perception. Our thoughts are governed by the information that the brain receives from the five senses. From this information – what we hear, see, taste, smell and touch – the brain creates a perception of the situation. This is a process of translating the different information from the senses into a more accurate representation. For example, the information that the eyes send to the brain is a two-dimensional upside-down image; the brain learns from other senses, particularly touch, that this is not an accurate representation and creates a better one (a three-dimensional image). This translation process happens amazingly quickly, so most people think that what they 'see' is simply the information from their eyes.

The rabbit/duck test

The rabbit/duck test shows how our brain translates the images that the eyes receive into meaningful representations. If you look at the image, you can see either a rabbit or a duck. While it is possible to see both, you will not be able to see both at the same time.

The rabbit/duck test

Attention and concentration

Attention and concentration are closely linked skills. When we notice something and focus our attention on it, we take in information more deliberately. In order to be able to notice something, the brain must be aroused by the information that it receives through the senses. Levels of arousal can fluctuate, for example, some people can sleep through storms.

A QUICK THINK!

Think of a time when you have been visually fooled. For example, walking into what appears to be a large room only to see your reflection and realise that there is a large mirror.

Concentration is the ability to sustain our attention. In order to concentrate, children's brains have to learn to filter out information that is not relevant. This is not an easy process, since the brain is constantly receiving information, for example, sounds from other children, feelings of hunger, the sight of people moving. The ability to focus and sustain interest develops with age, so while a toddler is easily distracted from an activity when shown another toy, an older child will be less distracted.

It is worth remembering, however, that for both adults and children concentration is easier to sustain when the activity is enjoyable and stimulates the senses. Thus, concentration spans are variable and dependent on the activity. A three-year-old may be able to spend 20 minutes playing in the sand, but find it hard to sit still at other times.

APPLYING THEORY TO YOUR PRACTICE

1 Which of these activities consistently hold children's interest for long periods in your setting?
   - Sand play
   - Dough
   - Water
   - Story time
   - Outdoor play
   - Snack time

2 In what ways do these activities stimulate the senses?

3 In what situations do you find it hard to concentrate?

POINT OF INTEREST

Attention Deficit/Hyperactivity Disorder (ADHD)

Children with ADHD find it hard to concentrate and settle on one activity. Their attention span is limited and they are often easily distracted. There are many theories as to why this may occur, but it would appear that for some children their brains are not sufficiently aroused to sustain attention. For other children, the opposite appears to be the case: the brain receives too much information, which the child is unable to filter out sufficiently. Treatment for ADHD is variable, but drug treatments to either stimulate or dampen arousal systems are generally used.

Memory

The role of the memory is to store information. If you could not store information, you would forget everything that you learned. As well as storing information, we also need to be able to retrieve it – this is what happens when you remember. Psychologists looking at memory believe that information is stored in different ways. It would seem that young children do not process information and store it in the same way as adults. This may be one reason why we cannot remember early childhood, although babies definitely have a memory of people, foods and smells.

In addition to storing information, we need to know what information is stored, and make connections between stored and new information. For example, if someone says that they have food poisoning, you might make a connection between that person and a programme you saw about food poisoning. Finding new connections and being able to locate our knowledge in this way is referred to as **metacognitive skills**. The absence of these skills in older children and adults is thought to cause learning difficulties.

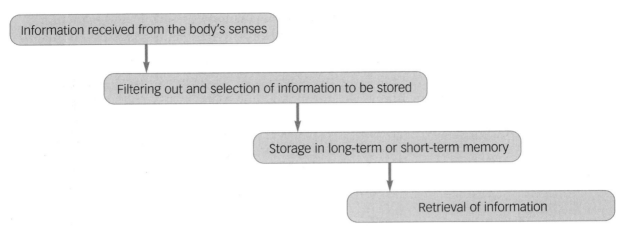

Memory flow chart

The role of language in cognitive development

The development of language appears to be extremely important in supporting cognitive development. As well as using language for communicating, language is used to organise our thinking. Many people know that they can hear 'inner speech' and this allows them to organise themselves or 'self-direct'. In young children, self-direction shows itself from around two or three years of age, although speech is not internalised. A young child often appears to be doing a running commentary on his or her activities, even while alone. It appears that while older children and adults can think inside their heads, young children need to vocalise their thoughts. This accounts for children's often unexpected remarks and questions, and why children appear to switch off if they cannot talk.

Learning concepts

Many of the concepts that children need to learn are those we take for granted. Some concepts, such as time, are very abstract – you cannot physically see

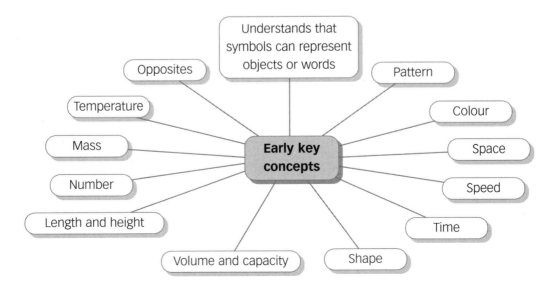

them. Children learn some concepts by playing with materials and exploring their world; others are learned by adults focusing the child's attention on them.

Stages and sequences of cognitive development

It is quite difficult to outline stages of cognitive development in young children because it is dependent on the stimulation and experiences they receive. For

Age	Probable sequence of tasks
0–1 years	▶ Looks for an object that has been removed ▶ Places an object in a container when asked ▶ Finds an object that has been seen and then hidden
1–2 years	▶ Takes out objects one by one from container ▶ Points to parts of the body ▶ Scribbles ▶ Points to a named picture
2–3 years	▶ Completes a three-piece puzzle ▶ Copies a circle ▶ Matches textures ▶ Is able to point to little and big – e.g. 'Which is the big teddy?' ▶ Matches three colours ▶ Stacks beakers in order
3–4 years	▶ Tells if an object is light or heavy ▶ Is able to repeat a simple story ▶ Matches one to one – e.g. putting a cup with each saucer ▶ Points to long and short objects ▶ Is able to sort out simple objects ▶ Knows primary colours ▶ Names three shapes ▶ Counts ten objects with support
4–5 years	▶ Picks up a number of objects – e.g. 'Find me four cubes.' ▶ Names five textures ▶ Names times of day associated with activities, e.g. bedtime, dinner time ▶ Names eight colours ▶ Matches symbols (letters and numbers) ▶ Is able to decide which object is the heavier ▶ Places objects beside, behind and next to ▶ Counts by rote up to 20
5–6 years	▶ Counts accurately up to 20 items ▶ Prints own name ▶ Arranges objects in order of size ▶ Names days of week in order ▶ Tells month and day of birthday ▶ Sight reads ten or more words ▶ Predicts what happens next ▶ Points to half and whole objects, e.g. half a cake ▶ Counts up to 100 by rote

Probable sequence of tasks in children aged 0–6 years

example, a child who has not heard or been shown the names of different colours may not have acquired these concepts. The table on page 27 therefore shows probable sequences and stages of cognitive development only; as with other normative charts, it should be used as a guide.

Effects of developmental delay

The effects of developmental delay can vary enormously from child to child as much will depend on the extent of the delay and how quickly the delay is identified. In some cases, a delay in one area of development may impact negatively on another. For example, a child whose language is delayed may find it hard to control their behaviour and so may find it harder to make friends. In the same way, a child who has difficulty with fine motor skills might avoid any activities where these skills are needed and so may miss out on some learning. Early identification is often seen as the key to helping children and is one of the reasons why all pre-school settings have to appoint a member of staff as a SENCO (see Optional Unit 1).

For many children, developmental delay is most likely to have some effect on their emotional development. This is because children's self-concept is still developing and they are learning about themselves. Sadly, some children come to the conclusion that because they are 'different' this means that they are not 'good' or 'clever'. If they have some physical delay, they may also become dependent on adults to help them with tasks and so lack confidence to use their own initiative. It is therefore essential that adults look at ways of boosting all children's self-esteem through praise and also by giving children choices and opportunities to 'shine'.

CASE STUDY

Griffin is four years old. He has difficulty in co-ordinating his hand movements. He rarely sits at the writing table and only shows an interest in painting when large brushes are put out. He is beginning to notice that other children attempt to write their names on their pictures. When asked if he wants to write his name on a painting, he says no and passes the pen to the adult.

1 Explain how Griffin's developmental delay might impact on other learning.

2 Suggest practical ways of helping Griffin to join in writing activities.

3 Consider ways in which adults might boost his confidence.

Theoretical perspectives of child development

Theories of child development often shape practice in the early years setting. They can provide insight into the way children learn, and explain specific behaviours and responses. Having a good understanding of child development theories and perspectives is therefore useful when working with children and their parents. This section looks at some of the key theories and perspectives of child development that relate to the five areas of development. These include:

- perspectives in psychology
- attachment theories
- theories of personality.
- theories of how children learn
- theories of language acquisition

Perspectives within child development

The academic subject whose focus is the way in which children develop is developmental psychology. Psychology is a relatively new social science that looks at what is going on in our bodies and minds. As people and children have different life experiences and we are generally not born or raised in laboratory conditions, it can be very hard for psychologists to prove their theories beyond doubt. This means that when considering psychological theories, we will see that there are often several approaches to, for example, the way in which learn.

Nature or nurture?

This is an ongoing debate in developmental psychology. The nature or nurture question centres on the extent to which behaviour, intelligence and personality are the result of life experience, or reflect inherited and instinctive characteristics. In the early days of psychology, people tended to hold very fixed positions with regard to this debate. Today, however, most psychologists accept that both are likely to be influential, although theories generally fall into either camp.

A QUICK THINK!

*Parents tend to hold **nativist** views of their children, seeing their qualities as inborn rather than acquired. You may hear parents say things such as, 'It's not surprising that he's no good at maths because his dad wasn't either.' Parents also tend to ascribe the differences between their children to various family members.*

Is this an inherited or learnt trait?

Attachment theories

Attachment theories consider the way in which babies and parents interact and develop special relationships or bonds. They also assess the consequences for babies and children when separation takes place, and when bonds are not developed sufficiently with parents and carers.

Attachment theories

▶ **Attachment/bond** – these terms indicate a close tie or special relationship between the carer, usually a parent, and the child.
▶ **Separation** – a temporary or permanent absence of the parent or carer.
▶ **Separation anxiety** – distress that is shown by the child when separation takes place.
▶ **Deprivation** – the permanent absence of the parent once a bond has been established.
▶ **Privation** – this term refers to situations in which the child has not been able to form an attachment because no adult or carer was present.

Cupboard love theories of attachment

The relationship between child and carer was originally thought to be one of 'cupboard love'. The idea was that the baby cared for the person whom they learned to associate with feeding them. This theory was discredited by many experiments, including one known often as Harlow's monkeys (see below).

POINT OF INTEREST

Harlow's monkeys

In 1959, two researchers – Harry Harlow and Robert Zimmerman – carried out an experiment to determine if there was more to attachment than food. Two artificial monkeys were placed in a cage. One was made from wire and the other was made from cloth. Baby monkeys were put into the cage. Half the baby monkeys were fed by the 'wire mother', the other half were fed by the 'cloth mother'. The researchers found that all the monkeys spent time clinging to and using the 'cloth mother', even those who had not been fed by her. This experiment showed that food alone is not the source of attachment.

Bowlby's theory of attachment

In the 1950s, a psychiatrist called John Bowlby was commissioned to look at the effects on children of being raised in orphanages. This was important work as many children after the Second World War were orphaned. Bowlby's report and later book had a great impact and succeeded in changing attitudes and practice. His theory of attachment has since been criticised and expanded on but it is still considered to be a landmark in child development theory.

- The importance of a principal attachment
  Bowlby concluded that babies need to form one principal attachment. He suggested in his early work that this would be with the mother; however, he later conceded that it could be with the father or another carer. Bowlby found that where a principal attachment was not formed, there were serious implications for the child. The child would sustain long-term psychological damage that would affect subsequent relationships.

- The critical period
  Bowlby suggested a timeframe in which the principal attachment should be made. He thought that babies need to form this attachment by 12 months of age, and that any separation from the principal carer during the child's first four years of life would have serious consequences for the child.

- Quality of attachment
  Bowlby also looked at the quality of the principal attachment, although subsequent research has studied this in greater depth. Bowlby felt that parenting is more than just feeding and caring for the physical needs of the child; the child also needs support and care.

- Patterns of distress
  Bowlby noted that babies and young children show a definite pattern of behaviour when they are separated from their principal carer. This pattern is known as **separation anxiety**. Children move from one stage of separation anxiety to another (see flow diagram below). Bowlby concluded that if a child

Protest

The child shows distress – cries loudly, screams and may even show physical protest by kicking and throwing him or herself on the floor. Children do not want to be comforted and want only to be reunited with the principal carer.

Despair

In this stage, the child appears to be calmer, even accepting of the principal carer's absence. The child may accept comfort from others, but his or her body language shows withdrawal and depression. He or she does not want to join in with others, and may cry quietly or show comfort behaviours, such as sucking his or her thumb or rocking.

Detachment

This stage is reached when the separation continues. The child appears to have come to terms with the separation, but has actually 'cut off' the relationship. If reunited with the carer, the child may ignore and show no signs of wanting a relationship with the carer.

Stages of separation anxiety

is left in the final stage of separation anxiety for long periods, he or she could suffer severe emotional disturbance.

▶ Stranger danger
Most babies and toddlers are very wary of strangers, typically from around eight months to three years of age. If held by another person or left alone with a stranger, children will automatically return closer to their carer and will cry. Bowlby felt that attachment behaviours such as this one are instinctive. He suggested that fear of strangers is probably a protective device designed to prevent young children from straying into danger by leaving their principal carer.

Criticisms of Bowlby's work and subsequent research

Bowlby's theory of attachment is widely acknowledged to have 'set the scene' for explaining the importance and consequences of children having a secure emotional base. However, his work has been criticised by many developmental psychologists, while further research has expanded on his understanding of children's early relationships.

▶ Quality of care
One criticism of Bowlby's work is that he failed to account for the quality of care provided. Subsequent research (for example, by the Robertsons in 1971) has suggested that where care is sympathetic to the child and surrogate attachments can be made, the effects of short-term separation are reduced.

▶ Babies and children can make more than one attachment
Bowlby's early work has also been criticised for failing to explore whether babies and young children can make more than one strong attachment. Bowlby emphasised the role of the mother, which led to some mothers being pressurised into staying at home rather than seeking employment. Later work suggested that babies and toddlers make a similarly strong attachment to those fathers who are involved with them.

▶ The strength of attachments
Bowlby's early work did not concentrate on the quality and strength of attachments; this area was expanded further by the researcher Mary Ainsworth (in 1971–8). Ainsworth noted that the quality of a baby's attachments affected his or her behaviour during separation. Children who are securely attached are more able to explore their environment, using their principal carer as a 'safe base'. Ainsworth suggested that a secure attachment is established as a result of the principal carer's sensitive and caring behaviour towards the child. Her research suggested three categories of attachment, as shown in the table opposite; the majority of children show type B attachments.

> **A QUICK THINK!**
> *Babies and children appear to use parents and other principal carers as a 'safe base'. Have you ever seen a toddler move behind his or her parent's legs and then peep out at a stranger?*

Category	Behaviours
Type A: Anxious Avoidant	The baby appears to be indifferent to its mother or principal carer, showing little or no distress during separation. The baby is easily comforted by others, and ignores the mother or principal carer on her/his return.
Type B: Securely Attached	The baby is distressed when the mother or principal carer leaves, and seeks immediate reassurance from the mother/principal carer when she/he reappears. The baby then calms down and can resume play. Other adults can comfort the baby during separation, but there are marked differences in how the baby responds to the stranger and the mother/principal carer.
Type C: Anxious Resistant	The baby is clingy and difficult when the mother/principal carer is present. He or she has difficulty using the mother/principal carer as a safe base (unlike types A and B). The baby becomes very distressed when the mother/principal carer leaves, and continues to show distress when she/he returns. The baby alternates between clinginess and resistance to the mother/principal carer; other adults cannot provide comfort.

Implications of attachment theories: settling in

For pre-school settings, there are several implications of attachment theories. Firstly, it is important to recognise that young children at two and a half or three years old are still likely to be affected by the '**stranger danger**' instinct. Their distress when left in the company of people they do not know is genuine, and ideally we should be looking for ways of preventing this from occurring. This means providing a **settling-in** process that allows the child to form an attachment to a member of staff *before* being separated from his or her parents. This is the idea behind a key worker or key person system. Once the child has settled in, he or she should go on to develop several attachments, both with his or her peers and other members of staff.

CASE STUDY

Jodie is two and a half years old. Today is her first session at the pre-school. She visited it yesterday with her mother for the morning and seemed quite happy. The play leader has told Jodie's mother to give her a quick kiss and then go. She says that all the children cry at first, but that they soon stop. Jodie cries and tries to run after her mother. She is picked up by a member of staff, but Jodie pushes her away and runs to the door. The play leader tells the member of staff to leave her, as she will soon quieten down. After half an hour, Jodie appears to cry less, but is withdrawn and not interested in joining the other children. The play leader tells the staff that she is just sulking. When Jodie's mother returns, Jodie rushes to her. The next day, Jodie cries as she approaches the door of the pre-school and refuses to let go of her mother's hand. Jodie's mother says that Jodie wet the bed last night for the first time in ages.

1 What are the signs that Jodie is showing separation anxiety?

2 Explain why Jodie showed no signs of distress on the preliminary visit the day before.

3 Consider the settling-in procedures of your setting. Do they allow the child to make an attachment to a member of staff before the child leaves his or her parents for the first time?

Loss and grief

Sadly, there are times when a child's main attachments are no longer available to him or her, possibly because of bereavement or a relationship breakdown. In such instances, children will grieve. There are several theories of grief, but it is generally accepted that there is a grieving process through which both children and adults go. The phases of this process, however, are not automatic and clear-cut. This means that a child who one day appears to be coping well, may on another day be particularly distressed. It is also important to be aware that there is no definite time scale to grief, so children may need continued support over several months and even years.

Phases of grief

1 Disbelief and shock
   This is the initial stage of grief in which the truth of the situation is hard to bear.

2 Developing awareness
   An acute stage of grief in which the realisation sets in that the person is gone. The implications are often hard to bear and strong feelings emerge, including guilt, anger and depression.

3 Resolution
   This is the final stage of grief in which the person begins to come to terms with what has happened and re-establish a pattern to life.

While the grieving process can be seen to have three distinct phases, some grief theorists focus on the components of grief. Ramsay and De Groot (1977) outline nine components of grief and their associated behaviours (see table opposite). The way in which children experience these components is widely variable.

Component	Features and feelings	Ways to support the child
Shock	Numbness, disbelief, apathy, disinterest.	Wherever possible, try to lessen the shock by preparing children ahead of time.
Disorganisation	Inability to cope, difficulty in thinking and organising, panic and anxiety.	Reassure the child. Make sure that he or she has plenty of time and support; keep to familiar routines and surroundings; provide close physical comfort.
Denial	Searching for the missing person, believing that there has been a mistake, refusing to accept that the person has gone.	Support the child but avoid false promises, especially in situations where parents have separated. Tell older children that this is part of the grieving process.
Depression	Yearning, pining, despair, intense sorrow, feelings of powerlessness.	Physically comfort the child. Be ready for the child to need objects and photos of the missing person, etc.
Guilt	Thinking that they are in some way responsible, assessing the ways in which they have acted.	Reassure the child that the loss or separation has not occurred because of them.
Anxiety	This can show itself in many ways: some children become concerned that the remaining people around them may also go.	Provide plenty of reassurance and understanding. Do not trivialise the child's concerns. Provide familiar routines and make sure that any changes are explained carefully to the child.
Aggression	Outbursts of anger against family and friends; anger and acts of aggression that may not have a particular cause.	Be understanding, but maintain boundaries. Avoid punishment, confrontation or negative comments. Be ready to provide physical comfort. Activities such as role-play may help the child to express hidden anger.
Resolution and reintegration	Beginning to accept the situation; feelings of grief are less frequent, although they continue to emerge.	Be ready to allow the child to set the pace, but encourage him or her to join in with activities. Be supportive when, from time to time, grief reappears; for example, an event may cause the feelings of yearning and pining to return.

Personality development

The term 'personality' is generally used to describe the differences in how people relate to others. There are several theories of personality development, which can be categorised into three major approaches:

- biological, or trait, theories
- behaviourist theories
- psychoanalytical theories.

Biological, or trait, theories

Biological and personality trait theories are based on the idea that there is a genetic or biological component to personality. These theories reflect the nature element of the nature versus nurture debate. They primarily look at how a child or adult behaves in certain situations or with other people. There are several variations of these theories, but most suggest that a child is in some way partly pre-programmed to respond in certain ways, and that the child's responses will in turn affect the way that others respond to him or her. For example, some babies are born with an easygoing temperament that encourages parents and other people to respond in a relaxed manner.

Trait theories suggest that personality can be measured in some way. This has given rise to the common practice of carrying out psychometric tests by employers.

Behaviourist theories

Behaviourist theories suggest that the child learns and develops his or her personality in response to others. There are two strands to this approach:

▶ Firstly, children repeat behaviours and responses such as smiling because they are encouraged to do so by adults around them. A mother, for example, may make more eye contact and smile back at a smiling baby; the baby thus learns to smile frequently.

▶ A second strand to the behaviourist approach is that babies and children subconsciously copy reactions that they have seen in adults. A child who often sees aggressive faces or is physically disciplined will repeat both these expressions and behaviour.

(For details of operant conditioning and social learning theory, see page 36.)

Psychoanalytical theories

Psychoanalytical theories view personality as the result of what is happening inside the mind. The two most famous theorists linked with this approach are Sigmund Freud (1856–1939) and Erik Erikson (1902–94). While there are considerable differences in their theories, they share the belief that personality is shaped during childhood and reflects the way in which basic inner conflicts have been resolved. Both theories suggest that these conflicts and resolutions occur at different times in childhood.

POINT OF INTEREST

Sigmund Freud – the father of psychoanalysis

Freud's work is considered revolutionary and has had a huge impact both on attitudes to parenting and the treatment of people with emotional problems. Freud was the first theorist to recognise that some of our actions and speech, and facets of our personalities, are not always deliberate and conscious. He suggested that we had a conscious and unconscious mind, and that our unconscious mind guides us in ways that we do not realise. Freud's work led him to believe that childhood is fundamentally linked to personality and behaviour.

Components of the unconscious mind

Freud suggested that the unconscious mind consists of three main components. While the id is present at birth, the ego and the superego develop during childhood.

▶ Id – this part of the mind is purely interested in obtaining pleasure and having its needs met. It therefore represents the selfish part of our make-up. Freud suggested that the id was the only part of the unconscious to be present at birth.

▶ Ego – Freud suggested that the ego starts to develop in babies after a few months. It is the 'planning' component of the mind. While the ego thinks about consequences, it does so only to satisfy the id's desires and is therefore focused on our own rather than other people's needs. The ego is therefore amoral. For example, a child sees a biscuit; the id wants it and the ego thinks about how best to get it. If the biscuit is snatched, an adult may confiscate it; therefore asking for a biscuit politely may be the best means of obtaining it.

▶ Superego – later on in childhood, the ego learns to take into account the needs of the superego. This is the moral part of the unconscious mind, and is subdivided into two parts: the conscience and the ego ideal. The conscience threatens the ego with guilt if it meets the id's desires in an amoral way, while the ego ideal rewards the ego if it acts properly.

Unconscious conflict

Freud argued that once all the component parts of the mind have developed, the ego is caught between the demands of the id and the potential punishment/rewards of the superego. The result is that the ego is trapped in a situation of great tension or anxiety, called unconscious conflict. Freud suggested that unconscious conflict causes people to have dreams, show neurotic symptoms and behave in certain ways.

Psychosexual stages

Freud also described how the personality develops during different stages of childhood. He suggested that both adults and children are driven by the biological instinct to procreate. This drive he called libido, or life force. Such ideas sexualised behaviour and were very shocking to Victorian society.

Freud argued that the libido develops through several distinct stages in childhood. Each stage is characterised by the ways in which the child gains pleasure from a different part of his or her body. The child's personality develops in line with this progression, depending on how the child adjusts to each stage. Interestingly, Freud's psychosexual stages link closely to the biological maturation of young children's bodies.

Children who have not satisfactorily passed through a psychosexual stage are likely to have part of their libido stuck or 'fixated' at that point. This in turn affects the development of the child's later personality and behaviours. Freud suggested that fixation occurs either because the child has not received enough pleasure, or because he or she has remained for too long in a particular stage. The reactions of the parents to the child are also seen to have an important influence.

Age	Stage	Area of pleasure	Features of stage	Effects on personality and behaviour if *fixation* occurs
0–1	Oral	Mouth	Babies are gaining pleasure from feeding and sucking. They will also be weaned during this stage.	Behaviour linking to pleasures gained in the mouth – e.g. overeating, smoking, thumb sucking. Also naivety: 'Swallows anything they are told!'
2–3	Anal	Anus	Children are learning to control their bowel movements. They learn that adults praise them when they master toilet training or can be angry with them if they do not.	Freud argued that if children were toilet trained too early and were too controlled, they would develop 'controlling' habits – e.g. extreme tidiness, meanness, stubbornness – while if children did not have enough encouragement to become toilet trained, they would become overgenerous, gushing in personality.
4–5	Phallic	Genitals	Children are exploring their bodies and are noticing their genitals. They are also learning about their gender. Freud felt that girls needed to adopt the gender role of their mothers, while boys had to separate from their mothers and follow the gender role of their fathers (see also Oedipus complex).	Vanity, recklessness
6–12	Latent	None	Freud felt that this was a resting period for children in terms of their emotional development.	None
13–18	Genital	Genitals	Children are developing into mature adults. If they have passed successfully through the other stages they will be able to make strong relationships with the other sex.	

Freud's five stages of personality development

The Oedipus complex

As part of the phallic stage, Freud suggested that boys have to deal with the 'Oedipus complex'. In the Greek tragedy by Sophocles, *Oedipus Rex*, Oedipus kills his father before falling in love with and marrying his mother. Freud suggested that this story mirrored a hidden reality – around four to five years of age, boys really do fall in love with their mother and become deeply jealous of their father. Freud argued that boys are therefore in competition with their father for their mother's love. However, they are also frightened that he will castrate them. This leaves the boy with an inner conflict: should he carry on loving his mother and risk his father's anger?

To resolve the Oedipus conflict, Freud suggested that boys attempt to befriend their fathers by copying their behaviour. While this part of Freud's theory has come under intense criticism, it is interesting to note that many boys do indeed hold onto their penises and begin to play in quite sex-stereotypical ways at this age.

Criticisms of Freud's work

Freud's work is seen as being revolutionary because he provided an explanation for dreams, phobias and conditions that appeared to have no medical cause. His work, however, has been widely criticised because his research consisted of subjective interviews and notes rather than comprehensive research. His work also involved adults rather than children, and he focused particularly on men rather than women.

Erikson's theory of personality development

Erik Erikson provides another key theory of personality development. He was originally a student of Freud, so his work was heavily influenced by Freud's theories. However, while Erikson agreed that childhood was crucial to personality development, he also suggested that aspects of personality continue to develop during adulthood. He suggested that, at key stages, our lives present us with different hurdles or 'dilemmas'. The way in which we cope with these dilemmas affects our ongoing personality development. For example, there comes a point when young adults have to decide whether they wish to settle down with a partner or whether they want to maintain their independence.

Age	Dilemma	Stage	Effects on personality
0–1	Basic trust versus mistrust	Babies have to decide whether the world and the people around them are safe and friendly, or hostile.	If babies do not have their needs met, they may decide their world is a hostile one. This can mean they find it harder to form relationships later.
2–3	Autonomy versus shame and doubt	Children are learning to explore their environment and develop some control over their bodies and bowel movements. They may try to do things for the first time – e.g. dressing.	If children are not given encouragement to explore or are made to feel guilty about toilet accidents, they may feel doubt about themselves. This can mean they will be less independent when older.
4–5	Initiative versus guilt	Children are increasingly able to plan and carry out activities. They also need to learn about their gender role – similar to Freud's phallic stage.	Children need to feel they are independent, although they also need to learn what the boundaries on their behaviour are. Too much control of the child may result in a

Age	Dilemma	Stage	Effects on personality
4–5 (contd.)			fearful, dependent child, whereas a very permissive attitude may leave the child without any guilt or conscience.
6–12	Industry versus inferiority	In these years, children are comparing themselves to other children.	Children who experience failure and notice that they are not as competent in some areas as their peers, may lose confidence and feel inferior. Children in this stage who meet only with success may become over-confident and lack humility and empathy.
13–18	Identity versus confusion	Adolescents need to consider their identity – sexual identity and also what they wish to become in the future.	Ideally, at the end of this stage, adolescents have a firm idea of who they are and what they want to go on and do. If they have not worked through this stage, they may 'drift'.
19–25	Intimacy versus isolation	This age group may be considering whether to live alone or find a partner to settle down with.	Adults must decide whether to form a couple or stay single. If this conflict is not resolved, they may find themselves unable to commit to a relationship.
26–40	Generativity versus stagnation	Adults in this stage are often having their own children or are making progress in their careers.	In this stage, adults are trying to make an impact on the future. Most people have children or try hard in their careers. If adults feel they have not left their mark on life, they may feel bitter and resentful.
41 plus	Ego integrity versus despair	Adults in this stage are thinking more about their mortality.	In this stage, adults are trying to come to terms with themselves and the way they have lived their lives. They may feel satisfied and accepting of themselves or they may feed depressed and bitter.

Erikson's stages of personality development

Learning theories

There are several theories of how children learn. Understanding how these theories work can be very helpful when thinking about how best to plan for children's learning.

Learning theories can be broadly divided into three major approaches:
- behaviourist theories
- constructivist theories
- theories of language development.

Behaviourist approaches to learning

Behaviourist theories of learning consider the ways in which we learn by responding to events and other people. This approach is quite different from the other two theories of learning. Central to this approach is the notion that children and adults are in some ways recipients of learning, and that learning is particularly tied to what we experience and what happens to us. There are two separate theories within the behaviourist approach

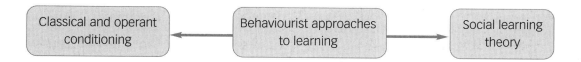

| Classical and operant conditioning | ← | Behaviourist approaches to learning | → | Social learning theory |

Classical conditioning

The key name associated with this theory is Ivan Pavlov (1849–1936). Pavlov was working as a physiologist looking at the digestive systems of dogs when he noticed that, at feeding time, the dogs would begin to salivate even though no food was present. Pavlov thought that this was because the dogs had learnt to associate certain noises with food, and thus would salivate just upon hearing the noises. He decided to investigate this effect further by carrying out a series of experiments. In one of his most famous experiments, Pavlov found that dogs that normally would not salivate if they heard a bell could be 'conditioned' to do so. By presenting the food and the bell together, the dogs learnt to associate the sound of the bell with the presence of food. After a short time, hearing the bell alone would make the dogs salivate.

POINT OF INTEREST

Classical conditioning and children

This theory of learning is not seen as having widespread use with children. It does, however, explain some phobias and reactions that children may have acquired – that is, learning by association. We should also remember that a child's first visits and early separations from his or her parents must be happy, otherwise a child will associate coming into a setting with being unhappy.

CASE STUDY

Jonathan's parents take him each week to the park. One day, while he is on the slide, he hears some very loud bangs. Some workers nearby are demolishing a wall. He cries. The next time he is in the park, he refuses to go near the slide.

1 Explain why Jonathan dislikes the slide.

2 Why will it be important to reassure Jonathan and to let him see gradually that the slide is harmless?

Operant conditioning

Put at its simplest, operant conditioning suggests that we learn and are influenced by the results of what we do. For example, if you try something and like it, you are more likely to do it again.

Thorndike's Law of Effect

The original idea of operant conditioning was put forward by Edward Thorndike, although he did not use the term operant conditioning. Thorndike showed through his experiments that the results of behaviour affected future behaviour. He called this 'The Law of Effect'. In his famous experiment, Thorndike put cats into boxes from which they could release themselves if they pressed a lever. He placed a piece of fish outside the box, which was visible to the cats. Gradually, the cats became faster at getting out of the box to get the fish.

Skinner's reinforcers

B.F. Skinner (1904–90) built on Thorndike's theory in the 1950s and shaped it into the widely recognised operant conditioning theory. While Skinner partly accepted the work of Pavlov, he suggested that humans and animals were actually more involved in their learning and that they drew conclusions as a result of the consequences of their actions. He called the consequences 'reinforcers'. He suggested that there are three types of reinforcers:

▶ Positive reinforcers

These meet a need or desire, for example, gaining a sticker, winning a prize or enjoying an activity. Skinner suggested that positive reinforcers are the best and most effective type of reinforcers.

▶ Negative reinforcers

These result in repeat behaviour in order to prevent something from happening. For example, we learn to wear an apron because otherwise our clothes are spoiled.

▶ Punishers

These are strong shocks that are designed to prevent us from repeating an action, for example, learning to not touch a hot iron again. Punishers were seen by Skinner as being the least effective way of working with people.

Effective positive reinforcers

In early years settings, a variety of positive reinforcers are often used with children. These include stickers, praise and certificates, as well as small rewards such as being the first to choose something. Food can be a strong positive reinforcer, but it should not be used as there is a danger that unhealthy attitudes towards food will develop.

Attention and recognition as positive reinforcers

Many early years practitioners find that children will often repeat activities and behaviours if they receive some kind of attention or recognition. A child who is praised is more likely to do something again. Unfortunately, an adult's attention is such a powerful positive reinforcer that it can also lead to children showing unwanted behaviour in order to get an adult's attention. Thus, in some cases, ignoring a child's unwanted behaviour may be the best strategy.

POINT OF INTEREST

Operant conditioning and children

Operant conditioning is a powerful means through which children learn. It is used particularly in shaping children's behaviour. In terms of early years practice, it might help us to remember the following:

▶ activities need to be enjoyable as this will encourage children to repeat them
▶ children find attention a positive reinforcer and learn how to do things to gain our attention. This may include behaviour that is inappropriate.

Differences between classical and operant conditioning

The key difference between classical and operant conditioning is timing.

▶ Classical conditioning takes place when two things are presented <u>at the same time</u> and are thus associated together.
▶ Operant conditioning stresses that learning occurs <u>after</u> an action or behaviour.

Social learning theory

Social learning theory, though simple, has widespread implications. At its heart is the idea that children learn by imitating the actions, gestures and words of others. The key theorist linked to this theory is Albert Bandura (1925–present). He showed through a range of experiments that children would remember and act out what they had seen.

The Bobo doll experiment

The most famous of Bandura's experiments is often referred to as the Bobo doll experiment. In this experiment, three groups of children saw a film in which an adult attacked a large inflatable doll (the Bobo doll). There were three different endings to the film.

▶ In the first ending, a group of children saw the adult being told off by another adult.

▶ In the second ending, a group of children saw the adult being rewarded with sweets and lemonade.

After watching the film, the children were put in a room with a range of toys including the Bobo doll. The children who had seen the aggression go either unpunished or praised were considerably more aggressive towards the doll. The experiment also showed that if the children were asked to be aggressive towards the doll, all of them could repeat the adult's actions they had witnessed.

Social learning theory and children
This theory has strong implications for our practice with young children.

▶ Behaviour
Social learning theory indicates that any behaviour we wish children to adopt should be modelled by us; for example, if we want children to share, they must see us being able to share. Equally, we need to be careful that children do not learn about inappropriate behaviour from us. An adult who shouts and whose tone of voice is aggressive is likely to find that children will learn this type of behaviour.

▶ Working with children
Social learning theory also reveals that children often learn how to do things by being alongside and involved with **role models**. In some ways, this is the traditional way in which children learned. Practitioners may, for example, sit with a group of children and play with dough; children will notice how the adult is handling the dough and be likely to copy.

Criticisms of the behaviourist approach to learning
Whilst most psychologists would agree that some of our learning takes place in the way that Skinner and Bandura describe, the **behaviourist** approach fails to account for why children's logic and conclusions about the world can be so different from those of adults. It is also a passive model of learning that relies heavily on adult input.

Constructivist approaches to learning

Constructivist approaches to learning consider children to be active learners and thinkers. There are three theorists in particular whose work has been very influential in terms of early years practice. Their work has been explored and developed further by others.

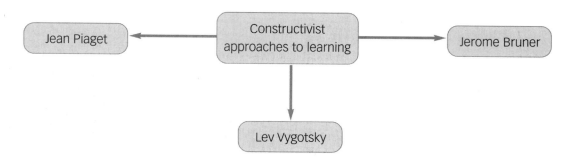

Jean Piaget (1896–1980)

Piaget's interest in children's thinking and logic began while he was working on intelligence tests. Piaget was fascinated by the way in which children regularly gave similar but wrong answers to some questions. He eventually concluded that children's logic is different from that of adults and began to explore why. Using his own children as a basis, Piaget wrote detailed observations about their development. He finally concluded that children 'construct' their ideas based on experience; this is why the term 'constructivist approach' is used in relation to his theory. Piaget used the term 'schema' to mean a child's conclusions or thoughts. Piaget felt that children's schemas would change as new pieces of information became known.

A QUICK THINK!

See if you can draw a person in under 30 seconds. If you can, this means that you have developed a schema – a quick way of doing or thinking something that no longer requires much thought.

Try to draw a person again, but this time start with the feet and work your way upwards. This is usually much harder because you have to change your schema for drawing a person.

Assimilation

Child constructs a schema based on what he or she knows.

The lady at the nursery stays there because I always see her there.

Equilibrium

The schema remains the same whilst the child's experiences seem to confirm his or her ideas.

Every day, the lady at the nursery is waiting for me in the room.

Disequilibrium

The child has information that seems to cast doubt on his or her schema or idea. Things do not add up any more!

I am in a shop, but I can see the lady from the nursery. What is she doing here?

Accommodation

Child adapts his or her thinking and constructs a new schema incorporating this new information.

The lady at the nursery doesn't stay there all the time.

The process by which children's schemas form and change

Stages of development

As well as trying to understand how children's thinking develops, Piaget looked at the different stages of children's development. Piaget believed that children's thinking processes are linked to their biological development – the process by which structures develop within the brain. (Recent work on brain development now shows that children's brains do actually grow and develop from birth onwards.) Piaget concluded that these different stages of development are influential in children's thinking.

Piaget grouped children's cognitive development into four broad stages. He identified each stage by ages, although he did suggest that not all children would reach the final stage. Note that subsequent work has suggested that he may have underestimated children's development. The table below outlines these stages.

Stage	Age	Features
Sensori-motor	0–2 years	The child develops physical schemas as he or she gains control of his or her movements. At around 8 to 9 months of age, the baby begins to understand that objects continue to exist even if he or she cannot see them. This is known as **object permanence** and may explain why most babies begin to protest when their carer leaves the room.
Pre-operational	2–7 years	Children begin to use symbols to stand for things, for example, a piece of dough represents a cake. Language is also a way of using symbols. Children also show egocentrism – believing that everyone sees the same things or has the same thoughts as them. Piaget felt that children in this stage were easily tricked by appearances (see, for example, his experiments on conservation below).
Concrete operations	7–11 years	Piaget felt that this stage marks a significant change in children's logic: they are less easily deceived by appearances and can apply rules and strategies to their thinking. The term 'concrete' is used because Piaget felt that children were helped in their thinking when they could do and see things in practical ways, for example, physically counting out items.
Formal operations	11–15 years	In this stage, children are able to think entirely in the abstract, for example, they can multiply numbers in their head or read maps without having to turn the page.

Conservation

One of Piaget's tests to identify a key stage in children's development centres on the child's ability to '**conserve**'. Conservation means understanding that certain things do not change in quantity or quality, even though their appearance does change. Piaget suggested that young children find it difficult to conserve because they are easily taken in by appearances. This explains why children reach different conclusions from adults. For example, a three-year-old may think that a man wearing a women's dress has become a woman, or that a volume of water has changed simply because it has been poured into a different sized container.

Animism – an example of how egocentrism works

Many children in the pre-operational stage draw pictures with human faces or believe that inanimate objects, for example, puppets and teddies, have real feelings. This is thought to be linked to egocentrism: children believe that because they have thoughts and feelings so do other things.

A happy dog!

How Piaget's work has affected early years practice

Piaget's work has had a huge influence on early years practice. Before his work was recognised, children's education was generally about getting them to remember knowledge; children were seen as passive rather than active learners. Piaget's work stresses the importance of encouraging children to learn from their direct experiences. This is sometimes referred to as active learning.

Criticisms of Piaget's work

While Piaget's work is hugely influential and highly regarded, his findings have subsequently been developed further. Key criticisms of his work are that he underestimated children's abilities, designed experiments that were difficult for children to understand, and failed to account for the ways in which adults influence a child's development. There is also some doubt as to whether or not children really follow the stages of development that Piaget described; some children master some elements of cognition but not others.

Vygotsky's theory of cognitive development

Lev Vygotsky (1896–1934) was a developmental psychologist whose work was influential in Russia in the 1920s and 1930s, but unknown in western Europe. His theory of children's cognitive development is similar to Piaget's; however, Vygotsky believed that children's learning takes place through the process of socialisation. He therefore placed great emphasis on the role of adults and other children in a child's learning. Because of the social aspect of Vygotsky's learning theory, it is often referred to as a social constructivist theory.

Vygotsky's view was that children are born to be sociable, and that by being with their parents and friends they acquire skills and concepts. He believed that learning is first done socially, but that the child is able to subsequently internalise his or her learning. Language, which Vygotsky saw as fundamental to learning, is one example of the internalisation of learning. Speech is at first used to communicate socially with others, but then gradually the child learns that he or she can use speech to direct him or herself; eventually this is done as an 'inner voice'. For Vygotsky, this explains why children often go through a stage of talking aloud, seemingly to no one in particular.

The role of the adult

For Vygotsky, those people surrounding the child play an important role in his or her learning. He saw the child as an 'apprentice' who learns by being helped and challenged by others. Vygotsky used the term **Zone of Proximal Development** (ZPD) to describe the relationship between a child's possible learning and his or her current abilities. The example below shows how a child's actual abilities and skills can be developed further through contact with others.

> **Current abilities**
> Terri is five years old. She has quite good fine manipulative skills and wants to do the zip up on her new coat.

> **Learning through socialisation**
> Terri's mum spends a few minutes showing her how to make the zip work. Terri has a go herself and is encouraged by her mum.

> **Development of skills and concepts**
> Over a few days, Terri becomes increasingly skilled at doing her coat up. She no longer requires her mum to help her. She has now learnt about how to do zips up. Her skills and knowledge have been developed during this process.

How Vygotsky's work has influenced early years practice

Vygotsky's strongest influence on early years practice has been making practitioners aware of the importance of their role in developing children's thinking. Piaget did not stress the role of the adult, which led to a feeling among practitioners that if they provided a stimulating environment, children would learn for themselves.

> ## APPLYING THEORY TO YOUR PRACTICE

Vygotsky and Bruner both saw responsive adults as being important in children's learning.
Try out the following observation:

1 Observe the way in which a child is playing.

2 Consider what skills the child has already acquired.

3 Think of a way of joining in the child's play and extending these skills.

4 Consider how you might be able to tell if your support has helped the child to learn.

Jerome Bruner (1915–present)

Jerome Bruner built on the work of both Vygotsky and Piaget. Bruner agreed with Piaget's view that children are essentially active in their learning and ready to explore their world. He also felt that some biological processes explain why children's logic develops in stages.

The importance of language in learning

In terms of Vygotsky's approach to learning, Bruner suggested that adults should adapt the ways in which they work with children to meet the child's immediate needs. The term 'scaffold learning' or '**scaffolding**' is often used to describe the support an adult provides in a child's learning. This term was first used by Wood *et al.* in 1976, but neatly sums up Bruner's approach to helping children learn. Bruner emphasised the way in which an adult may help a child to use language, for example, by asking questions that allow the child to solve a particular problem.

Modes of learning

While Piaget considered learning in terms of stages of cognitive development, Bruner considered learning according to the ways in which information is represented or stored.

Mode	Age	Description and use
Enactive	0–1 year	Learning and thought takes place because of physical movements.
Iconic	1–7 years	Thoughts are developed as mental images.
Symbolic	7 plus years	Symbols are used to help thinking, for example, language.

Bruner's modes of learning

Enactive mode

We often learn a skill by repeating physical movements, for example, learning to tie our shoelaces. Bruner suggested that this is the first cognitive skill that babies are able to use. Bruner's enactive mode mirrors Piaget's sensori-motor stage in which children are learning to control their bodies (see page 46).

Iconic mode

An icon is something that is visual. Bruner suggested that the iconic mode involves building in our mind pictures of things we have experienced. We may, for example, shut our eyes and imagine the room. Bruner's iconic stage relates to Piaget's pre-operational stage during which children concentrate more on appearances; this is what confuses children during Piaget's conservation test (see page 46).

Symbolic mode

Like Piaget, Bruner believed that, at around seven years of age, children's thinking changes dramatically. Bruner linked this change to the child's ability to use symbols, and thus the use of language. In symbolic mode, thinking occurs without needing to have direct experience. For example, you may listen to the news on the radio and retain this information, even though you have not directly witnessed the events mentioned.

Bruner's work and memory

Bruner's work shows significant parallels to information processing theories (see pages 23–6). These highlight the way in which memory influences our ability to process information. In symbolic mode, we use language as a tool to trigger information stored in the memory. For example, the words 'Treaty of Rome' may help us to remember about that period of history, even though we were not present at the Treaty of Rome!

How Bruner's work has influenced early years practice

Bruner expanded on Vygotsky's work by showing how adults can stimulate children's thinking. Bruner's emphasis on the importance of language has also been influential. Bruner felt that the development of language is central to the child's ability to move from the iconic to the symbolic mode. This has meant that, for example, in the Foundation Stage curriculum, there is considerable emphasis on the importance of language.

> **A QUICK THINK!**
>
> *Many European countries do not begin the process of formal reading and writing until children reach six or seven years. This is because it is thought that children will find it hard to remember symbols and use them efficiently. Based on the constructivist approaches to learning, why do you think they have reached this conclusion?*

Theoretical perspectives on language development

We have already looked at the way in which children develop language (page 20). There are several different theories relating to language development that are useful to consider.

The behaviourist approach to language development

The behaviourist approach considers that the environment in which the child is brought up is critical to language development. B.F. Skinner, whose learning theory we considered on pages 42–3, suggested that language develops through positive reinforcement. He suggested that when a baby makes a sound, the parent is likely to respond. This in turn prompts the baby to continue to make sounds. Skinner used this process to explain why babies who at first make the same type of sounds regardless of their home language, will eventually learn which sounds to use. He suggests that parents will respond more to sounds that they recognise, for example, when a baby says 'dada' or 'mama', the parent is likely to smile more and pay greater attention to the baby.

There are many difficulties with the behaviourist approach to language development. Firstly, it fails to explain why children make 'mistakes' when they first speak. If the child is only learning to repeat language that he or she hears, then why do all children make similar mistakes? Secondly, this theory does not adequately explain why children's first sounds and words tend to be similar.

Is the ability to learn language instinctive?

Nativist approaches to language development consider that our ability to learn language is in some ways instinctive. A key nativist theory is that proposed by Noam Chomsky (1928–present). Chomsky suggested that a cognitive structure enables language acquisition; he called it the Language Acquisition Device. Chomsky argued that there must be some type of cognitive structure to enable humans to work out the rules or grammar of language however complex they are. This theory explains why all babies make the same babbling sounds regardless of where they are born. It also explains why children all over the world seem to learn language in a similar way. Chomsky's view is widely recognised, but the role of adults in helping children to speak is still considered a major influence.

Is there a critical period in which language must be learnt?

It has been suggested that if children are not exposed to language in the first ten years of life, they will never develop the ability to speak. This idea points to a '**critical period**' for language development. There is some evidence for and against this idea.

- Teenagers and adults who have been brain damaged as a result of an accident find it harder to regain language they have lost, whereas younger children with similar injuries find it much easier. This would support the idea of a critical period.
- Children who have suffered severe deprivation have still managed to acquire some language. One of the most famous examples of this is the case of Genie. Genie was 13 years old when, in 1957, she was rescued from an upbringing characterised by extreme deprivation. She had spent her childhood in appalling conditions: she was punished for making any sounds and was strapped and bound. When she was found, Genie could understand only a few words and essentially had no speech. Although she made progress in learning to speak, Genie struggled with the rules of language. The case of Genie casts doubt on the idea of a 'critical period' for language development, as Genie was able to develop some speech.

The constructivist approach to language development

The constructivist approach to language development centres on the use of language in helping children to think rather than on how language is learned. Piaget, Bruner and Vygotsky all agreed that language and thought are linked, although Piaget differed in his views because he viewed language as a tool.

In contrast, Vygotsky and Bruner both suggested that language organises and drives our thought process (see also page 50 on language and thought).

Links between behaviour and development

Children's development can shape their actions and reactions. It is important to be able to understand the links between behaviour and development, as this allows us to consider how best to meet a child's needs. (See also page 77 for strategies to help children learn about social behaviour.)

Understanding the term 'behaviour'

An important starting point is to consider the term **behaviour**; it can be used in more than one way.

▶ In common speech, 'behaviour' often refers to socially acceptable or unacceptable behaviour. Expressions such as 'just look at that child's behaviour' are usually negative and quite judgemental.

▶ Psychologists use the term 'behaviour' to refer to the responses that people show, i.e. their actions and reactions. This way of using the term is neutral and often more helpful when considering children's needs.

Children's responses are affected by their development

The way in which children act is heavily influenced by their stage of development. Babies in the first few weeks cry because it is their only way of gaining attention. From around six weeks, crying usually decreases as parents become more skilled at understanding their babies' needs. The baby also learns to smile, coo and laugh.

Because of the link between development and behavioural responses, early years practitioners need a good understanding of each area of development and how it is reflected through a child's behaviour. The charts below shows some of the behaviours that can easily be misunderstood, but that are directly linked to the child's stage of development.

Physical development

Physical development is about gaining control of movements. This allows the child greater independence. As well as learning to use and control movements, children also learn about their bodily needs.

Behaviour reflecting the needs of the child	Link to development
A young child may prefer to stand rather than sit during activities.	The child can see what he of she is doing more clearly. Standing over an activity may also increase the amount of strength that the child can apply, for example, when rolling out dough.
A child suddenly declares that he or she is too tired to walk any more.	Young children are not aware of their body's needs and so do not realise that they are getting tired until the body sends out 'exhausted' messages. Children cannot pace themselves in the same way as adults.
A child runs instead of walks.	Young children enjoy the ability to move, and running makes them feel good. An awareness of safety develops only later.

Cognitive and language development

Children's ability to digest and make sense of information is directly linked to their cognitive development. Language acquisition is also linked to cognitive development; thus, significant changes to the way in which children think and act occur as they learn to use language effectively.

Behaviour reflecting the needs of the child	Link to development
The child may flit from one activity to another.	A child's attention and concentration span develops with age, and is directly linked to the way in which he or she processes information. Sensory activities usually help young children to concentrate for longer periods.
The child may fiddle when he or she is meant to be listening.	A child's ability to sit still and process the spoken word is limited until language is completely mastered. The child will respond best to active situations in which they can absorb information through a variety of senses. Children fiddle in order to meet their sensory needs.
The child may forget what he or she has been told to do.	Children are better at processing information visually rather than through words. Children may also find it hard to apply information to a different situation. Young children find it hard to think through the consequences of their behaviour. A child's understanding of the effects of his or her behaviour on others will develop much later.
The child may show impulsive behaviour, such as snatching.	Young children find it hard to think through the consequences of their behaviour. A child's understanding of the effects of his or her behaviour on others will develop much later.
The child may have a tantrum or outburst.	Tantrums and unexpected outbursts are usually linked to frustration and difficulties in expression. Once children can use language effectively and understand what is happening, these outbursts tend to diminish.

Emotional and social development

At the core of the child's emotional and social development is the need to feel settled and secure. Whether this need is met depends on the child's ability to form relationships with others. In addition, communication is essential to developing relationships. Children usually become more skilled at developing relationships with others when they have acquired some skill in language.

Behaviour reflecting the needs of the child	Link to development
A child protests when his or her carer leaves, or becomes very clingy to one member of staff.	Separation anxiety is powerful in young children and is marked by strong emotions. In order to cope with these feelings, the young child needs to form a close attachment to adults in the setting. The more settled and attached a child becomes, the more able he or she is to become independent.

Behaviour reflecting the needs of the child	Link to development
A child takes things from another child.	Young children do not necessarily understand the notion of 'possession' and are quite impulsive. As a child's cognitive understanding and language develops, he or she is able to understand the concept of possession.
A child does not take turns.	Turn-taking and co-operation is a skill that gradually emerges from around three years of age. It is linked to children's language development and their experiences of socialising with other children.
A child does not make friends.	While babies can be aware of other babies, many children do not play with other children of the same age until their language and communication skills are quite developed. Thus, many children under three years old will not automatically play with other children.

CASE STUDY

Amanda is two years and six months old. She has started at her local pre-school. At the start of each session, she tries to stay near the play leader and follows her around the hall. She does not appear to be interested in joining in with other children, and will often just stand and watch.

1 Explain how Amanda's actions are based upon her stage of development.

2 Why is it important for staff to understand her needs?

3 Give one suggestion as to how Amanda's needs might be met.

Influences on development

We have seen in earlier sections that development is a process. There are many factors that can influence this process, so it is useful for early years practitioners to have some understanding of them. This section looks at the major influences that can affect a child's development.

Stereotypes and judgments

While few people would dispute that children's development is influenced by a variety of factors, it is actually a complex area of study. Therefore, early years practitioners must not fall into the trap of assuming they can pinpoint how a child's development is affected by, for example, his or her home circumstances. To do this can result in early years practitioners labelling children and failing to meet their needs (see also pages 133–144).

CASE STUDY

Davina is a supervisor at the Busy Bee nursery. She is concerned about Kyle's language development. She tells a pre-school assistant that she believes that Kyle's difficulty is connected to his family circumstances. Kyle has two older brothers and lives in a single-parent family. Davina thinks that Kyle may not be getting enough attention at home.

The next week, Kyle's mother pops in to say that she has had Kyle's hearing tested because she is worried about his speech. It turns out that Kyle has a conductive hearing loss.

1 Explain why the supervisor came to the 'wrong conclusion'.

2 Why is it important not to make assumptions about children?

Environmental and social factors

The place in which a child grows up can influence his or her development in a multitude of ways.

Housing

On a basic level, children need to live somewhere that provides warmth and shelter, and is clean and well ventilated. Sadly, these basic requirements cannot always be met because poor housing and poverty go hand in hand. Research suggests that poor housing can effect children's physical development because repeated infections stunt a child's growth. Higher levels of colds, lung infections and asthma are associated with poor housing.

Access to safe outdoor environments

Children need fresh air and large-scale physical activity. This promotes good bone development, lung capacity and muscle strength. Vigorous outdoor activity also helps children to develop independence and confidence through learning to balance, jump and run. While some children are lucky enough to have a garden or access to a nearby park, other children are not as fortunate. They may be unable to take outdoor exercise frequently. Children who do not have access to a safe outdoor environment may be less physically skilful than other children, and may feel less confident in large spaces.

Outdoor activity helps a child develop

Pollution

Ideally, all children need to breathe in clean air. We are only just learning about the effects of pollution on children's health. It is now thought that the increase in childhood asthma may be related to levels of air pollution.

Safe environments

All children need to be kept safe, although they also need opportunities to explore their environment. This balance is quite hard to achieve, but most parents are aware of potential dangers and are able to provide adequate supervision and equipment to keep children safe. In some instances, children may be exposed to environments that are inherently dangerous. Where accidents occur, children's development may be affected; for example, a head injury can cause cognitive delay.

Cultural factors

Each family lives in slightly different cultural circumstances, with different approaches to parenting. It is very hard to quantify the influence that culture has on individual children, which includes exposure to music, arts, language and food. Thus, some children will learn more than one language, while others will listen to music traditional to their culture. The way in which culture affects a child's overall development is therefore virtually impossible to identify as, even within a culture, families have their own traditions and individual differences.

Family values and beliefs

Attitudes and beliefs change from family to family, and from generation to generation. This can contribute to the development of children in often very subtle ways, most notably in terms of social behaviour. Codes of social behaviour are partially learnt at home. For example, while some families eat around the table, others prefer to eat while watching television; some children have a very specific bedtime routine, others do not. It is important to remember that the 'ideal' family does not exist and that, as children get older, they learn to adapt their social behaviour to suit the situation.

Some families will have their mealtimes around the table

As well as social behaviour, families play a major part in stimulating children and helping them to learn particular skills. A child whose family enjoys board games may learn to roll dice at an early age, while a child whose family goes swimming every day may quickly learn to swim.

Genetic influences

There are strong links between genetic make-up and physical development and growth. Scientists are increasingly finding out about they ways in which genetic make-up affects our development. It has been shown that genes are responsible for children's height and other physical characteristics, such as eye colour and hair type. In addition, scientists are learning about the ways in which an individual's genetic make-up may predispose him or her to certain types of disease and illness. Asthma, for example, is thought to have some sort of genetic component.

While there is a clear genetic influence on physical development, there remains fierce debate as to whether or not personality and particular aptitudes and skills are genetically influenced. This reflects the nature versus nurture debate (see page 29). Many scientists are reaching the conclusion that while genetic make-up predisposes us towards certain qualities, environmental triggers also play a role. For example, a child may be genetically predisposed to play music, but also needs to be encouraged to sing or play an instrument.

Chromosomal disorders

As well as inherited influences on development, some children have chromosomal disorders that affect their development. Many chromosomal disorders have no inherited component and are a chance occurrence – a result of nature's lottery. Normally, 23 chromosomes from the mother are combined with 23 chromosomes from the father. In some cases, chromosomes are damaged or missing, or a new variation occurs. Changes to the usual chromosomal pattern can result in children's development being affected, although the extent to which this happens varies enormously.

Economic factors

The financial situation of a child's family can have some impact on his or her overall development. A child growing up in poverty is statistically more likely to have accidents, poorer health and leave school with a lower level of qualifications. It is for these reasons that organisations such as the Child Action Poverty Group campaign for an end to child poverty. The reasons behind the statistics are quite complex, but a low income essentially means that a child has less access to those factors that contribute favourably towards the achievement of his or her potential, such as access to safe environments, good housing, diet and nutrition. Poverty also puts many emotional pressures on parents, and these should not be underestimated. In a society that values material goods, living in poverty can undermine a person's self-confidence, which in turn affects the person's relationship and parenting skills.

Mario has recently come to this country with his family as asylum seekers after a solider shot his brother, who died as a result. The family has been housed in a one-bedroom flat and are living on a tiny weekly income. The children are aged three and four years and have few toys, outings or chances to play.

Consider the effects of living in cramped accommodation have on a child's physical development.

1 How might attending pre-school help children who live in poverty?

2 Why might a supportive pre-school benefit the whole family?

As with all influences on development, it is important to remember not to 'stereotype' a child who may come from a low-income family. Some parents are able to provide favourable conditions for their children despite their financial situation.

Nutrition and diet

Our bodies are a complex balance of chemicals and water. Food therefore plays an essential role, providing our bodies with the chemicals required to sustain health and well-being. Ideally, good nutrition should begin before conception and into pregnancy, as it is now known that the mother's and even the father's diet can have some affect on development. For example, it is thought that the mother taking folic acid supplements during the three months before conception and the first few weeks of pregnancy can prevent spina bifida.

In terms of a child's development, a balanced nutritious diet helps the child to fight off infection and provides his or her body with the nutrients or chemicals necessary for growth. A balanced diet will also provide children with sufficient calories, or energy.

In this country, very few children are under-nourished, i.e. receive insufficient food. However, a surprising number are malnourished, which means they fail to receive the appropriate balance of nutrients. Ironically, while some children are overweight or even obese, they are not necessarily getting the right nutrients. The number of young children who are either overweight or obese has risen in the past few years. This is a worrying trend: in addition to not getting the nutrients they need, the extra weight may prevent the children from taking part in physical activity. The need to ensure that children eat five portions of fruit and vegetables a day has meant that many settings now offer fruit and vegetables instead of biscuits as snacks.

Carbohydrates	Vitamins and minerals	Protein	Fat
Provides energy (kilojoules/calories) for the body. Found in foods such as pasta, rice, potatoes, pulses and bread.	A range of vitamins and minerals are required in small quantities to assist the maintenance of the body. Whilst vitamins and minerals are vital, they are usually gained in sufficient quantity when children are given a varied and balanced diet that contains food from the other three nutrient groups as well as plenty of fresh fruit and vegetables.	Essential for growth and maintenance of the body. Found in foods such as meat, fish, eggs, nuts, lentils and dairy products.	Provides energy for the body and allows absorption of vitamins A and D. Found in foods such as dairy products, meat, fish and margarine.

Nutrients and their role

Lifestyle

There is wide variation in the way that people live. Again, it is worth remembering that the 'ideal' family does not exist, but that there exists a range of family structures. The nuclear family consisting of married parents and their children is no longer the 'norm', despite the way in which the media portrays families. In addition, contrary to popular myth, the majority of single parents are not teenagers but older parents, some of whom are widows and widowers.

Politicians and public figures often give the impression that one style of family structure is better than another style. Statistics to provide evidence in support of these ideas can be very misleading. A good example is that of single parents. While it may be true that children from single-parent families do less well academically, many people believe that the cause of this is not the family structure but the economic circumstances of the parent, or the conflict caused within the family by the breakdown of the parents' relationship. Thus, perhaps the key point is not to consider the family structure of the child but to look at the support that a child gains from within that structure. Children who feel secure are likely to thrive, regardless of the circumstances in which they live.

APPLYING THEORY TO YOUR PRACTICE

Mrs Patel is worried about the behaviour of one child in her group. She is sure that her lack of concentration is a result of her being raised in a single-parent household. She is surprised a week later when the child's parent tells her that her child has just been diagnosed with a hearing loss.

1 How might Mrs Patel's previous thoughts have affected her behaviour towards the child?

2 Why is it important for practitioners not to draw conclusions about children's family lifestyles?

Observation and assessment of development

As professionals working with children, we need to find out about their strengths, weaknesses and interests. This information allows us to plan activities that will help them to develop; it also helps us to identify children who need extra support. This section looks at the reasons why we observe children, and the range of observation methods that are used to identify children's progress.

The **National Standards**, which are used to inspect pre-school settings before registration is awarded, emphasise the role of observations and record-keeping. This means that you will need to show that you plan and record activities based on observations of children.

Methods of assessing development

The words observations and assessment are often used together. It is helpful to understand the differences between them.

▶ An observation is a record that is kept while children are being watched. It is a tool for assessing children. The key advantage is that it provides you with your own picture of the child.

▶ Assessment can take many different forms, for example, a written test for children or a survey involving parents and other professionals.

Why observe and assess children?

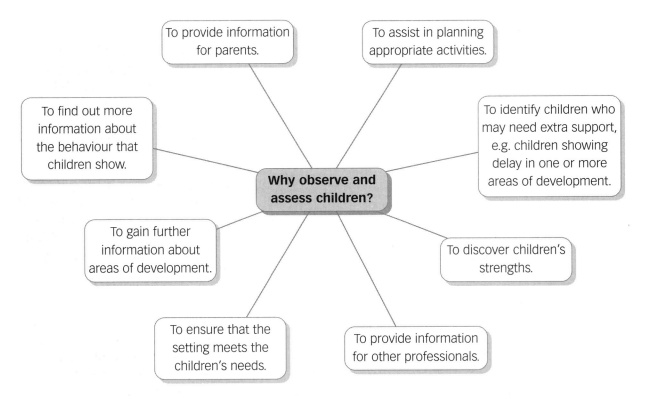

There are many reasons why it is important to observe children. Firstly, it can help us to check that the provision in the setting is right for the child. We may see that a child finds it hard to play alongside other children, and from this realise that the child needs more adult support. Observations can also help us to notice whether a child is making progress or has particular strengths or difficulties. In this way, we can identify those children who need additional support (see also Optional Unit 1).

As well as helping us to be aware of children's development, observations encourage us to talk to parents and share particular highlights or concerns with them. In day care or extended sessions, this feedback is particularly vital, as parents will need to know what their child's day has been like.

In addition, observations can provide information for other professionals when concerns about a child's development or behaviour have been expressed. Pooling information from both the child's parents and pre-school setting will help professionals to get a more rounded picture of the child's needs.

Considerations for the use of observations

Limitations

A good starting point is to remember that observations and assessments have serious limitations. We must never assume that we 'know' the child based solely on a few observations. Children will show different skills and attitudes in a range of situations. Observing a child in only one situation will fail to provide a rounded picture of that child. Thus, while observations have an extremely important role in helping us to learn about children, you should remember that they are a tool only.

Parental permission and the Data Protection Act (1998)

Years ago, parents had few rights in relation to what was written about their children. Fortunately, this situation has now changed, reflecting the trend that parents should be seen as equal partners in the care and education of their children. It is now accepted practice for parents to give permission before observations are carried out on their child. Information gained from these observations should be shared with parents, so that a proper exchange of information and views can take place.

The law regarding information that is held about people has also changed. The Data Protection Act (1998) at first applied to personal information that was held on a computer only. This Act has subsequently been amended so that anyone can ask to see any type of written personal information, including handwritten notes. This means that parents have a legal right to look at and, if necessary, challenge what has been written about their child.

Confidentiality

As well as checking that parents are happy for their child to be observed, it is important to understand that any records or information about individual children is **confidential**. Breaching this confidentiality is a breach of trust, which is treated as a disciplinary matter in many settings. Thus, records of observations should be stored securely and shared only with those who should have access to them. Parents' permission should always be asked before any information is passed on to people outside of the setting, for example, speech and language therapists.

Factors to consider when carrying out observations

Several factors may influence both the type of observations that are carried out and the way in which this is done. It is important to understand these factors as they can affect the validity and objectivity of the observation.

Participative versus non-participative

It is important to understand that a person's performance changes when the person knows that he or she is being observed. In some cases, being watched can improve and enhance performance; in others, it may adversely affect performance. Children, too, react differently when they are being observed. Thus, methods in which the observer asks the child to do something or interacts with the child may produce slightly different information from other methods in which the adult is unobtrusive or non-participative.

In terms of observation methods, there are advantages to the adult being present with the child. The adult can clarify what the child is trying to do, or ask the child to do a particular task in which he or she may not otherwise choose to engage.

A QUICK THINK!

Do you like being watched by other adults when you are working? How do you think it affects you?

Open versus closed data

Observing children is not quite as easy as it may seem at first glance, since there is potentially much to watch. Because it is impossible to note everything down about a child, the observer will have to be selective. This means that two people watching the same child at the same time may note down very different things.

Some observation methods are designed to make the observer more objective by providing closed data; a checklist is a good example of a closed data method. These methods focus the observer on specific things that a child does, for example, noting whether a child can build a tower of three bricks. The observer is not required to note down any additional information, for example, how the child is doing the task or whether he or she is enjoying it.

Open data methods allow more freedom for the observer to note down what he or she believes to be relevant. This has the advantage of providing a larger pool of information. However, the disadvantage of open data methods is that they are likely to be more subjective.

Methods of observation

There are several methods of observing children. Each method has particular strengths and weaknesses. There is no 'perfect' method, so when choosing a method it is important to think about the type of information you want to collect. It is also important to remember that a single observation does not provide a comprehensive picture of a child. Rather, several observations using a variety of different methods are the best means of learning more about a child.

Checklists and tick charts

Checklists and tick charts are a popular method of observing children. This is because they are easy to use and understand. They are used in many early years settings and form the basis of most systems of record-keeping on children.

Using checklists and tick charts

Checklists and tick charts are very simple to use. A sheet is prepared with a list of statements. The observer needs to read carefully through the tasks or skills and note whether a child is able to do them; a tick or remark is recorded on the prepared sheet accordingly. The observation can be done unobtrusively, by simply watching the child and hoping that he or she will show the skills to be recorded, or as a participant, by asking the child to do the required tasks.

Child's name .... Date ....

Date of birth .... Observer ....

Developmental checklist

By 12 months	Yes	No	Sometimes
Walk with some help?			
Pick up objects with finger and thumb?			
Transfer items from one hand to the other?			
Look for an object hidden under a beaker?			
Look at a person who is speaking to him or her?			
Make tuneful babbling sounds such as Da-da?			
Respond to different sounds e.g. drum, bell?			
Imitate gestures such as pat-a-cake and bye-bye?			
Hold beaker using two hands?			
Use fingers to eat finger foods such as squares of bread?			
Pick up dropped toys?			
React to the word 'No'?			
React to own name?			

An example of a checklist

Designing checklists and tick charts

Many settings have commercially prepared checklists and tick charts, which are often based on developmental milestones. It is possible to design your own checklist or tick chart, but you will need to think carefully about what information you wish to collect. Designing your own checklist or tick chart has many advantages, as you can put in more detail.

Advantages	Disadvantages

Advantages

- Checklists and tick charts provide a closed method of recording information. The observer is directed to observe certain features of a child's behaviour, for example, the child's hand preference.
- The checklist or tick chart can be used again later to see if the child has made progress.

Disadvantages

- This method, although closed, is still subjective because the observer may decide that a child can 'almost' do a task or skill.
- The design of the checklist or tick chart can be vague; there is not necessarily a guide to say how well the task should be done. For example, statements such as 'can wash hands' are open to wide interpretation.
- Checklists and tick charts do not give any indication of the child's feelings or attitudes.
- Checklists and tick charts may focus the observer and the child's parents on what the child cannot do rather than what he or she can do.

Narrative or written records

This type of observation method is known by several names, including free description, naturalistic, narrative and written records. The method itself is quite simple: the observer records what he or she sees. It is a popular method because it allows the observer to produce a 'snapshot' of a child's activity.

Using this method

The narrative records method is simple to use. You will need to decide what aspects of a child's development, play or responses you wish to focus on. This decision is essential because this is an open method of recording; without an aim, you are likely to find it hard to know what to record.

Make a note of the time that you begin the observation. Note down what the child is doing at the start of the record and who else, including other children, is present. Write down what you see as you see it, including the actions and response of others towards the child. This should mean that you write in the present tense, almost like a sports commentator. Each time you stop or pause, you should note down the time. Most observers carry out this observation as non-participants so that they can be more objective. It is hard to monitor and write down your own responses.

KEY POINTS

- Record only what you see, not what you suspect the child is thinking.
- Make your notes as detailed as possible.
- Note down body language and facial expressions.
- Try to 'catch' speech as well as movements.

Advantages	**Disadvantages**
▶ Narrative records is an open method of recording. This means that you should have a large pool of information from which to draw.	▶ Narrative records is a subjective method of recording. Since it is impossible to 'catch' everything, the observer will continuously be making choices about what to focus on.
▶ This method provides a fuller and more detailed picture of the child.	▶ This is a tiring method of recording, so the observer will need to stop from time to time.
▶ This method does not require any special equipment or prepared sheets, so it can be carried out quite spontaneously.	

Time sampling

Time sampling is a useful method of recording because it allows the observer to look at a child for longer periods. This method can also be adapted to focus the observer on particular areas of development.

Using this method

A time sample records a child's activity at regular points during the observation, for example, every five minutes over an hour or every ten minutes over a session. You will need to begin by preparing a sheet.

At its simplest, time samples are just the times followed by a short narrative about what the child is doing. At the allotted time, you simply write down what the child is doing. You can adopt the 'running commentary' style used in free descriptions (see above). However, as the idea behind this method is literally to 'sample' what the child is doing, you should keep your observations brief so that they provide a 'snapshot'.

Using a more structured sheet

Time samples can be made more focused by adding columns that record specific behaviours, for example, speech, activity and social grouping. This type of time sampling has the advantage of focusing the observer on specific behaviours, which is likely to make the observation more objective.

Advantages	**Disadvantages**
▶ Time sampling is a simple method that provides an easier way of noting down what a child does over a longer period than, for example, free description. It allows you to build up a picture of what a child does over a day or a session.	▶ If you use the simplest form of time sampling, the observation is likely to be subjective: it depends on what the observer focuses on.
▶ This method provides you with a range of information across several developmental areas, for example, you may see the child engage in social activity, speech and physical movements.	▶ The key disadvantage to this method is that, because you should stick to the times on the sheet so that the child's activity is 'sampled', you may 'miss' a particularly interesting activity or behaviour.

Event samples

Many settings use event samples to look at the circumstances and patterns of a child's unwanted behaviour. However, this method is also used to look at other aspects of a child's activity.

Using the method

This is not a 'traditional' observation as recording takes place only when a child shows a particular behaviour – the 'event'. Thus, if you want to look at how often and in what circumstances a child talks to an adult, you will record only when this happens. This method is therefore used to look in detail at a child's specific activity or behaviour.

Begin by identifying what information you need to collect to find out more about the 'event'. You may wish to

Event	Time	Situation	Social group	Dialogue
1	9.16 am	Curren is hovering near the painting table	Susan + 2 children	A–C 'Do you want to come and paint a picture too?' C–A nods head
2	9.27 am	Curren is finishing painting	Susan + 2 children	A–C 'Have you finished?' C smiles 'It's a lovely picture. Tell me a little bit about it.' C–A 'It's my mum. Can't take my apron off.' A–C 'Wait still, I'll do it.' Curren hands apron to Susan and runs over to sand area
3	10.12 am	Curren is waiting for his drink at snack time	Curren is sitting next to Ahmed. Jo is handing out drinks	A–C 'Milk or squash, Curren?' C–A 'Milk.' A–C 'Can you remember the magic word?' C–A 'Thank you.' A–C 'Good boy.'
4	10.19 am	Curren is putting on his coat in the cloakroom area	Jo + 5 children	C–A 'Can't put coat on.' A–C 'Keep still. There you are. You can go out now.'
5	10.36 am	Curren is waiting for his turn by the slide	Jo + 2 children	A–C 'Good boy. It's your go now.' C smiles C–A 'I go fast down now.'

This event sample sheet was prepared to collect information about a child's speech and language after concerns were expressed that the child was very quiet. This sheet allows the practitioners to note down to whom the child talks, the situations in which the child talks, and the length of time spent communicating

record the time when the 'event' occurs, whom the child is with, and where it happens, as well as other information specific to the aim of the observation. Next, prepare a sheet on which to collect the information. For each type of information to be recorded, add a column on the sheet. It can also be useful to add a comments column, because you may wish to record additional information.

Advantages

▶ Event samples are a useful way of doing some 'detective work' about a particular aspect of a child's behaviour or activity.

▶ This method assesses the frequency with which the chosen 'event' occurs; it can therefore be used over time to see whether strategies or support for that child have been effective.

Disadvantages

▶ This method may require the assistance of other people as you may not have seen the 'event' yourself. In this way, the observation's validity and objectivity are called into question.

▶ Event samples do not work well if the prepared sheet has not been thought through carefully. You will need to adapt the sheet and the columns according to the type of information to be collected.

Longitudinal observations

Sometimes it is helpful to build a picture of a child over time to see the rate of developmental progress that child is making. It can also help to see whether strategies and support provided for that child have been effective. When observations are completed regularly over a number of weeks, the term 'longitudinal' is used. Ideally, alongside a regular pattern of observations, a range of observation methods should also be used.

GOOD PRACTICE

What makes a good student observation?

Many qualifications require that students present observations and assessments of children. The reason behind this requirement is that it shows whether students have a good underpinning knowledge of child development. So, what makes a good observation?

▶ **Clear aims and relevant method**
The more focused you are as an observer, the more accurate and detailed your observation record will be.

▶ **Open methods of recording**
To show your skills, the best methods of recording tend to be open methods. This is because you can collect a wide pool of information about a child. Closed methods, for example, a checklist, provide less information about the hows and whys of a child's responses.

▶ **Detail**
The more detailed your information, the easier it is to support your conclusions with evidence.

Using the information provided by observations

Once an observation has been carried out, it is essential that the recorded information is collated. This means looking carefully at the recordings and considering what this means for the child. As a student, you should also think about how the information relates to child development theories and perspectives.

Assessing children's development against milestones

A good starting point when analysing observations is to look at children's normative development or milestones. This is particularly useful when developmental delay has been suspected. It also provides a context in which to think about the needs of the child. However, it is important to remember that charts of normative development are a guide only and that children's development can show variations.

Identification of developmental delay

In some cases, you may suspect that a child's development is very different from what is expected for his or her age. The SEN Code of Practice states clearly that you should at this point work in partnership with the child's parents. This means talking to the child's parents about your observations and your analysis of them <u>before</u> contacting any outside professionals. Talking to a child's parents about developmental delay requires tact and awareness, and it can be helpful to agree with the parents that further observations are undertaken. Where parents also believe that a child is showing signs of developmental delay, they may wish to consult their health visitor or GP, who will then refer the child to the appropriate services (see also pages 240–2).

Reflecting on practice

In addition to thinking about the information gained directly about the child, it is important to consider your own and your setting's practice. It is a good idea, especially when considering a child's concentration, distraction levels or communication, to think about whether the activities and layout of the setting influence what the child does. This is not always easy to do when working in a setting, because you grow accustomed to a particular routine or approach.

Considering children's developmental needs

Observations and the information they provide can help us to focus on the support and challenges that children need. Identifying developmental needs is about thinking of activities, support and equipment that will be of benefit to the child. A good approach when thinking about how best to meet these needs is to work out what the next steps will be in the child's development. For example, a child who is able to complete a small jigsaw puzzle may enjoy the challenge of something more complex; a child who has learnt to put on his or her coat may need support and encouragement to put it on a hanger.

Thinking about children's developmental needs allows us to check that activities are suitable or are adapted to meet the needs of individual children. This is very important, because across a group of children of the same age, there will be variations in each child's developmental needs.

Applying theories of child development during observations

As a student, you should try to make links between what you have seen in the setting and child development theories. The table below gives some common examples of children's behaviours that can be linked to child development theories.

Behaviour	Theory	Explanation
A young child looks to see if an adult is near; there is, so the child smiles and continues playing.	Attachment theory (Bowlby/Ainsworth)	Young children often use adults as a 'safe base'. Knowing that an adult is around can help a child to feel relaxed.
An adult praises a child for helping to tidy up; the child carries on tidying.	Operant conditioning (Skinner)	The adult's praise acts as a positive reinforcer and so the child learns to repeat the action.

Behaviour	Theory	Explanation
A child is throwing sand; the child next to him also begins to throw sand.	Social learning theory (Bandura)	Learning has taken place through imitation: the second child has noticed the action of the first child and copied his or her behaviour.
A child talks aloud to him or herself as he or she draws a picture.	Social constructivist theory (Vygotsky)	The child is using speech to help organise his or her thoughts.
Story time has been moved to earlier in the afternoon. A child is crying because he or she was expecting to go home afterwards.	Constructivist learning theory (Piaget)	The child has developed a schema about going home. He or she has reached the conclusion that home time follows story time.

→ **APPLYING THEORY TO YOUR PRACTICE**

Look the following snippets taken from observations. Consider how the behaviours shown might link to theories of child development.

1 Jacob is ten months old. He is sitting in his pushchair. He throws out his rattle. He looks down to where it has dropped.

2 Sudeshni is two years old. Every time she comes into the pre-school, she goes directly to the sand tray.

3 Jenny is four years old. She goes into the home corner and begins 'tidying'. As she does so she makes a loud sigh and says, 'more mess again!'

The role of adults

The role of adults in children's development is critical. This section looks at the ways in which adults can support children's development and learning.

Working in partnership with parents

Parents are crucial to a child's development. They are often unsung heroes: many of the things they do are taken for granted by both family members and professionals. As well as meeting children's physical needs for food, clean clothes and a safe environment, parents also contribute to their child's development by spending time playing and communicating with them.

Recognising the unique role that parents play in their children's lives, and building upon this recognition, is therefore essential. When early years practitioners and parents are able to share information and show respect for each other's role, the child benefits. In terms of development, parents are uniquely placed to notice what their child does in the relaxed and usually unstructured environment of home. This information should be used by early years practitioners to gain a fuller picture of each child and, in this way, more effectively target support.

The importance of play

Traditionally, play was seen as a trivial pastime in which babies and children indulged. Our understanding of play is now more sophisticated: play is generally recognised as being essential to a child's growth and development. This understanding of play is the reason why the Foundation Stage and other early years curricula emphasise the importance of providing play environments and activities that encourage children to learn through play (see also Unit 2).

Play and physical development

Play is a great motivator for babies and children. As part of their play, children enjoy running around, chasing, crawling and climbing. During such play, children automatically build up their muscles, stamina and physical skills. In the same way, children playing with, for example, duplo, jigsaws and dough, build up hand–eye co-ordination and fine manipulative skills.

Play and cognitive development

Children learn about their immediate environment through play. Babies, for example, often drop objects from their high chair to see what happens, in a playful way. Older children create games and play them, and in this way learn about rules. Play of all kinds appears to stimulate the brain and expose it to new sensations. This in turn helps children to formulate ideas or schemas about what is happening.

How play supports children's overall development

Play and language development

While cognitive and language development are interlinked, play often allows children to practise speech and communication. An early example of practising speech is the toddler talking seriously to a teddy or doll. Later on, we see that children practise their speech and communication skills on each other, quite often through role-play.

Play and social and emotional development

Play is one of the mediums through which socialisation takes place. Babies gain a sense of security as well as enjoyment through simple games, such as peek-a-boo, and from being hugged playfully. As children become older, they are able to play alongside other children and in this way learn about relationships. Role-play, in which children pretend to take on different roles, helps children to explore feelings and the dynamics of different relationships.

The role of the adult in providing for play

There are some key principles that adults should remember when supporting children's play.

Supporting children's play

▶ Make sure that children have sufficient time in which to enjoy their play.

▶ Avoid constantly intervening and directing children during play.

▶ Provide materials that are stimulating and attractive to children.

▶ Make sure that a range of play opportunities are available.

▶ Look out for equipment and materials that are versatile.

▶ Encourage children to make choices and take responsibility for their play.

▶ Make sure that equipment is appropriate to the child's age and developmental stage.

▶ Avoid making assumptions about the way in which children may wish to play.

Activities to promote development across the age range

In some ways, it could be argued that all play activities promote development. This is because any activity that engages children's thinking and physical activity will be beneficial. There are, however,

Play that involves thinking can be very beneficial

some activities that work well with children across the age range to promote development, and as such are always worth providing. This is because they are sensory and provide children with open-ended challenges.

Water play

Water play is enjoyed by babies, toddlers and children of all ages. Water play encourages physical development, but also develops concepts of capacity, space and measures.

Paint and mark making

Mark making can begin as early as 15 months. The feel of making marks with crayons, paints, chalks and charcoals is enormously powerful. Children develop fine motor control, learn to express themselves and communicate through their marks.

Making dens and houses

Small spaces have enormous appeal for children of all ages. Tents made from sheets or curtains draped across structures provide children with an opportunity for role-play. As children's social skills develop, den making can become a co-operative exercise.

Cooking

Not only is this a good life skill, but children of all ages benefit by learning about measuring, making choices and also mastering tools. For cooking to be truly beneficial, it is important to choose recipes that allow children to do plenty of things for themselves.

Risk and challenge versus protection

Adults play an important role in keeping young children safe. Young children are not always aware of risks and cannot be expected to predict the consequences of their actions. Working with children means that adults have to take responsibility for keeping children safe. This is particularly vital because, for example, a head injury could have major consequences for the child's subsequent development.

While understanding the need to keep children safe, adults must also understand that children need to explore their environment, learn to make choices and have some measure of independence. Thus, adults working with children need to achieve a balance between over-protectiveness, which is restrictive, and negligence in their duty of care. The key to getting this balance right is being aware of the potential hazards in the environment and thinking about the ways of evaluating and managing the risks.

Ways in which risks may be managed in settings

▶ Safety equipment

A range of safety equipment may be used to minimise risks, for example, blunt-ended scissors, safety gates and door catches.

▶ Supervision

Close supervision of children during potentially hazardous activities is one way of managing risks, for example, during outings, outdoor play and cooking.

▶ Layout

An evaluation of the layout of a setting can reduce the possibility of accidents, for example, moving equipment so that children are less likely to bump into it.

▶ Procedures

Safety procedures during, for example, home time and toileting, help staff to understand their role and prevent accidents.

Intervention

How and when to intervene in play and activities is one of the most important skills that adults need to learn when working with children. High levels of intervention can result in children failing to learn social skills, or how to take the initiative or solve problems. On the other hand, failure to intervene at critical moments may result in accidents or in children becoming frustrated by an activity.

A good approach when looking at intervention is to consider how adults might intervene on different levels. Choosing the level that is the most appropriate for the situation helps to avoid occasions when adults 'swoop in' on children's play and change it. If adults are constantly changing children's play, it can undermine the children's confidence and their ability to learn and explore.

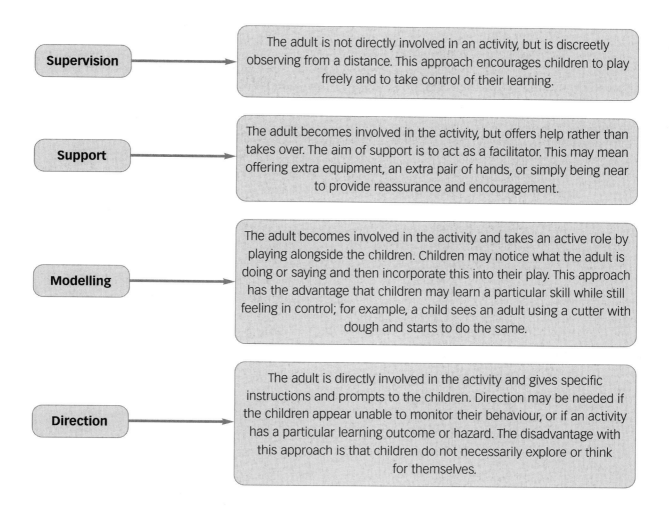

Supervision → The adult is not directly involved in an activity, but is discreetly observing from a distance. This approach encourages children to play freely and to take control of their learning.

Support → The adult becomes involved in the activity, but offers help rather than takes over. The aim of support is to act as a facilitator. This may mean offering extra equipment, an extra pair of hands, or simply being near to provide reassurance and encouragement.

Modelling → The adult becomes involved in the activity and takes an active role by playing alongside the children. Children may notice what the adult is doing or saying and then incorporate this into their play. This approach has the advantage that children may learn a particular skill while still feeling in control; for example, a child sees an adult using a cutter with dough and starts to do the same.

Direction → The adult is directly involved in the activity and gives specific instructions and prompts to the children. Direction may be needed if the children appear unable to monitor their behaviour, or if an activity has a particular learning outcome or hazard. The disadvantage with this approach is that children do not necessarily explore or think for themselves.

Use of materials and equipment

To promote their development, young children need to be stimulated and provided with opportunities to play. An important role of the adult therefore is providing children with materials and equipment for play. The key when doing this is to check that materials and equipment are suitable for the child's stage of development. However, most manufacturers identify equipment and materials by age group, as this is an easy way to give potential buyers some idea of the product's suitability. The difficulty here is that children's development varies across the same age group. Thus, while one four-year-old may be ready to play with a material, another four-year-old will not.

Early years practitioners therefore need to use the information from their observations when deciding the developmental needs and interests of each child. Providing materials and equipment that are beyond a child's skill or developmental level can leave the child feeling frustrated and lacking in confidence. Conversely, providing materials and equipment that are not challenging enough for a child can limit his or her development.

The charts below give some indications of the types of materials and equipment that can promote different areas of a child's development. While the charts indicate some broad age bands, remember that you will always need to consider the needs of the individual child.

Equipment and materials that promote children's physical development

Age	Examples of equipment and materials	The role of adults
1–2 years	**Gross motor**: sit-and-ride toys, brick trolleys, large cushioned bricks and shapes, swings, rockers. **Fine manipulative**: pop-up toys, stacking beakers, large crayons, bricks, cuddly toys.	Children are likely to learn how to walk at this time, and will be unstable at first. Close supervision is therefore essential, as children are likely to bump into objects and fall over. Children's fine manipulative skills are still developing, and a child may continue to use his or her mouth to explore new items. Close supervision of what a child places in his or her mouth is essential. Adults can help children to learn how to use toys by playing alongside them.
2–3 years	**Gross motor**: soft balls, sit-and-ride toys, tricycles, push-and-pull toys, small climbing frames, rockers. **Fine manipulative**: simple jigsaws, pop-up toys, duplo, toys cars and trains, dough, sand, paint, tea sets.	Children need to have enough space in which to run and explore their environment. They will need careful supervision and encouragement. Children often know what they want to achieve, but may not quite have the physical skills to achieve it. Adults should look for signs of frustration and provide support where appropriate.
3–4 years	**Gross motor**: balls of different sizes, bean bags, obstacle courses, tricycles, pushchairs, climbing frames, slides. **Fine manipulative**: dough, sand, scissors, floor puzzles, dressing-up clothes, cooking activities, construction toys.	A child's sense of balance and general control is increasing. This means that many children are ready for new challenges, for example, walking on small walls or trying out an obstacle course. Children's fine manipulative skills are developing, which means that they require increasing opportunities to be independent and make choices.
4–5 years	**Gross motor**: bicycles with stabilisers, roller skates, stilts, tricycles, wheel barrows, pushchairs, see-saws, balls, hoops, play tunnels. **Fine manipulative**: junk modelling materials, paint, small construction kits, jigsaws, dough, water and sand, collage materials, board games.	Children are beginning to enjoy co-operative games and may copy each other's behaviour. Supervision is still important, but should be unobtrusive. Children's fine manipulative skills are fairly developed and they enjoy setting themselves challenges, for example, making a house out of a box or building a bridge for a train. Aim to offer support and help, rather than direct these activities.

Equipment and materials that promote children's cognitive and language development

Age	Examples of equipment and materials	The role of adults
1–2 years	Toy telephone, pop-up toys, lift-up jigsaw puzzles, picture books, items for heuristic play such as corks, wooden hoops, baskets, metal containers, plastic bottles.	Adults need to acknowledge children's communication by smiling, talking to them and engaging them in simple rhymes. Children should be encouraged to explore their environment and to enjoy seeing the effect they have on materials. Heuristic play helps children to learn many concepts by playing with everyday materials.
2–3 years	Jigsaw puzzles, construction bricks, picture books, pop-up books, water and sand play.	Adults need to listen carefully to children and act as their 'language partner'. Adults should not correct mistakes in pronunciation or grammar, but recast the sentence using the same words. Books, nursery rhymes and songs also help children's language. Children need time to explore and will enjoy making simple structures, either by themselves or with a little support. Adults need to be careful not to intervene too quickly, as children will want to learn by trial and error.
3–4 years	Tape recorders, picture books, role-play, dressing-up clothes, floor puzzles, construction bricks and toys, interlinking train sets, objects to sort, magnifying glasses.	Children's language should be increasingly fluent and recognisable. Adults need to model vocabulary in context, so that children can eventually add it to their repertoire of words and expressions. Adults should also share stories with individual children and small groups. Opportunities to make marks and 'pretend' writing should be built into play sessions. Adults should seek out interesting objects for children to touch and feel, so that they can explore the properties of materials.
4–5 years	Memory games, activities where children can set their own challenges, large range of books and stories, feely bags, junk modelling, board games that encourage counting and symbol recognition.	Adults need to look for ways of developing children's vocabulary so that they can express their ideas and feelings. Adults should provide games and activities that encourage children to do some simple problem solving. Adults must be aware that very directed activities will not give children scope to explore their own ideas.

Equipment and materials that promote children's social and emotional development

Age	Examples of equipment and materials	The role of adults
1–2 years	Toys that are familiar to children. Rockers, see-saws and swings, which give children a physical sense of being rocked.	Adults need to recognise a child's need for routine and security. A child will need to form a strong relationship to one or more members of staff. Children should also be allowed free access to comforters, as this helps them to feel secure.
2–3 years	Cuddly toys, pushchairs, tea sets and other props for role-play, so that children can act out their feelings.	Children can get very frustrated; this may show itself as tantrums or tears. Adults need to look for ways of giving children choices and opportunities to be independent. Adults will need to be patient, and think ahead to prevent situations from arising in which the child becomes upset.
3–4 years	Dressing-up clothes and small-world toys, such as farm sets and play people. Materials such as sand, water, dough and paint.	Adults should continue to look for ways of helping children to feel independent. This may mean encouraging children to, for example, tidy up, pour out drinks or prepare snacks. Malleable materials can help children to play out their feelings. Adults should also model descriptive words for feelings, for example, 'upset', 'angry', 'jealous', so that children can learn gradually to talk about how they feel.
4–5 years	Stories and books to help children talk about how they are feeling; dressing-up clothes and props; simple games and activities in which children can play together, for example, cooking, playing cards.	Adults need to encourage children to understand their feelings and learn how to describe and manage them. Friendships between children are beginning to emerge. Adults can help children to play together by creating situations that foster teamwork.

APPLYING THEORY TO YOUR PRACTICE

Children of a similar age can have different play preferences. It is important to observe children to find out what they most enjoy doing.

During the course of a session, observe three children in your setting who are of a similar age. For each child, note down what is played with and for how long.

1 What individual play preferences did you observe?

2 Are there any activities that all the children are drawn to?

3 Why is it important to provide a wide range of play opportunities?

Strategies for managing behaviour

A good starting point when thinking about how to promote behaviour is to remember why it is useful. Social behaviours are like codes or passwords. Behaviour that is very different from that expected by others can result in a person becoming marginalised or isolated.

Children need to learn the different codes that are used in a variety of situations; for example, the code for behaving at home is different to that for a library. In order for a child to be accepted by other children and adults, he or she will need to learn the 'unwritten' codes of behaviour.

Understanding different perspectives

The term 'managing behaviour' is often used in early years settings, although you should be aware that the focus currently lies with promoting children's positive behaviour rather than only noticing and reacting to unwanted behaviours. This shift in emphasis is quite important. The phrase 'managing behaviour' might give the impression that adults are simply controlling children. However, promoting positive behaviour is about finding ways to help children take responsibility and show appropriate behaviour. Promoting positive behaviour means that adults in settings are pro-active, looking ahead in order to prevent confrontation.

Providing a positive environment

Children are more likely to show appropriate behaviour when their needs are met. Tantrums and aggressive behaviour are often linked to a child's stage of development or an underlying need that has not been recognised. Adults therefore need to think carefully about whether the setting's activities, layout and routine meet the needs of the individual child.

GOOD PRACTICE

Providing a positive environment

- Are activities provided that meet the individual child's developmental needs?
- Are activities built upon children's interests?
- Are activities sufficiently stimulating and challenging?
- Does the child have a good relationship with the key worker?
- Are children encouraged to make choices?

Expectations

One of the ways in which we can help children to understand what is 'wanted' behaviour is to give clear messages about what is expected of them. This is best done at the start of sessions and activities rather than afterwards. Expectations should be positive rather than negative, for example, 'we will need to walk' rather than 'don't run'.

Checking that expectations are fair

While helping children to be aware of expectations is a very effective strategy, it works only if the expectations are fair and reasonable. This means that the age and more particularly the stage of development of the individual child should be taken into account. For example, a child who is developmentally working at around two years of age is likely to find co-operating with other children quite difficult; the child may therefore not cope in situations in which turn-taking is expected.

Concentration and attention

It is important that we have fair expectations of a child's ability to listen, concentrate and sit still. The key to this lies in understanding that young children find it hard to process information when they are not being active. Listening is quite hard for young children as their ability to process the spoken word is still developing. This means that story time can be difficult for many children unless it is quite short or they can join in. Fidgeting and moving around is the child's way of coping with a lack of sensory stimulus.

GOOD PRACTICE

Concentration and attention

- Make sure that 'waiting times' are kept to an absolute minimum.
- Organise story times according to the children's language levels so that children whose language skills are still developing do not become frustrated.
- Look for ways of providing sensory activities, since these will 'hold' a child's attention.

Ways of helping children to understand expectations

The way in which we help children to understand our expectations is important. Again, we need to be aware of the stage of development of the child. Long explanations may be too difficult for very young children, so communication will need to be brief and to the point. An effective way of helping children to understand what is expected of them is to demonstrate what is required, for example, by pointing out another child who is waiting for his or her turn, or by indicating where toys are put away after play.

GOOD PRACTICE

Communicating expectations

- Tell children what they need to do.
- Use visual methods, for example, to show the child what he or she needs to do.
- Be concise in your language.

Adult: Of course, you can get out the jigsaw puzzle. Remember to put it back in its place though when you have finished. Can you show me where it goes?

Child: It goes there. (child points)

Adult: That's right. We put the jigsaw back just there. (adult taps the shelf) That means that we can find it quickly if we need it out again.

Reminding children of expectations

While adults are often good at transferring and using information from one situation to another, young children may find this difficult. A child may know that he or she must wait his or her turn before going on a slide, but may push past another child to get to a tricycle. Thus, some children will need gentle reminders or prompts. For the adult, this means thinking ahead and predicting possible difficulties that children may encounter.

CASE STUDY

Sunita is about to get the box of bricks out for play. The pre-school are keen for children to make their own choices while playing, so most of the items are accessible to the children. The play leader comes along and gently reminds Sunita that she will need to return the bricks when she has finished playing with them. She offers to help Sunita to do this, if Sunita wants her to.

1 Why is it a good idea to tell children about your expectations at the start of an activity?

2 Explain the advantages of the supervisor offering to help Sunita tidy away.

3 Why is it important that children learn to tidy away?

Using humour and non-confrontational strategies

Children respond well to a positive atmosphere. Using a sense of humour can therefore be an invaluable strategy. It avoids possible confrontation and helps children to change direction without them hearing any negative messages. Puppets and cuddly toys can also be used to help children show wanted behaviour. For example, children can show a teddy how to tidy up, take turns or ask politely for something.

CASE STUDY

Mark is three years old. He has just tipped a box of toys onto the floor. Jamila smiles and says to Mark, 'I think that you are playing tricks on me. See if you can surprise me by popping them back into the box when my back is turned.'

1 Consider how typical Mark's behaviour is for his age.

2 Explain why this approach might help Mark to tidy up.

3 Why is it important to avoid children frequently hearing negative messages about their behaviour?

Understanding the importance of role models

We have seen that social learning theory (see pages 43–4) draws attention to how children learn from watching and copying the behaviour of others. Adults will therefore need to show the behaviour that they wish children to imitate. This means, for example, asking children if you can join in their play so that they learn how to do this for themselves.

Did these boys learn this caring behaviour from watching adults?

GOOD PRACTICE

Being a good role model

▶ Make sure that you listen to children – this will encourage them to listen to others.

▶ Show children how to take turns.

▶ Make sure that your tone of voice and overall actions are gentle rather than aggressive.

Providing feedback

It is helpful for children to be given feedback about their behaviour. Feedback may mean praising or acknowledging a behaviour that a child has shown. For the child to be able to repeat the wanted

A QUICK THINK!

What behaviours must adults model to children?

behaviour, he or she will need to know what it is that he or she has done. This means using phrases such as, 'You waited for your turn. That's fantastic, because it meant that Jade didn't get hurt.' These acknowledgements are more effective than comments such as 'good girl' or 'good boy', which do not teach the child about their behaviour.

Children should also be given feedback about behaviour that is not appropriate. Feedback works best when it is immediate. A simple 'look' can be enough for some children to desist from some activities, followed by a smile and recognition when the child shows more appropriate behaviour. In other instances, an adult will need to talk to a child. It is best if children are given clear messages about what they should be doing, as there is always a danger that children will learn that adult attention can be gained by displaying inappropriate behaviours.

GOOD PRACTICE

Providing feedback

- Make sure that children understand which element of their behaviour is not appropriate.
- Focus on giving information to children about what they should be doing instead.
- Avoid lengthy explanations in situations where you suspect that children are attention seeking.
- Praise and encourage children as they begin to show more appropriate behaviour.

Working with other professionals

A range of other professionals can be involved with early years settings. In some cases, their role is to support children either by giving information to the setting or by directly working with the child. It is important to remember here that parents should give consent before other professionals are contacted. When other professionals are involved in supporting the child and/or family, it is useful to make sure that you understand the scope and nature of their role. It is also helpful to find out how you can support each other.

TEST YOUR KNOWLEDGE

1 What is the difference between classical conditioning and operant conditioning?
2 Name the three stages of separation anxiety.
3 What is the difference between expressive and receptive language?
4 Name one type of observation method that will provide open data.
5 Explain the importance of observing children's development.
6 Explain one theory of how children acquire language.
7 Consider ways in which a practitioner can develop children's language skills.
8 Describe factors that might have an effect on a child's development.
9 Analyse the limitations of using milestones to assess children's development.
10 Evaluate how the social constructivist theories have affected practice in pre-schools.

PRACTICE ASSIGNMENT TASK

Choose one of the following areas of development:

◗ physical
◗ cognitive
◗ language
◗ emotional
◗ social.

Produce a guide for volunteers in pre-schools, which contains the following information about this area of development:

◗ expected states of development in this area for children aged 3–5 years
◗ the role of the adult in promoting this area of development
◗ ideas for observing and assessing this area of development.

Further reading and references

Bee, H. (1999) *The Developing Child*, London: Longman

Bentzen, W. (2000) *Seeing Young Children: A Guide to Observing and Assessing Behaviour*, New York: Delmar publishers

Lee, V. & Das Gupta, P. (1995) *Children's Cognitive and Language Development*, Oxford: Blackwell

Lindon, J. (2003) *What does it Mean to be Three? A Practical Guide to Child Development in the Foundation Stage*, Leamington Spa: Step Forward Publishing

Meggitt, C. & Sunderland, G. (2000) *Child Development: An Illustrated Guide*, Oxford: Heinemann

Rich, D. (2002) *More than Words: Children Developing Communication, Language and Literacy*, London: British Association for Early Childhood Education

CORE UNIT 2

Early Learning

Children's learning and development is closely linked to the support and stimulation they receive from adults. This is clearly recognised by the National Standards. Thus, as a professional working with children, you will need to plan effectively. To do this means understanding the curriculum models that are currently in use. It also means knowing about ways of monitoring children's progress.

This unit is divided into three sections:

▶ Planning an appropriate curriculum for children aged 1 to 5 years

▶ Providing an early years curriculum that enables children in the Foundation Stage to achieve the Early Learning Goals

▶ Recording and reporting children's progress

Planning an appropriate curriculum for children aged 1 to 5 years

Why is planning important?

Before you begin to work with children, it is important to understand why planning is so important.

Firstly, there is a link between planning and children's development. Children thrive when they feel secure and when they are provided with stimulation. In childcare settings, this combination of emotional security and stimulation does not simply 'happen'. Staff need to think ahead about the ways in which they can create this environment. It means actively planning a good **routine** and layout as well as activities, equipment and toys that will encourage children to play and explore.

Planning is also needed to help staff teams work together effectively to meet children's needs and interests. A good system of planning should create some focus for how staff time is spent so that each member of staff understands his or her role. This role may be working with individual children or being responsible for particular activities.

What is meant by the term 'curriculum'?

The term '**curriculum**' is used when a series of learning intentions or activities are set out. As well as the term curriculum, you may also come across the term 'framework', which has a similar meaning. The idea behind having a curriculum for young children is that practitioners and parents know which skills, attitudes and knowledge are being promoted.

Models for planning the curriculum

A single curriculum for young children does not exist. This is because of the different views as to how children best learn and how to plan for their learning. It is also worth noting that even settings that are following the same curriculum model may work with children in entirely different ways. For example, one pre-school may encourage children to play outdoors, while another may not have a garden and may therefore work with children mostly indoors.

Differences between curriculum models

There have been many different views on how to promote young children's learning. Most curriculum models today emphasise the need for children to learn through play, but this has not always been the case. A further key factor that distinguishes between different curriculum models is the role of the adult. In some curricula, the adult is very directive and leads the child's learning, while in other models the role of the adult is to follow the child's learning and provide support.

A further difference between curricula is the balance between knowledge and skills. Today, most curricula focus heavily on the acquisition of skills, especially cognitive skills, rather than knowledge. Thus, an activity might be planned, for example, to encourage children to talk rather than to learn specific words.

Using different curriculum models in the pre-school setting

Whilst the basis of our work in the pre-school will take its direction from the Foundation Stage, it is useful to learn about different approaches to delivering the curriculum. One of the best ways to do this is to visit other pre-schools and nurseries. This is easier now than before because many pre-school staff meet at training days and at meetings organised by their local early years service. You might also be able to ask your early years advisory service for contacts and advice as to which settings might be of interest. To make the best of a visit, it is worth reflecting afterwards on key features of the approach and to consider ways in which they might work in your setting. Learning about different practices in this way can help to enrich the opportunities that your pre-school offers.

You could ask the following questions:

▶ How are staff deployed in the setting?
▶ What are the key features of the routine of the setting?
▶ What is the balance between adult- and child-directed activities?
▶ How is the setting laid out?
▶ How do staff encourage children to play and learn?
▶ What is the planning system?
▶ How do staff keep records of the children's progress?

Birth to Three Matters

'Birth to Three Matters' is a curriculum produced by the DfES and Sure Start to help practitioners plan for and focus on the needs of children under three years old. This framework has been well received because many practitioners found it hard to know how best to plan for very young children. It is a good idea to familiarise yourself with this document, especially if you work with this age range. Copies are free from DFES Publications Order Line: 0845 60 222 60.

© Crown Copyright

The framework takes as its focus **the child** and steers away from subjects. It identifies four aspects:

▶ a strong child
▶ a skilful communicator
▶ a competent learner
▶ a healthy child.

Suggested skills and activities are divided into four components, as shown in the table below.

Aspects	Components			
A strong child	Me, Myself and I	Being acknowledged	Developing self-assurance	A sense of belonging
A skilful communicator	Being together	Finding a voice	Listening and responding	Making meaning
A competent learner	Making connections	Being imaginative	Being creative	Representing
A healthy child	Emotional well-being	Growing and developing	Keeping safe	Healthy choices

© Crown Copyright

Montessori

Montessori is an approach to early children's learning that was pioneered by Maria Montessori in the late nineteenth century. The Montessori approach is a structured educational programme that is tailored to suit the child's individual needs. Montessori schools have differentiated equipment to help build children's skills. They also place great emphasis on the child learning by being given the opportunity to learn at the right time. Play without structure was seen by Montessori as a wasted opportunity.

Highscope

Highscope is a curriculum model that aims to give children significant responsibility for their own learning. Highscope originated in the United States, and was initially designed to help children who live in traditionally disadvantaged areas.

Individual learning plans

An **individual learning plan** is a way of tailoring the curriculum to meet a child's specific needs. As with other areas of planning, there is not a standard format for an individual learning plan and many settings use different terms to describe this type of planning. The key is to remember that within any large group of children, there will be a range of needs, strengths and interests.

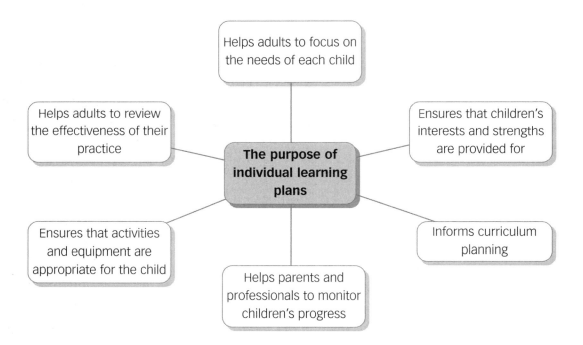

Individual learning plans are required to ensure that each child's learning is catered for. In settings that take babies and toddlers, an individual learning plan may be drawn up for each child. Some settings call these 'play plans'. This is because the focus is to ensure that each child has access to the play and equipment that is necessary to his or her stage of development. For example, a baby who is not mobile will have slightly different play needs from a child who is walking.

Individual learning plans are also used to help staff work with children who have specific needs in one or more developmental areas. These plans will focus on the child's developmental needs and consider strategies and activities to promote his or her development. For example, an individual learning plan may be created in order to help a child learn English when the child has a different home language. Without an individual learning plan, adults working in the setting may be unclear as to the best way in which to work with the child; the child may therefore not get as much out of the activity. In the same way, individual learning plans are used to help children with special educational needs; these plans are now referred to as Individual Education Plans or IEPs (see page 213).

Some settings automatically write individual learning plans for all their children, regardless of any specific difficulty or support needs that each child has. This approach may seem daunting, but is actually very effective when combined with record-keeping and providing feedback to parents. The idea is that each child's progress is noted down and, at the same time, working goals, often linked to the curriculum, are recorded. This provides a focus for staff when they work with each child and allows the child's progress to be recorded in detail.

How to create and use individual learning plans

The starting point for any learning plan is to consider the developmental needs and interests of the child. Children learn best when their play, activities and types of adult interactions are linked to their stage of development. This means beginning by observing closely the child and talking to his or her parents. Individual learning plans that are drawn up specifically to help a child in one particular area of development, such as language, usually have goals or targets attached to them. The idea of having such targets is to provide a tight focus for the adults.

There are many different formats for individual learning plans, although the best ones have a well-defined structure and provide the adults in the setting with clear guidance as to what they need to do. The best person to create an individual learning plan is the person with whom the child has the most contact and who has also observed the child. From this person's knowledge of the child, he or she should be able to consider what the child enjoys doing and the best type of learning situations for the child.

Individual Learning Plan

Name of child: Anne M.   Child's age 3:6

Key worker: Jane

Date of Plan: 14/4/03   Date of review:

Target	Strategies to be used	Date	Comments
Personal Social and Emotional To take part in self-chosen activities To select resources independently	Show Anne the range of play options Encourage Anne to talk through what equipment and resources she will need		
Communication, Language and literacy To join in rhymes To recall simple stories	Read rhymes and stories to Anne individually Encourage Anne to hold and use props Encourage Anne to point to pictures and to tell the story		

A sample format for an Individual Learning Plan

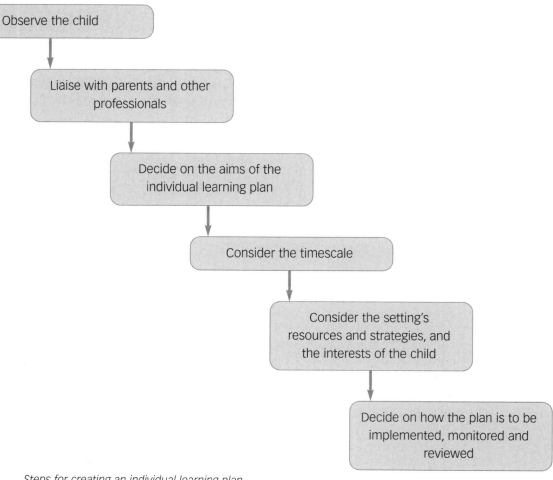

Observe the child

↓

Liaise with parents and other professionals

↓

Decide on the aims of the individual learning plan

↓

Consider the timescale

↓

Consider the setting's resources and strategies, and the interests of the child

↓

Decide on how the plan is to be implemented, monitored and reviewed

Steps for creating an individual learning plan

▶ **Observe the child**

The starting point when drawing up an individual learning plan has to be observing the child. You will need to think carefully about each child's needs and interests. Ideally, this should be done as part of your recording system. In order to get a feel for the child's progress, you should refer to normative development charts (see Core Unit 1).

Parents are a good source of information about a child's skills, strengths and interests

▶ Liaise with parents and other professionals

It is always good practice to involve parents when drawing up individual learning plans. In terms of a child who may have special needs, this is a requirement of the SEN Code of Practice 2001. Parents should be able to provide you with their perspective on their child, which includes information about his or her skills, strengths and interests at home. An exchange of ideas and information is needed in order to set realistic and useful targets.

In addition to working with parents, it is important to involve colleagues and sometimes professionals working outside of your setting. For example, a speech and language therapist may already be working with a child, and the details of this work might be incorporated into an individual learning plan. The idea behind involving parents and other professionals is to provide the setting with as much information as possible about the child's needs.

▶ Decide on the aims of the individual learning plan

The aim of the individual learning plan gives the plan its focus. Many individual learning plans contain targets, and these should ideally be limited to three or four. For the plan to succeed, it is important that targets are chosen carefully. The latest approach is to choose targets that are realistic and, if necessary, quite small; for example, to point to and name three parts of the body. This means that when the plan is reviewed, new targets can be set.

It is good practice to agree with parents on the type of targets to be set. It is worth remembering that parents can have very different feelings about what is important for their child to achieve. For example, a parent of a two-year-old may be focusing on toilet training, while the practitioner's focus may be on language.

▶ Consider the timescale

Once the targets have been set, it is worth considering the timescale. It is important that the timescale is not too long, as there is a danger that those involved in implementing the plan will lose their focus. Timescales ranging from one month to six weeks are therefore quite popular.

▶ Resources, strategies and interests

The next step is to consider how the targets are to be achieved. Practitioners should think about the role of the adult as well as specific activities that might appeal to the child. For example, a child who has not been interested in coming to listen to stories may have a favourite book at home or enjoy sitting close to an adult at story time.

▶ Implementing, monitoring and reviewing the plan

Ultimately, a plan is simply a piece of paper; it is the practitioners who will make the paper come to life. Thus, decisions should be taken while drawing up the plan as to who will be responsible for implementing it. It is also important that times are set as to when the plan will be monitored and, if necessary, amended.

Finally, to complete the process, the plan should be reviewed. If all has gone to plan, the targets will have been met and some new targets for focusing on can be drawn up.

CASE STUDY

Dina is four years old and has just moved to the area. She is new to the setting and she is settled in the company of her key worker. However, she is not yet joining in with the other children.

1 Why might it be important to draw up an individual learning plan for this child?

2 What information might Dina's parents be able to provide?

3 Why is it important that the plan is based on Dina's interests?

Creating curriculum plans

Curriculum plans are documents that outline the learning that will take place and its expected timescale. It should link to the curriculum document you are working with. It is worth noting that there are not only different approaches to curriculum planning in the early years sector, but also a range of formats. It is important to understand your pre-school plans, its format and the length of time that they plan for.

The process of planning

Most settings begin by producing an overview of their work. This is usually referred to as a long-term plan. The long-term plan shows how each part of the curriculum is to be delivered over a period of time – normally a minimum of six weeks and a maximum of a year. Many settings will also indicate the themes, events and visits that they will be using as a focus for their work with children. Using the long-term plan as a guide, more detailed plans need to be drawn up which will include: actual ideas for activities, resources and the ways in which individual children's needs will be met. To achieve this, settings may be divided into medium- and short-term planning.

Medium-term plans, whilst not used by all pre-school settings, can provide a bridge between broad long-term plans and short-term plans. They build on the long-term plan as they describe in detail the ways in which any theme, visit or event will be planned for within the setting. Quite often these will be presented in a spider diagram format to show how the areas of the curriculum are to be covered. The length of these curriculum plans can vary, but many settings expect their medium-term plans to cover a month or half-term.

Short-term plans are essential tools in the day-to-day running of pre-schools and implementation of the curriculum. They are usually drawn up on a session or weekly basis. They should show how the children's individual needs are to be met, as well as the focus of the activities and play opportunities. Most settings also find it helpful to identify the adults who will take responsibility for implementing the activity.

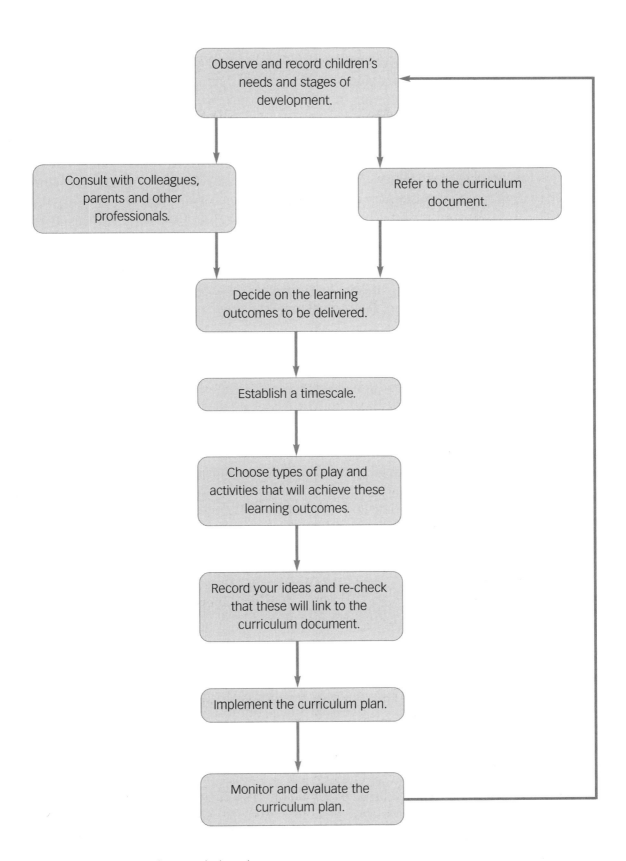

The steps to creating a curriculum plan

Important steps in planning

Creating a curriculum plan is a process that is best done with other colleagues: they may have information about particular children or specific ideas they would like to incorporate. It is also good practice to involve parents and to think carefully about the interests of each child.

Observe and record children's needs

Children should be at the heart of any curriculum plan. This means that you will need to find out as much as possible about children's needs and interests. Parents and colleagues will play an important role in this respect. As part of this process, you should also refer to children's individual learning plans (or individual education plans for those children with identified special needs). If you are inexperienced, it is worth looking at charts of normative development to give you an indication of the skills that children are developing. This is important because children learn best when activities are planned that are interesting and meet their developmental needs.

Consult with colleagues and parents

Parents and colleagues will provide you not only with information about children, but also with ideas and thoughts based upon their own experiences. The best curriculum plans are often put together by whole staff teams. This has huge advantages, as particular members of staff may have suggestions for certain areas of learning or development.

Refer to the curriculum guidance

This next step is crucial, even when you are familiar with the curriculum. Referring to the curriculum guidance ensures that you stay 'on track' and do not overlook any particular learning outcomes. The curriculum guidance for the Foundation Stage and Birth to Three Matters contains ideas for practitioners and is worth looking at.

Decide on the learning outcomes to be delivered

Once you have looked at the curriculum guidance, you will begin to get a feel for the learning outcomes to be planned. You should at this point also look back at previous curriculum plans, to see what has already been covered. It is worth considering how effective previous curriculum plans have been; it may be that some of the learning outcomes need to be repeated or reinforced.

Establish a timescale

You will need to consider the period that your curriculum plan will cover. This is likely to depend on your session times and the way in which the setting works. For example, schools often have curriculum plans that last a term or half-term, while some day nurseries produce monthly plans. Once you have a timescale in mind, you will be able to decide more easily how much of the curriculum's learning intentions will be covered.

Choose types of play and activities that will achieve these learning outcomes

The next step is to think about the activities that will enable children to access the learning outcomes. Choosing the right activities is essential. Curriculum plans can be successful only if the ideas for the activities are interesting and

Area of learning	Activity
Personal, social and emotional development	▶ *Activity plan: Teddy's seaside holiday.* ▶ Using shells to decorate an area of the garden or a plant tub. ▶ Making a frame with shells for a special photograph. ▶ In pairs, look at these shells – do you have the same favourites?

Communication, language and literacy	▶ *Activity plan: Mark making in the sand with shells.*
	▶ Stories:
	   ▶ *The Hare and the Tortoise*
	   ▶ *Meg at Sea*
	   ▶ *Smelly Jelly, Smelly Fish*
	   ▶ *Snail Trail*
	   ▶ *Turtle Bay*
	   ▶ *Who are You in the Sea?*
	▶ Nursery rhyme: 'Mary, Mary, quite contrary, how does your garden grow?'
	▶ Role-play area: Souvenir and gift shop.
	▶ Hard and soft – feely bag game.
	▶ I am describing a shell – can you work out which one?
	▶ Kim's game: Which shell is missing?

Mathematical development	▶ *Activity plan: How much water does this shell hold?* ▶ Count shells. ▶ How many shells will fit into this little box? ▶ How many shells in the feely bag – one, two, three or more? ▶ Sort shells into sizes. ▶ Which is the best size of box for this shell?
Knowledge and understanding of the world	▶ *Activity plan: Pebbles and shells.* ▶ Shells in the water tray – can you make any shells float? ▶ Look at these shells with the magnifying glass – can you see the ridges on the shells? ▶ Can you use the remote-controlled car to go in and out of an obstacle course with shells? ▶ Let's look outside – can we see any snails? – Snails have shells. ▶ Look at this snail on the window outside – can you see how it moves?
Physical development	▶ *Activity plan: Follow the line with the shell.* ▶ Can you find the shell hidden in the sand tray? ▶ Parachute games – cockles, whelks and mussels. ▶ Shell prints in the dough. ▶ Shell and spoon obstacle races. ▶ Which of these shells can you make roll? ▶ Hunt the shells that are hidden outside. ▶ Scoop water with flat shells.
Creative development	▶ *Activity plan: Can you make a box for teddy's favourite shell?* ▶ Dancing and making spirals and twists like the conch shells. ▶ Making shell shakers. ▶ Make shell people – stick faces onto shells. ▶ Collages with various materials including shells. ▶ Observational drawing and painting of shells.

An example of a medium-term plan

rewarding for children. Try hard to think about how children play and what excites their curiosity. Look for sensory activities and play experiences that allow children to be active, rather than activities that are very adult-directed and structured. You should also think about how the activities can be extended or simplified to meet individual children's needs.

Record your ideas and re-check that these will link to the curriculum document

The look of curriculum plans can vary from setting to setting. Many pre-schools find it helpful to organise their curriculum plans for children aged three and above according to Areas of Learning in the Foundation Stage. Whatever format you choose, it should be easy to read and understand. You should also show how the activities link to the curriculum guidance. Doing this means that you can double-check that you are covering the learning outcomes and that you have evidence of doing so.

Monitoring the plan

As well as implementing the curriculum plan, it is vital that the plan is monitored. It is important here to emphasise that it is good practice for plans to be changed if needed. Young children's interests do change, and while we may try to plan for their needs, we should realise when an alternative approach is required. In the same way, we may find that an activity that we have planned is a huge success and begins to develop a life of its own. The key here is to remember that the curriculum plan is a tool, not a promise! If children are enjoying learning by a different means to that planned, all is not lost. We simply need to record the changes as they happen. This may require attaching a separate sheet of paper to the curriculum plan, which allows any changes to be noted along with the reasons for them.

Using themes

Some pre-school settings use themes as a basis for their curriculum plans. This can be helpful as it acts as a focus for ideas. If you decide to use a theme, it is a good idea to consider whether it will really appeal to and have meaning for the children. Very young children are far more interested in the quality of the emotional environment and their play than in an abstract theme. Thus, many early years experts believe that themes are irrelevant when working with two-year-olds. For slightly older children, however, themes can be one way of providing interlinked play experiences.

Interesting colours, shapes and textures can be introduced under a 'shell' theme

Activity	Activity focus	Organisation	Resources	Notes – Individual children	Evaluation/comments
Gift shop – role play	Role play and fine manipulative skills	Mary – facilitator	Wrapping paper, sticky tape, scissors		Mark stayed for 20 minutes! Add in tissue paper tomorrow
Box for Teddy's shell	Problem solving – which box will fit best?	Robin + small groups	Teddy, boxes, scissors, glue, paper and collage	Left-hand scissors for Aiden Encourage Anna to chat	Anna enjoyed about beaches More small boxes needed
Shells in sand tray	Exploring textures and printing	Mary – facilitator Role model printing and pouring	Different sizes of shells, containers, wet sand and dry sand	David may want to wear gloves	Kylie enjoyed printing and noticed that dry sand did not show sand prints
Kim's game	Memory Playing alongside others	Helen – small groups Change to number of objects to extend	Tray, tea towel, shells, bucket and spade, other objects		Children took turns taking objects off the tray. Ahmed could point to and count the objects (8)
Shells in the garden	Visual discrimination, counting shells	Jennie – small groups Hide shells outdoors. Put some shells in groups of four	Magnifiers, boxes to collect shells	Encourage Rachel to join in with other children	A huge success. Children enjoyed hiding them back again for other children. James noticed he could spot those in groups of four

Example of a short-term plan for a session

It is therefore important to make sure that the theme has meaning for the children; some of the best themes are based on experiences and objects that are familiar to them. You should also be aware that it is not necessary for every activity within the setting to fit in with the theme: children need a variety of experiences and will have definite preferences. If a theme is used, it is best to begin by referring to the curriculum document to ensure that particular learning outcomes are not missed.

Ensuring that curriculum plans are not discriminatory

It is easy to forget that children do not just learn those things that we intend them to learn. They can learn other things as well, including underlying attitudes. The term 'hidden curriculum' has been used to describe the unintended learning that often occurs. We should therefore step back and think about the messages children might learn from the activities that we devise for them. A setting that emphasises only Christian festivals, such as Easter and Christmas, may send out the message that the festivals and traditions of different faiths are not important. In the same way, settings that have a competitive atmosphere may teach some children that they are not as highly valued as others are.

In addition to thinking about the hidden messages that might be gleaned from children's activities, it is important to consider whether all the activities are accessible. This means checking that all children can both physically take part, and benefit and learn from the activity. For example, a cake-making activity might discriminate against a child with diabetes; in order to make it accessible for that child, the recipe might need to be adapted or changed.

KEY POINTS   **Preventing discrimination**

> Have activities been chosen that build on children's interests?
> Do activities reflect and build upon children's home experiences?
> Can activities be adapted, extended or simplified to allow all children to participate?

THINKING AND RESEARCH

Compare two curriculum plans from different pre-schools.

> Is each pre-school using the same format?
> Are curriculum plans organised around areas of learning?
> Are activities linked around a theme?
> What are the advantages of the format that is used?
> Are there any disadvantages?

Working in partnership with parents

Today, it is recognised that parents play an essential role in both the care and education of their children. A key message to all practitioners is therefore: learning does not stop at the doorstep of the setting! Thus, curriculum plans should be shared with parents, and practitioners should look for ways of involving parents in curriculum planning. Parents can offer ideas and resources; by sharing our knowledge of the curriculum with them, they will be able to contribute.

Some settings include on their curriculum plans suggestions for parental involvement. This approach needs to be handled carefully because not all parents will have the time or the inclination to follow the suggestions. We should also be aware that parents may have varying access to transport and resources; thus, any suggestions for parental involvement should (ideally) be reasonably straightforward. We may also choose activities that can be continued at home if the child is interested. For example, dough that a child has made in the setting can go home with the child, while a book that a child has enjoyed might be lent overnight.

Creating a curriculum plan

Q. Should everyone in the pre-school be involved in planning?

A. Ideally, everyone should know what is going on in order to widen the pool of ideas and experience. However, some pre-schools find it hard to get everyone together. In this case, the person who is responsible for putting the plan together should talk to staff members individually and collate suggestions. This saves time at the planning meeting.

Q. Is it acceptable to use the plans from the previous year?

A. While you might be able to adapt a plan or use it as a reminder, it is unlikely that you can simply use a previous year's plans. This is because children's interests and needs change. It is also important for staff to feel 'fresh' about what they are doing; simply repeating a plan is not likely to be a great motivator.

Q. How can we incorporate children's individual needs into the curriculum plan?

A. You should begin by choosing activities and ideas that build on children's needs, strengths and interests. You can also use codes to identify those children who will particularly benefit. It is worth using activity sheets, however, which describe in detail how to adapt and extend activities or strategies when working with individual children.

Providing an early years curriculum that enables children in the Foundation Stage to achieve the Early Learning Goals

Understanding the principles behind the Foundation Stage

It is worth understanding the background to the Foundation Stage. The Foundation Stage was introduced in September 2000 and replaced the previous early years curriculum, known as Desirable Learning Outcomes. The previous curriculum had been heavily criticised because many practitioners delivered it using very formal and inappropriate activities. The Foundation Stage curriculum differs significantly because it encourages the use of play to develop children's skills and learning. It also places significant emphasis on the importance of identifying children's needs and planning appropriately, and on working in partnership with parents. The aim of the Foundation Stage is to provide all children from the age of three years with a range of experiences that will help them to develop the skills and attitudes they need for later learning.

POINT OF INTEREST ★

Links to National Standards

Standard 3 of the National Standards is about care, learning and play. Inspectors will be wanting to see that children are making progress towards the Early Learning Goals.

Structure of the curriculum guidance

A major resource in delivering the Foundation Stage is the curriculum guidance folder. While every early years setting should have at least one folder, you should consider having your own copy. These are available free of charge from the DfES (see the number at the end of the chapter). The folder is divided into the following sections:

The Foundation Stage

This section looks at the aims for the Foundation Stage and the importance of working with parents.

Principles for early years education

This section looks at the overarching principles upon which the Foundation Stage is based. It also considers the importance of including and making the Foundation Stage accessible to all children. The last pages in this section look at teaching and learning, and the importance of play.

Areas of learning and Early Learning Goals

This is the largest section within the folder in which six **areas of learning** outlined. Each area of learning is designed to develop particular skills or attitudes. It is worth noting that personal, social and emotional development comes first. This is no coincidence: it is thought that this area of learning underpins a child's development. The six areas of learning are:

▶ Personal, social and emotional development
▶ Communication, language and literacy
▶ Mathematical development
▶ Knowledge and understanding of the world
▶ Physical development
▶ Creative development.

Early Learning Goals and Stepping Stones

Each area of learning includes targets for children to reach, which are referred to as '**Early Learning Goals**'. These have been written with the end of the Foundation Stage in mind, by which time most children are five years old and finishing their first year at school. Most early years practitioners are comfortable with the level of these goals, but it must be stressed that they have not been written for the under three's.

To help practitioners identify the best way to reach these goals with the children in their setting, a series of steps are given, known as '**Stepping Stones**'. These break down the skills that children will need to develop in order to achieve the eventual goals. Thus, the experiences and activities of most children in pre-school settings will have been planned according to the Stepping Stone that best

These are the steps that children need to pass on the way to the Early Learning Goal.

This section is designed to help you think about children's stages of development. You may see children in your group playing in the same kind of ways.

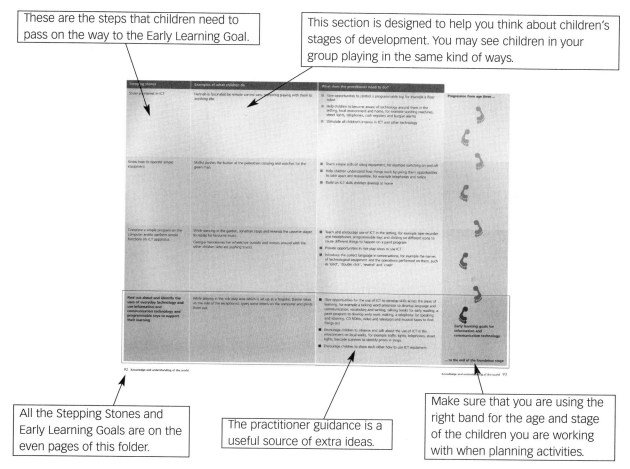

All the Stepping Stones and Early Learning Goals are on the even pages of this folder.

The practitioner guidance is a useful source of extra ideas.

Make sure that you are using the right band for the age and stage of the children you are working with when planning activities.

Left-hand page – This shows the Stepping Stones and Early Learning Goals together with accompanying examples of what children in each stage might do.

Right-hand page – This gives some examples of how practitioners might work with and support children.

Arrows – Stepping Stones – These show the underlying skills that are necessary for children to acquire and practise

matches their development. As a practitioner, it is therefore important to refer to the Stepping Stones closely while 'having an eye' on the eventual goal.

The role of the Early Learning Goals

The Early Learning Goals play an immensely important part in the Foundation Stage. The idea is that children will all be able to start the National Curriculum in Year 1 with the skills they need already in place. The Early Learning Goals also provide a benchmark so that children who need further support can be identified easily. Reception teachers complete a profile at the end of the school year that shows how children are progressing.

How children's learning at the Foundation Stage links to their previous learning and to the National Curriculum

It is worth remembering that children's learning does not happen in a vacuum; they do not know automatically how to do something. Most children are continuously learning or practising skills that will eventually lead them to acquire new skills. This is reflected in the concept of the Stepping Stones. Ideally, you should look at each child and consider the skills and knowledge he or she has gained, then plan to build on the existing skills. The Early Learning Goals for children at the end of the reception year link closely to Year 1 of the National Curriculum. In theory, this should mean that children's transition from reception class to the more formal National Curriculum is smoother.

Area of learning	Aspects of learning	Curriculum guidance page
Personal, social and emotional development	Disposition and attitudes	32
	Self-confidence and self-esteem	34
	Making relationships	36
	Behaviour and self-control	38
	Self-care	40
	Sense of community	42
Communication, language and literacy	Language for communication	48, 50, 52, 54
	Language for thinking	56–8
	Linking sounds with letters	60
	Reading	62
	Writing	64
	Handwriting	66
Mathematical development	Numbers as labels and for counting	74
	Calculating	76
	Shape, space and measures	78–80
Knowledge and understanding of the world	Exploration and investigation	86, 88
	Designing and making skills	90
	Information and communication technology	92
	Sense of time	94
	Sense of place	96
	Cultures and beliefs	98
Physical development	Sense of space	104
	Movement	106,108
	Health and bodily awareness	110
	Using equipment	112
	Using tools and materials	114
Creative development	Exploring media and materials	120
	Music	122
	Imagination	124
	Responding to experiences, and expressing and communicating ideas	126

The areas of learning covered by the Early Learning Goals and the expectations for children's achievement in each area

There are six areas of learning within the Foundation Stage. Each area is subdivided into sections known as 'aspects of learning'. When planning, it is helpful to use these aspects of learning as a starting point; they will enable you to be sure of covering the whole curriculum.

For each aspect of learning, one or more Early Learning Goals are given. By the end of the reception year, it is likely that most children will achieve these goals. Thus, while we need to keep an eye on the eventual Early Learning Goal, daily work with pre-school children will be focused on the Stepping Stones. This approach may need to be explained to parents, who may not realise that many of the Early Learning Goals are neither relevant nor appropriate for their young child.

The range of experiences that can be provided by pre-schools to progress children towards achievement of the Early Learning Goals

Some of the best learning materials for children have a sensory component. This allows a child's brain to process information more effectively and thus concentrate more easily. Worksheets and adult-directed activities in which children are passive recipients are not a recommended mode of delivery for the Foundation Stage curriculum.

POINT OF INTEREST

Links to National Standards

Standard 3 of the National Standards states clearly that children should be engaged and active in their learning. Inspectors look for opportunities that are provided for children to explore and investigate. They also want to see that children are able to make their own choices and decisions.

Outdoor learning

A good starting point when considering the type of experiences we should provide for pre-school children is outdoor learning. Traditionally, children spent considerable time outdoors; however, because of increased levels of traffic and other dangers, children are now kept inside more frequently. This is thought to have led to reduced levels of physical activity in children, and hampered their learning about space and risk-taking. Concerns about a lack of opportunities for children's outdoor play have resulted in pre-schools being encouraged to take children outdoors during session times. Thus, activities should be planned for outdoor learning, and children should be encouraged to play and use equipment outside. Ideally, pre-school settings should allow children to move freely from indoors to outdoors rather than having pre-arranged times. However, the ability to plan for this will depend on the type of outdoor access available to your setting.

Children gain from being outdoors

Children's outdoor play may involve:

- wheeled equipment, such as tricycles, prams and trucks
- equipment to encourage climbing and balancing skills
- natural materials, such as mud, water and sand (which can be provided in small containers)
- areas for planting, digging and scooping.

Role-play

Many children learn through imaginative, or **role-play**. This form of active learning also develops children's language skills. There are many different ways of providing role-play opportunities, including the long-established home corner and dressing-up area. Traditionally, many settings have considered role-play to be an 'indoor' activity, but you should aim to provide materials that children can also use outdoors.

Children's role-play may involve:

- small-world toys, such as play people, train sets, garages and dolls' houses
- dressing-up clothes, shoes and other props
- home corners and tents
- materials, such as sheets and tablecloths, so that children can make their own dens.

Construction play

Most pre-school settings provide for construction play. This type of play allows children to solve problems, negotiate and learn practical skills. It is important that construction play is not seen simply as using commercial toys and equipment – the Foundation Stage curriculum states clearly that a range of tools should be provided for this type of play. This may mean looking carefully at the equipment available in your setting, as well as thinking about how adults will supervise the children. As with other play experiences, children should be able to engage in construction play both inside and outdoors.

Children's construction play may involve:

▶ construction toys, such as Duplo, Lego and wooden bricks
▶ cardboard boxes, including large boxes for outdoor play
▶ a selection of paper, wood and fabrics
▶ joining materials, such as masking tape, different types of glue and staplers
▶ a selection of tools, including scissors, sewing equipment, hammers and screwdrivers.

Malleable and natural materials

Sand, water, dough and other natural materials, such as mud and gravel, are long established tools for children's learning. These are particularly sensory materials, which help children to concentrate. Many settings find that children's attention span and behaviour as a group improve if there are plenty of sensory activities on offer. Thus, we should avoid situations in which only one type of material is provided. If storage is a problem, consider using containers that are smaller and easier to lift and carry, for example, several washing-up bowls of water if a separate water tray is not available. While this situation is not ideal, it will allow children to have access to some provision rather than none. In addition, small containers of sand and water can be placed outdoors overnight.

Children's construction play may involve:

Sand and water (use play sand, not builder's sand):

▶ sand and water trays
▶ buckets, washing-up bowls, plastic trays
▶ funnels, scoops, spoons, jugs, hosepipes, guttering, sieves
▶ toys, such as dinosaurs, cars, boats and tea sets.

Dough and other malleable materials:

▶ a selection of doughs, including cooked and non-cooked types
▶ items for playing with, such as scissors, cutters, tea sets, rolling-pins and forks.

Mud, gravel and other natural materials (use peat or other materials from environmentally sustainable sources):

▶ containers, such as barrels, buckets, washing-up bowls and trays
▶ implements, such as spades, trowels, wooden spoons and scoops.

Mark making area

Mark making covers everything from drawing and painting through to children's early writing. It can also include collage or 'sticking and cutting'. The idea of having a combined approach to mark making is that children can express themselves using a variety of media. Thus, some children will want to both draw and attempt writing.

It is worth noting that, in general, it is no longer considered essential to make children sit down to carry out activities. Many children prefer to stand as they write, draw and paint, because this allows them greater control over their work.

Mark making encourages vivid imaginations

In addition to tables, children will therefore need access to boards or easels that enable them to work in an upright position. It is also recommended that writing materials are made available as props in role-play areas.

Children's mark making may involve:

▶ blackboards, white boards and paper of many different sizes
▶ real-life forms, such as driving licence and passport application forms.

A QUICK THINK!
How does mark making link to children's physical skills?

Information and communication technology (ICT)

This is a new area for many pre-school settings. The idea is that children are familiarised with technology from an early age. Fortunately, for the computer-phobic, this is not necessarily about computers. The emphasis in the Foundation Stage is on the use of gadgets and programmable objects, including household ones such as microwaves. Children are encouraged to learn about safety as well as how to turn items, such as tape recorders or telephones, on and off.

Children's ICT play may involve:

▶ remote-controlled items, for example, cars and trucks
▶ tape recorders

- toys that use a microchip.
- keyboards and redundant phones for the role-play area.

Story and book area

Most settings have an area in which children can enjoy books and hear stories. Today, many story and book areas are also equipped with audio tapes. The story and book area works well when it is comfortable, quiet and relaxing. Ideally, an adult should be available to read to children, either individually or in small groups. This area may also contain story sacks, which are very popular with children as they contain a book and some key props to the story.

A story and book area may involve:

- a good range of fact and fiction books for children
- audio tapes and tape recorders
- cushions, beanbags, comfortable chairs or a sofa
- story sacks.

The importance of play in enabling children's progression and learning

Play is emphasised as a key way in which children learn. There are many reasons to support this rationale, as the diagram below shows.

There are many different views as to what constitutes 'real' play and the role of adults in children's play. With regard to the pre-school environment, it is likely that a continuum of play should be provided for. Thus, some play will be quite child-led, with children initiating play and choosing resources and equipment with minimal adult assistance and supervision. It also means that some play will be more adult-directed, with adults providing resources and offering some direction. However, it is essential to realise that activities in which children have little control or choice are generally the least effective in terms of their learning.

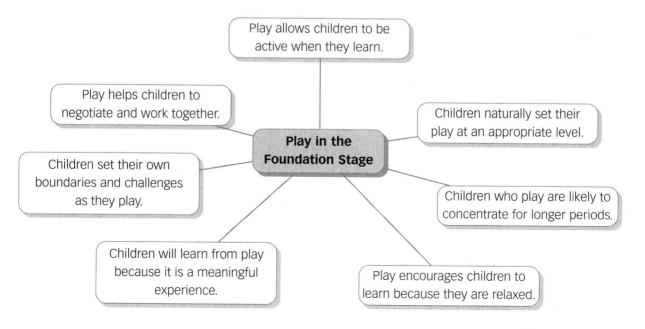

Children who are passive or unable to explore materials are likely to concentrate for shorter periods and have little memory of the activity.

THINKING AND RESEARCH

With a study partner, design a booklet to help parents understand the benefits of play. Suggest three activities the parents could do at home with their child.

How to create and implement curriculum plans that promote children's achievement of Early Learning Goals

As previously discussed, there is a large variation in the way that curriculum plans are presented. Some pre-school settings begin with a theme, while others focus on specific areas (such as those described on pages 107–118). It is also possible to construct curriculum plans that look at individual areas of learning. However, regardless of the approach, it is essential to refer throughout to the curriculum guidance. This means that you should establish a system that enables you to check that all aspects of learning (and hence Stepping Stones leading to the Early Learning Goals) are covered regularly.

Coverage of aspects of learning – adult focused activities

Area of development	5 Jan	12 Jan	19 Jan	26 Jan
Personal, social and emotional development	Pages 32, 34, 36, 38, 40, 42	Pages 32, 34, 36, 38, 40, 42	Pages 32, 34, 36, 38 40, 42	Pages 32, 34, 36, 38, 40, 42
Communication, language and literacy	Pages 48, 50, 52, 53, 56–8, 60, 62, 64, 66	Pages 48, 50, 52, 53, 56–8, 60, 62 64, 66	Pages 48, 50, 52, 53 56–8, 60, 62, 64, 66	Pages 48, 50, 52, 53, 56–8, 60, 62, 64, 66
Mathematical development	Pages 74, 76, 78–80	Pages 74, 76, 78–80	Pages 74, 76, 78–80	Pages 74, 76, 78–80
Knowledge and understanding of the world	Pages 86, 88, 90, 92, 94, 96, 98	Pages 86, 88, 90, 92, 94, 96, 98	Pages 86, 88, 90, 92, 94, 96, 98	Pages 86, 88, 90, 92, 94, 96, 98
Physical development	Pages 104, 106, 108, 110, 112, 114	Pages 104, 106, 108, 110, 112, 114	Pages 104, 106, 108, 110, 112, 114	Pages 104, 106, 108, 110,112, 114
Creative development	Pages 120, 122, 124, 126	Pages 120, 122, 124, 126	Pages 120, 122, 124, 126	Pages 120, 122, 124, 126

Instructions: Circle or highlight aspects of learning that have been covered each week via the planned adult focused activities

Example of a planning system

Ways to promote children's communication, language and literacy skills

There are six separate aspects of learning within this area of learning.

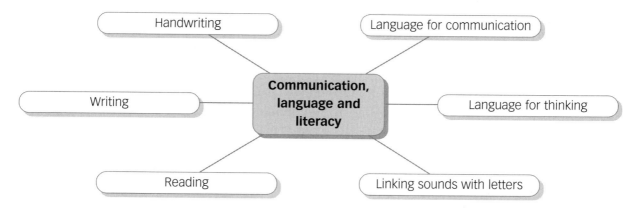

Language for communication

This aspect of learning is about helping children to develop the skills and vocabulary they need to socialise. Adults will need to model the skills of communication with children. This means actively listening to children and making sure that they get plenty of one-to-one time with a supportive adult. Experiences should be planned so that children can hear new vocabulary in context. There are various ways to plan for this aspect of learning; however, the key is to make sure that children have plenty of personal contact with a friendly and responsive adult.

Language for thinking

While many children 'chatter', they may actually find it hard to express their thoughts or understand concepts. This is because thinking is linked to language (see page 48). This aspect of learning emphasises the importance of children using language to organise their thinking and express their ideas. Activities need to be planned that will give children the vocabulary that is linked to concepts, and provide opportunities for them to explain their thoughts. For example, a child may guess what is in a box, but the next step is to ask the child what has made him or her come to this conclusion. Young children will also near to hear adults' model thinking language. This can be literally sharing your thoughts with a child, for example, 'I think that I will collect up all the buttons made from metal'.

Linking sounds with letters

In order that children can learn to read using a phonic method, they need to listen to letter sounds. In the earliest Stepping Stone, this is simply about encouraging children to discriminate between different types of sounds, for example, a shaker from a chime bar. As well as identifying differences in sounds, children also need to learn nursery rhymes. This is because rhymes help children to identify the sounds in words. Ideally, you should plan for children to learn a repertoire of traditional and modern rhymes and songs over a period of time.

Examples of rhymes that link sounds with letters include:

- Diddle diddle dumpling, my son John
- Jack and Jill went up the hill
- Five little ducks went swimming one day
- Five little peas in a pea pod pressed

Reading

It is important in pre-school settings to refer to the Stepping Stones for this aspect of learning. Young children are not expected to have reading books or to practise learning to read! Rather, this aspect of learning is about developing a desire in children for reading, and to enable them to learn about books and how to handle them. This means that story times should be pleasurable for children. Interestingly, the curriculum guidance states that, for young children, the size of the story group should be very small. You should also plan to have an adult available, with whom individual children can 'snuggle up' and share a book.

Writing

As with reading, this aspect of learning is not about children being able to compose sentences. The aim is to make sure that children enjoy the experience of making marks, and that they learn about writing. One of the best ways of encouraging children to write is to make sure they get a reply! In this way, children can begin to understand the point behind writing. They are often happy to have a go at writing, even if this means just drawing a picture and putting down some marks.

Can you see how this child is beginning to make marks similar to the letters in his name, Ted?

To help children write, you should make sure that there are plenty of examples of print for them to see. It is also important that children are able to sit near and witness adults who are writing. The starting point for most children will be putting down a mark that bears a resemblance to a letter in their name. Thus, children will benefit from playing games in which they can see their written name. In pre-school, it is important not to correct children's writing, as this usually results in children losing confidence and becoming less keen to try.

Handwriting

Handwriting is the physical skill that allows us to write using pens or other marking equipment. In the Foundation Stage curriculum, stress is laid on developing children's fine manipulative skills in preparation for their eventual writing. Thus, adults need to consider activities that will encourage children to use their hands, such as sorting and pouring activities.

Activities for communication, language and literacy:

- games that encourage children to listen out for sounds
- regular opportunities to learn new nursery rhymes and songs
- exploring sounds made by musical instruments
- role-play, with adults sometimes joining in
- sharing stories and books with small groups of children or individual children
- putting out story sacks for children to recall and enact stories
- making chalk marks and messages outdoors
- large-scale painting, to help children's manipulative skills
- writing notes and messages to Teddy.

Promoting children's numeracy and mathematical understanding

In the Foundation Stage curriculum, this area of learning is known as 'mathematical development'. It is designed to develop in children a meaningful sense of numbers, shape and measurement. The emphasis throughout the

Role-play enables children to practise their communication and language skills

Foundation Stage is making the child see that mathematics is relevant and practical. Thus, worksheets or formal methods of recording are not considered relevant to pre-school children. Rather, the idea is to emphasise the practical side of mathematics so that children gain confidence and insight into what numbers are about. Developing confidence and understanding is now considered very important; previously, many children were taught mathematics formally, which did not necessarily result in confident mathematicians. Mathematical development is further divided into three aspects of learning, as shown in the diagram below.

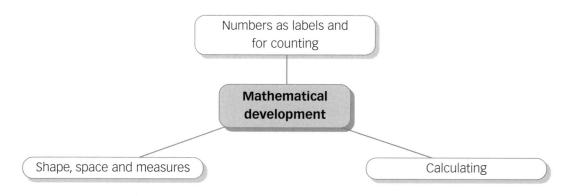

Numbers as labels and for counting

A child's first experience of mathematics often comes through hearing the 'labels'. For example, an adult may count out the number of plates needed for dinner, or may tell the child that she can have only one biscuit. This aspect of learning is designed to help children learn the 'labels' and then understand what they represent. Thus, children need to hear number rhymes and counting songs as well as hearing adults counting in context. Gradually, children will start using the 'labels' for themselves, although it is normal for pre-school children to mix them up a little. (You may hear lovely snippets of conversations in which a child reveals that he needs 'twenty hundred'.) It is therefore important for us to work with parents so they understand that, just because a child knows the 'labels', it doesn't mean that he or she is ready to do sums or other formal recording work.

> **A QUICK THINK!**
>
> *Think of three rhymes that involve counting.*
> *Why might it be helpful to include props when using counting rhymes?*

Calculating

This aspect of learning is the starting point for later formal recording. It is about helping children to see how mathematics is used for problem solving. In the earliest Stepping Stones, we need to provide plenty of fun opportunities for children to learn 'more' and 'less', for example, by comparing groups of objects. It is important that children see this in a way that is both practical and meaningful for them. For example, a child may help Teddy to decide if he has enough pots of honey for each of his five friends. Children also need to see how mathematics is used to solve problems. For example, a child may help Teddy to add together all his pots of honey that are scattered around the room.

Shape, space and measures

This aspect of learning helps children to notice shapes and use measures. In pre-school, this learning also happens practically. One of the best ways for children to gain a feeling of shape, space and measure is through constructing things or by problem solving. For example, children may wish to make a car for Teddy to sit in or a hat for him to wear. As well as making things, we can also help children learn some of the positional language they need to acquire by playing games such as 'Hunt the thimble'. The aim of this type of game is for children to learn to ask questions such as, 'Is it on top of ...?', or 'Is it beside ...?'

Activities that promote mathematical development:

- stories that involve numbers, for example, 'Teddy goes shopping'
- counting rhymes and songs
- sorting objects into groups
- simple board games that involve rolling dice
- dominoes
- using counting as part of everyday routines, for example, the number of chairs and beakers
- magnetic numbers on metal surfaces
- feely bags containing a set number of objects
- cooking activities in which children measure ingredients, for example, counting out scoops.

THINKING AND RESEARCH

Ask five adults about their experiences of mathematics at school.

- How confident did they feel?
- How does the advice to do practical mathematical activities with young children link to theories of child development?

APPLYING THEORY TO YOUR PRACTICE

Practical games that involve rolling a dice can be a good way of helping children to enjoy numbers. Children can, for example, roll a dice and then put spoonfuls of sand into a cup. The first to fill up his or her cup is the winner and can make a sandcastle.

1 Explain why this type of activity will help children to enjoy mathematics.

2 Describe how you might adapt this game to meet the different levels of mathematical understanding of the children you work with.

3 Carry out the game with one or two children and evaluate its effectiveness.

Promoting knowledge and understanding of the world

This area of learning is perhaps the most diverse in the Foundation Stage because it encompasses early science, design and technology, as well as the beginnings of history, geography, and cultures and beliefs. The key to delivering this aspect of learning is to remember that it is very child-centred. It is also worth noting that the practitioner guidance throughout this area of learning stresses the importance of developing children's language. This is reflected clearly in the Stepping Stones and Early Learning Goals.

There are six aspects of learning within this area of development:

- exploration and investigation
- designing and making
- information and communication technology
- sense of time
- sense of place
- cultures and beliefs.

Exploration and investigation

This aspect of learning is about encouraging children to notice differences, patterns and change. It is the beginnings of early science. To deliver this aspect of learning, you will need to make sure that children regularly get opportunities to handle and sort objects.

They will also need opportunities to look at how things work and see things grow. You can contribute to this learning by:

- providing children with different collections of objects, such as keys, buttons and haberdashery
- using magnifying sheets and glasses to help them explore these objects.

Beans can be used to help children notice different shapes, patterns and sizes

Designing and making

This aspect of learning encourages children to solve problems, use tools and learn about textures and materials. As well as the usual construction type of toys, children should be encouraged to use boxes, paper, fabric and other materials. It is also important to show children how to use tools safely. The practitioner guidance lists tools that children should learn how to use, including stapler, scissors, grater and a junior hacksaw!

In addition to construction and junk-modelling type activities, children will also benefit from cooking activities, provided they can use tools and are designing in some way. For example, making sandwiches or salads can be useful cooking activities because there is scope for children to make choices.

Information and communication technology

A good starting point for this aspect of learning is to understand that a computer is not necessary in the pre-school. Rather, the focus in the early Stepping Stones is to help children understand about gadgets and the way in which we use technology in our daily lives. Thus, activities such as encouraging children to turn a tape recorder on and off, or watching what happens when a mobile telephone rings, will cover the outcomes. You should also look out for programmable toys such as floor robots and remote-controlled cars, which teach children about 'cause and effect'.

Sense of time

Interestingly, this aspect of learning is closely linked to cultures and beliefs. Both these aspects of learning in the early Stepping Stones are designed to encourage the child to talk about significant events in his or her life, and the lives of his or her family and friends. Thus, we need to plan activities that encourage children to think about their experiences both in and out of the setting. A good way of doing this is to use photographs and bring in objects to trigger children's memories. It is also important that we find the time to listen to children, either individually or in small groups.

Sense of place

This aspect of learning focuses on children's local environments, which may include shops, play parks and buildings. The key is to think hard about what children actually see and experience. For example, if you live in an inland town or city, focusing on a topic such as the seaside or farms will not be relevant. Rather, the focus for children's learning is to talk about where they live, and begin to notice things that they like and dislike about their local environment. It can be very helpful to take photographs of local landmarks, buildings and other sites, because young children find it easier to talk about things that they can actually see.

Cultures and beliefs

This aspect of learning has links to 'sense of time'. It is essential to read the Stepping Stones very carefully because they give clear guidance about the child-centred nature of this aspect. The earliest Stepping Stones are focused on helping children to talk about their families, and the feelings and events that are important to them. This represents a significant departure from previous approaches, in which it was expected that children would talk about other faiths and cultures. Thus, activities involving festivals will be appropriate only when they have meaning and relevance for children.

Promoting imagination and creativity

In the curriculum guidance, these experiences are under the 'creative development' area of learning. Creative development is designed to help children to explore different materials and textures, and encompasses music and dance. There are four aspects of learning within creative development:

▶ exploring media and materials
▶ music
▶ imagination
▶ responding to experiences, and expressing and communicating ideas.

Exploring media and materials

For this aspect of learning, children should be given a wide range of materials, such as paint, dough, clay and fabric, in order that they can learn about them. This aspect of learning should allow children to explore, rather than being adult-directed. For example, you may put out a tray of primary colour paints for children to use and encourage them to mix colours. The focus is not about children producing an 'end product' to take home but rather that children learn and enjoy using a large range of materials.

Music

Most children are naturally keen to enjoy and use sounds. To deliver this aspect of learning, you will need to provide a range of instruments, including homemade shakers and rattles, and be ready for children to explore the sounds that they make. Activities that encourage children to sing and even make up their own songs are also vital. Look out for music that has a strong beat so that children can learn to play in time to music.

Imagination

Role-play and dressing-up is one of the many ways in which imagination can be cultivated. This aspect of learning is designed to help children use their imagination in a variety of ways, including dance. Look out for props that will help children to move to music, and provide a selection of small-world and dressing-up clothes for them.

Responding to experiences, and expressing and communicating ideas

In many ways, this final aspect of learning is a culmination of the first three. The idea is that children will be able to choose a medium for expressing themselves and focus on creating. This aspect of learning is also about helping children to evaluate and talk about what they are doing. We therefore have to make sure that children hear the necessary language from us.

Promoting personal, social and emotional development

This is the first area of development within the Foundation Stage curriculum guidance. This is not accidental: it is recognised that children's emotional well-being and social skills are key ingredients in their later formal learning. Settled, confident children are likely to be able to control their behaviour and be ready for learning.

There are six aspects of learning within this area:

- disposition and attitudes
- self-confidence and self-esteem
- making relationships
- behaviour and self-control
- self-care
- sense of community.

Disposition and attitudes

This aspect of learning is about maintaining and developing children's natural curiosity and motivation. The key to delivering this aspect of learning is to ensure that all activities are enjoyable and stimulating for children. The ability to plan carefully for children's individual needs is therefore important because if a child finds an activity too difficult, he or she may lose confidence and motivation.

Self-confidence and self-esteem

This aspect of learning is about children's inner confidence and sense of identity. Children with self-esteem are more likely to socialise with others, persevere with challenges, and try new things. The earliest Stepping Stone is about ensuring that children are able to leave their main carer. We therefore need to think about settling-in policies and organising the routine of the pre-school to help children feel comfortable. Later Stepping Stones focus on encouraging children to talk about their homes and themselves. This means planning activities and times in which adults spend time with children on a one-to-one basis.

Making relationships

This aspect of learning is about children learning to socialise with other children and with adults. The focus of our work is to look for activities that

Plan games that encourage children to play together

naturally encourage children to collaborate, negotiate and enjoy each other's company. Plan games such as picture lotto or activities in which children can play alongside each other. It is also important to realise that true co-operation will not generally occur until children enter the reception class. Adults will therefore need to support children when they are playing together.

Behaviour and self-control

This aspect of learning is about helping children to think about their own as well as other people's needs. It is not about getting children to 'do as they are told'. In terms of working with children, this aspect of learning is about helping children to understand the need and reason for boundaries and limits on their behaviour; for example, saying to a child, 'We need to tidy up so that no one falls over'. To deliver this aspect of learning, practitioners need to think about the daily routines of the pre-school. Ways in which children can learn about behaviour and self-control include tidying up, helping to mend items and clearing away beakers after snack times.

Sense of community

This aspect of learning is about children learning to feel part of a group and respect other people's needs. It is linked with the 'cultures and beliefs' aspect of learning from 'Knowledge and understanding of the world'. The focus is about helping children to appreciate and realise that other children have different needs, interests and strengths. Activities that encourage children to find out more about each other are therefore important, for example, putting up a display that shows photos of children at home enjoying birthdays and family celebrations.

Promoting physical development

An increasing knowledge of how children's brains develop means that this area of learning is particularly important. Physical movements are now known to affect children's cognitive skills and information processing. This area of learning links to many aspects of learning within the Foundation Stage, including handwriting, designing and making, responding to experiences, and expressing and communicating ideas.

There are four aspects of learning within this area:

- sense of space
- movement
- health and bodily awareness
- using tools and materials.

Sense of space

Many young children find it hard to get a sense of their position in relation to other people and the objects around them. This aspect of learning therefore focuses on helping children to develop spatial awareness. For some children who spend many hours in confined spaces, this is particularly important; it is one of the reasons why outdoor learning is considered so important. When providing activities, it is important to check that all children are trying out a variety of movements as sometimes individual children might be reluctant to try out an activity. This may mean thinking about ways to adapt the activity to ensure that it appeals, e.g. asking a child who never goes on a tricycle if he or she would like to take Teddy for a ride.

This aspect of learning is about children enjoying space and developing a range of movements. A good starting point is to provide a range of activities that will help children to experience different sensations, for example, balancing, climbing, squeezing into tight spaces and running in large ones. When providing activities, it is important to check that all children are trying out a variety of movements and, if necessary, to think about ways of making them attractive to all children.

Movement

This aspect of learning looks at developing children's fine motor as well as gross and locomotive skills. Activities that encourage children to try out different movements, such as climbing, swinging and using wheeled toys, will help to cover the Stepping Stones. It is important to check that activities can boost children's confidence, so observations of children's physical development are important. There is also some evidence to suggest that helping children to use cross-lateral movements – those that encourage children to use a left limb at the same time as a right limb, such as marching or crawling – may be beneficial in developing some parts of the brain.

Health and bodily awareness

This aspect of learning is simply about children becoming more aware of the needs of their bodies. It means that we should help children to think about

Learning how to wash their hands helps children to be independent

what they should do if they are feeling tired, hot or cold. It is important not to focus too much on food, because this is an area that is not in children's control. Other useful activities include working out how best to wash hands when very dirty, and inviting a dentist or other health practitioner to talk to children.

Using tools and materials

This aspect of learning focuses on developing children's hand–eye co-ordination and fine motor skills when using tools. The starting point is therefore to make sure that children have access to a variety of tools. You should also think about the support children may need so that they do not become frustrated. This aspect of learning is likely to be covered while children are involved in designing and making, or creative development. Look out for adaptations to help children who have particular fine motor difficulties, for example, scissors that work by squeezing. Consider, too, the needs of children who use their left hands.

> **A QUICK THINK!**
>
> *Think of three tools that you use in everyday life.*
>
> *Why is it important for children to develop the skills to use tools?*

Role of planning in achieving the Early Learning Goals

Planning is an extremely important way of ensuring that the curriculum is delivered and that children do get a range of opportunities in order that they can make progress. Whilst the Early Learning Goals are not intended for children in pre-school, it is important to look at the curriculum guidance and consider where children are in relation to the Stepping Stones. Ideally, over the period of time that children are with us, we should see how their development, skills and knowledge have progressed and this should be reflected in our planning. The Foundation Stage curriculum guidance can help practitioners with their planning, as for each of the stepping stones ideas are provided as to how adults might develop children's learning.

APPLYING THEORY TO YOUR PRACTICE

Being able to use a pair of scissors is a useful skill for all children, but one that also develops gradually.

1 Using the Foundation Stage curriculum guidance, write down which aspects of learning relate to using tools such as scissors.

2 Observe three children in your setting and consider the level of skill that they are showing.

3 Plan three different activities that will help children to develop and extend their scissor skills.

Recording and reporting children's progress

As well as planning for children's learning, it is important for settings to have a system in place for monitoring progress. Ideally, planning and recording systems should be interlinked so that plans can be adjusted according to the individual needs of children. Recording children's progress can also help us to recognise children's particular strengths and identify whether they need any specific help in an area of development.

Methods for recording children's progress

As with other areas in the early years sector, there are many different ways in which a setting may record a child's progress. Most settings keep a file for each child and usually have a range of strategies for recording progress.

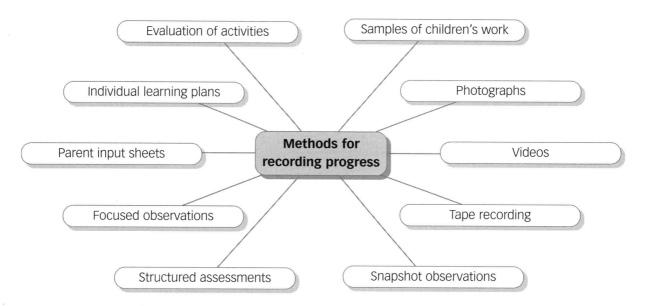

Video

Advances in technology mean that video records can provide a good way of collecting information about a child. As with other forms of records, it is essential that parents give consent. It is also important that, at the time, some analysis of the tape is made and notes are taken.

Parent input sheets

Parents know their child at home and are therefore likely to see his or her different strengths and weaknesses. For example, a child who is uncommunicative in the setting may be very talkative at home. This means that comments and input from parents should play an important part in any record-keeping process. Some pre-school settings ask parents to contribute regularly, and their comments are recorded.

Snapshot observations

Observations do not always need to be planned when working with children. Sometimes we might see something of interest that needs to be recorded, so many practitioners find that it is useful to have a notepad or some 'post-it' notes nearby at all times. This allows the practitioner to simply jot down the child's name and the date, and then later put the note on file.

Snapshot observations have a variety of uses. You may note down a child's reaction to another child or a new situation, or write down a new skill or interest that a child has developed. If you decide to use this as a significant way of monitoring children, it will be important to set aside regularly some time to carry out collation of your notes. Snapshot observations have a huge advantage as anyone in the setting can jot things down about a child.

For example: Sophie in role-play area. Sophie is collecting plates one by one and putting them in sink. Now asking Daniel to wash up. Daniel brings over a cup. Sophie smiles. 'You go out now. You come back in when I tell you.' Sophie sings happy birthday and puts plates in shopping bag. She takes shoes off and goes out. Gets dressing-up shoes and waves at Daniel. Both enter home corner. 'Want to come shopping?' Daniel nods. She gives Daniel shopping bag and gets another one out.

Structured assessments

There are a variety of schemes that adopt mainly a checklist approach. These have the advantage of allowing children's development to be considered over several areas, but they do have some significant disadvantages.

These children are showing their co-ordination skills

- Assessments that require the adult to ask the child to 'perform' may not always capture a child's 'true' performance.
- It can be hard to remain objective when carrying out assessments.
- Relying solely on a checklist-based scheme is not recommended because it gives a one-dimensional view of the child.

For these reasons, many practitioners will use a range of methods when looking at a child's progress.

Focused observations

As well as snapshot observations, many settings carry out more focused observations. While a range of methods can be used, the aim of focused observations is to consider specific areas of a child's development or progress. This may mean carrying out an event sample that looks at how often a child interacts with others, or a 'target child'-type observation to see which play activity a child most enjoys. Focused observations allow practitioners to reflect beforehand on the specific areas to be observed.

Tape recording

It can be very hard to assess children's speech using traditional pen and paper methods. Short tape recordings allow us to record a child's speech, in turn enabling us to analyse more easily their speech and therefore their progress. A good way of getting children relaxed enough to talk into a tape recorder is by turning it into a playful situation, for example, saying to a child, 'Teddy's mum was hoping that you might tell her about what you do in pre-school. She can't come in and so I thought we could send her your message.'

As with other methods of monitoring children's progress, you should always write a note of the date and the context in which the recording takes place. It is also important to spend a moment listening back to the tape and writing down the language skills the child shows. This saves time later; otherwise, you will be faced with a collection of tapes in a child's folder.

Photographs

Many settings use photographs as part of their strategies for record-keeping. You can use photographs both to show children at play and as a way of recording what they have done; for example, a den the child has built or a model the child has made from Lego bricks. It is important to date and briefly describe the context in which the photograph was taken. It is also important to write down what the photograph is intended to show because you may forget later why you took the photograph.

Samples of children's work

Many settings will regularly collect examples of a child's work. Children's early mark making can help us to find out about their physical fine motor movements, language and creative development. It is a good idea to date children's work and add a few brief notes about how the child produced it. Consider writing comments about the child's enjoyment, the choices he or she made, and the child's intentions for the drawing or mark making.

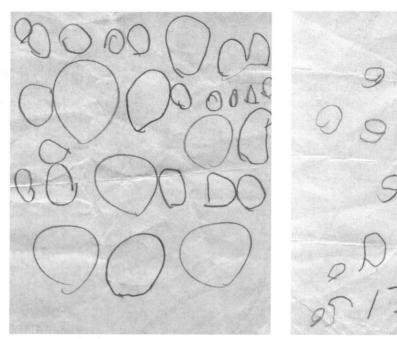

Can you see the development in symbol use that the child has made over three months?

Individual learning plans

Individual learning plans are ways of planning for children's progress. They should also help us to consider children's development. By keeping individual learning plans and regularly reflecting upon them, we should be able to see how children have made progress.

Evaluation of activities

Some settings design their activity sheets so that comments can be made about individual children's responses. This can be another effective way of gathering information about children.

A QUICK THINK!

Find out if your EYCDP or local education department has a record-keeping system to record children's progress in pre-school.

POINT OF INTEREST

Foundation Stage Profile

A system of recording known as the Foundation Stage Profile has been introduced for reception class teachers to use with children. Previously, children entering the reception class were assessed using a system known as 'base line' early on in their first term. With the advent of the Foundation Stage, this assessment system became redundant. This is because it was felt that final assessment should take place at the end of the Foundation Stage.

In the Foundation Stage Profile, teachers are given a booklet for each child, which they fill in during the course of the reception year. This means that by the end of the reception year, a profile on the child's achievement of the Early Learning Goals can be passed to Year 1 teachers. The profile looks at each of the areas of learning and puts great emphasis on personal, social and emotional development.

At the time of writing, there is some disappointment over the introduction of the Foundation Stage Profile. Some practitioners working with pre-school children feel that the profile should have been continuous from the age of three years to allow for their input when compiling the record. There is also concern that a scoring system has been put in the profile. Some practitioners feel that this changes the purpose of the profile from being a potentially diagnostic tool to a system of providing 'scores' for bureaucrats.

Systems for maintaining records

Parental consent

Information about children is very sensitive. It is therefore essential that systems designed to maintain records are carefully devised with confidentiality in mind. A good starting point is to consider the rights of parents and children. This means that no records can be kept without parental consent. It is also important to understand that, under Data Protection legislation, parents have the right to see any information that is being stored about their child. Particular methods of recording, such as videos and photographs, might be sources of concern for some parents; therefore, consent must be sought.

Confidentiality

As well as seeking parental consent, it is important that records are stored securely. Systems are needed to identify those adults who should have access to the records. It is therefore usual for records to be kept in locked filing cabinets or cupboards when they are not needed. Staff should also understand that talking about a child's progress to people other than that child's parents or other identified adults, is a breach of the child's right to confidentiality.

Sensitivity in comments

The language that we use to talk about children needs to be carefully considered. Records always carry the possibility of creating a 'label', so practitioners must be thoughtful in their comments. A good rule of thumb is to consider the effect of any comment on a reader. We should therefore be careful to write about a child's strengths and interests as well as his or her needs. Where a child's development is a cause for concern, it is important to make specific rather than general comments, and to focus on the support that needs to be in place for the child.

> **A QUICK THINK!**
>
> *Look at these two comments. Which comment do you feel is the more sensitive? Why? What wording has made the difference?*
>
> ▶ *Daniel cannot concentrate very well. He often fidgets and is disruptive when in a large group at story time.*
>
> ▶ *Daniel concentrates best in situations when he is active. He benefits from being in a small group at story time.*

Accuracy

The nature of records and the way in which they may influence other adults working with a child means that it is especially important to check that they are accurate. Therefore, pre-school staff should check before making a comment such as, 'Sara finds sharing difficult.' because this behaviour might be quite usual for a child of her age. It is also important that records are kept up to date and that comments are amended if necessary. Most pre-school settings therefore have a regular schedule of reviewing and updating children's records.

Involving parents in the creation of children's records

Over the past few years, the role that parents play in the care and education of their children has become increasingly recognised. Parents are able to provide pre-school practitioners with significant amounts of information about their child, and will have developed views as to how their child best learns. Thus, as part of the record-keeping process and as a matter of good practice, parents need to be involved in their child's records.

Most settings usually begin this process by asking parents to fill in a form and talking with them before their child joins the pre-school. The information gathered usually forms the starting point for the child's records. It is important, however, that this information is expanded on because parents may be able to tell us about the changing interests and activities that their child enjoys outside of the setting. Since all records on children should be available to parents, it is also worth sharing observations, notes and photographs with parents as and when they occur. This can prevent a situation arising in which parents disagree with what has been written about their child. It is also worth noting that should you have any concerns about a child's development, you should share these with the child's parents at the earliest opportunity.

Involving children in the creation of records

While adults play a significant role in the creation of a child's records, it is also worth considering whether the child should play a role. After all, the child is the subject of his or her own records! Involving children in records is a growing trend at all levels because practitioners are beginning to acknowledge that children's views and interests should be taken into account. In terms of involving children in the creation of records, you might consider asking children to choose a sample of their work for inclusion, or ask a child about his or her interests and the activities that he or she most enjoys.

Methods for using records to inform future curriculum planning

We have seen that in order for all children to access the curriculum, thought has to be given to their needs. Thus, while planning a curriculum, we should refer back to individual children's records. For example, we may wish to consider which children would benefit from a name treasure hunt because they are still learning to identify their name. Ideally, each person responsible for a group of children's records needs to spend some time reviewing the children's needs and interests before carrying out the curriculum planning. In this way, activities are more likely to meet the children's needs.

My Child at Home

Name of child _____

Date of birth _____

My child's favourite food is...	My child's favourite toys are...
My child makes me smile when...	My child's favourite play mates are...
My child finds it hard to...	My child needs...

I will be pleased when my child can...

I think it would help you to know...

Signed .... (Parent/Carer)

Date ....

Parents can become involved by completing a 'My Child at Home' form

Methods of incorporating records into reviews

Information may need to be collated from children's records for a variety of purposes.

▶ It is good practice to provide parents with a written review of their child's progress. Some settings do this monthly; others may choose to do this quarterly or even half-yearly. Reviews for parents are extremely important, particularly in day care settings where a child might spend a significant proportion of his or her day. Reviews for parents are also vital tools to ensure good communication between home and setting, especially if parents are unable to take and collect their children from sessions.

▶ Information about children may be collated to help other professionals, although parental consent is required first. For example, when a child is moving to another setting or going on to school, information should be forwarded to help the child settle in and ensure that his or her needs are met.

▶ Some information might be collated in order for professionals, such as speech and language therapists or educational psychologists, to learn more about the child in the pre-school environment.

Writing effective reviews

As we have seen, reviews can be written for a variety of purposes. It is important that care is taken when writing reviews so that a child is not 'labelled' or presented in a negative light. This can seem daunting, especially when a child has a specific area of difficulty. The starting point before you write a review is to consider its purpose: what information does the reader actually need? It can also be helpful to refer to reviews that have been written in a similar style. This will provide you with a template for language and format. Finally, a good piece of advice is always to ask colleagues to check your work, especially for errors in spelling or grammar.

Name of child	Rachel Glover
Date of Report	23/2/04

Personal, social and emotional development	Communication, Language and Literacy
Rachel has settled in well and has made one particular friend. She enjoys helping and tidying up.	Rachel loves story time and particularly enjoys puppets. She has started to use questions more widely.
Mathematical Development	**Knowledge and Understanding of the World**
Rachel knows five counting rhymes. She has just started to point to objects as she counts. She can also match pairs.	Rachel enjoyed making beds for Teddy and also working out the old toys from the new. She can use the remote control car. She can tell us what she enjoys doing at the weekend
Physical Development	**Creative Development**
Rachel can now use scissors to snip with and is keen to snip everything. She can also ride a tricycle well and enjoys kicking balls.	Rachel loves the home corner and plays imaginatively. She also sings several songs by heart and can use the shakers rhythmically

Overview

Rachel has settled in well and appears happy in the mornings. She has made one special friend, although is happy to play on the edge of larger groups.

Comments from parents

Staff Signature.....~~JohnThom~~...... Date 23/2/04

Parent Signature.......................... Date

An example of a parent report

GOOD
PRACTICE

Writing effective reviews

▶ Think about the purpose of the review.
▶ Check whether a format already exists.
▶ Make sure that your statements and comments are accurate.
▶ Prepare a draft review.
▶ Be accurate, specific and as concise as possible.
▶ Consider asking a colleague to check your work.
▶ If appropriate, gain the parents' perspectives.

Reflective practice

Reflective practice is the term used to describe the process by which practitioners review the effectiveness of their work. It is largely an internal process, and is increasingly seen as the way in which practitioners can improve their skills.

The trend to encourage practitioners to learn the skills of reflective practice can be seen on many levels. OFSTED increasingly ask settings to fill in a self-assessment form, while students are encouraged to think about the effectiveness of their activities and apply this knowledge when writing assignments. The concept behind reflective practice is that we learn to be aware of our own strengths and weaknesses, and can consider how to change our ways of working. This approach is considered far more effective at improving practice than waiting for others to judge our performance and make suggestions for improvement.

Why it is important for pre-schools to monitor and review their practice

Working in the early years sector is hugely exciting: while learning more and more about child development, we also work with individual children. This means that our practice cannot remain static over time if we are to respond to both the needs of children and the trends in early years education. A planning system that was effective ten years ago may no longer be considered useful today, while the routine of a setting that met the needs of its children when first created might now require adjustment.

Inclusion and the need to review practice

Inclusion is not only about meeting children's needs; it is also about making sure that this is done in such a way as to allow for them to join in with other children. Thus, settings and practitioners need to think about the ways in which they work, and consider whether the layout, routine or their own practice is creating a barrier for children.

Reflecting on practice by noting behavioural responses

Children's responses tend to be a significant indicator of how well the setting meets their needs. Behaviour in this context needs to be seen as wider than just 'good' or 'unwanted' behaviour; children's responses are more complex. For example, you might notice that a child spends a large proportion of his or her time 'wandering' and looking uncertain, or that a child has spent 15 minutes concentrating on pouring water using a variety of containers. Thus, you need to take time to think about children's responses in the setting. A group of children who seem to run everywhere may do so because the layout invites them to, or the routine of the setting does not provide sufficient opportunities for vigorous physical activity.

Using observation as a way of monitoring practice

An effective tool that can be used to check whether the provision's activities, layout and routine are promoting early learning, is a tracking type of observation. This type of observation focuses on several children at the same time and considers whether their needs are being met. The focus is not on individual children because the observation is designed to look at the effectiveness of the provision. Ideally, after discussion, one member of staff carries out the observation with an aim in mind. For example, the aim may be to observe how much interaction occurs between children and adults, or how many children are truly engaged at story time. After the observation has taken place, staff need to meet to think about what the observation may reveal.

Factors to consider when reviewing practice

Providing an early years environment that will meet the needs of all children is a tall order. However, it can be done. Observing groups of children across the setting should help teams to reflect upon their provision. Below is a list of questions that can be useful to consider when observing the provision.

Time	Child 1 Grey Top	Child 2 Silver Shoes	Child 3 Pink Doc Ms	Child 4 Red T Shirt	Child 5 Ginger haired	Child 6 Yellow top
9.40	Water + 4 children Pouring, scooping ⑤	Stickle bricks →Ⓐ Painting	←stickle bricks →A → helping A Ⓐ	Water +4 Hangs apron →Ⓐ drawing (R.H) ③ Ⓐ++	Stickle bricks →A →A → helping Ⓐ →Ⓐ	Painting ④
9.45	Shark ⑤ +3 children	Water ②	→Ⓐ watching water 9.47	Drawing A	Changed jumper Ⓐ →water 9.46	Wash hands ④ 9.49 Dry hands
9-50	Shark ⑤ Teapot + shark	Water ② Apron away →A Tool table ②	Hangs up apron 10.51 →A Ⓐ Painting	Puts picture away lego 9.51	↓hang up apron 9.51 → change room → computer A	9.50 Hang up apron Suck thumb →A
9.55	↓Shark ⊕+1 c⇄→ ℝℍ	Ⓐ Hammer + nail ②	↓Painting ⑤	↓Dough A ⑤ ↓Seat change RH		Hammer + nails Ⓐ 9.57-9.58
10.00	Shark ⊕+1 10.02 Ⓐ 10.03 Apron off	window →→ ↓ Tool table ②	wash hands ⑤ 10.04 →A	Dough small pieces ④ 10.01→A Tool table → window - birds→	Computer ② 10.07 watching A → stays with A	Tools ② Window 10.03
10.05	Change clothes Ⓐ	window →	→help A →Ⓐ	sand 10.05 →A → →suck thumb	Suck thumb	window ②

Ⓐ = Adult interacts with child
→ A child moves to adult
→ Child is moving or standing + watching
A = adult is present. No interaction
①②③④⑤ = levels of concentration 5= highest
R.H / L.H = Handedness

Tracking sheet

Key questions when observing the provision

- How many children are actively engaged in play at different points during the session?
- Do any children consistently spend time looking bored or distressed?
- What types of unwanted behaviour are shown and why do these occur?
- What levels of adult–child interaction exist within the setting?
- Do children interact with each other?
- Are children able to initiate activities?
- What body language is shown by both individual children and groups of children?
- How easily do children separate from their main carers?

Meeting as a team

Practice can be improved in a setting only if the team works well together. Reviewing practice should not be seen as a way of 'blaming' others; this approach is counter-productive. The focus of any team meeting should be to consider ways of driving forward quality within the setting. This means that team members need to be very careful in their use of language and respectful of others' ideas. Ideally, it is worth spending time on a weekly basis in thinking about how the curriculum plans are being implemented and, if necessary, making adjustments.

It is best to meet on a weekly basis

Reviewing your own effectiveness as a practitioner

As well as the whole staff team reviewing their work, you should also reflect on your individual practice. Again, it is worth focusing on the responses of children and thinking about the reasons for these responses. For example, what was it about the activity or the way in which you interacted with the children that created favourable responses? In the same way, we must think carefully about children who did not show an interest or exhibited some aspect of unwanted behaviour. It is easy to want to 'blame' these children rather than evaluating our own responses and considering how we could best meet these children's needs in the future.

CASE STUDY

Camilla prepared an activity to help a small group of children with their scissor skills. She was especially hoping that one child in particular would join in. He stayed for less than a minute despite her attempts to encourage him. Afterwards, Camilla observed what he did during the session and noticed that he was playing with the more sensory activities, especially the dough. This made her think about the nature of the activity that she had organised, and she wondered whether it was sufficiently sensory in nature. The next day, Camilla put several pair of scissors on the dough table.

1 Why does this provide a good example of a practitioner showing reflective practice?

2 Explain how reflective practice can help practitioners to meet children's individual needs.

3 Consider other reasons why the child might not have participated in the original activity.

Ideas for continuous professional development

Once you have thought about your own strengths and weaknesses, you may need to seek further support. Colleagues within your own setting can sometimes provide a useful soundboard, but do consider getting in contact with other early years practitioners. A visit to another setting can prove inspirational, providing you with the opportunity to see new solutions and strategies in action.

GOOD PRACTICE

Promoting your professional development

▶ Talk to other colleagues.
▶ Visit other settings.
▶ Ask early years advisers for support.
▶ Look out for training opportunities.
▶ Subscribe to an early years magazine.
▶ Read specialist professional books.

Recording your training

You should always keep a note of any training courses that you have attended. Not only will **OFSTED** be looking to check that staff are up to date, but you may wish to change employer in the future. You should write down the title of the course, the day on which you attended, and a brief summary of what it covered. It is also a good idea to keep course materials – for example, certificates of attendance, course notes and handouts – in a folder.

THINKING AND RESEARCH

▶ Begin to develop your own professional development folder.
▶ Consider whether there are any areas of the curriculum or practice in which you need further training, for example, child protection and first aid.
▶ Contact your local EYCDP. Find out about the type of courses they offer.

TEST YOUR KNOWLEDGE

1 List the six areas of learning within the Foundation Stage curriculum.
2 By what age will most children be able to achieve the Early Learning Goals?
3 Explain why it is important to plan activities for young children.
4 Explain why it is important to adapt plans to meet the needs of individual children.
5 What is the Foundation Stage Profile?
6 Describe an everyday routine that might provide a learning opportunity for children.
7 Explain why it is important to monitor plans against the Foundation Stage curriculum.
8 Analyse the importance of working in partnership with parents when planning activities.
9 Evaluate the importance of planning activities based on children's interests.
10 Consider the role of play in helping children to learn.

PRACTICE ASSIGNMENT TASK

Write a leaflet for parents that explains how your pre-school develops and helps children to learn. The leaflet should contain information about:

▶ the Foundation Stage curriculum
▶ how the pre-school plans for children's learning
▶ how learning is assessed.

Further references and reading

Broadhead, P. (2004) *Early Years Play and Learning Developing Skills and Co-operation*, London: RoutledgeFalmer

Bruce, T. (1991) *Time to Play in Early Childhood Education and Care*, London: Hodder Arnold

Hucker, K. & Tassoni, P. (2000) *Planning Play and the Early Years,* Oxford: Heinemann

Lindon, J. (2001) *Understanding Children's Play*, Cheltenham: Nelson Thornes

Pascal, C. & Bertram, T. (2001) *Effective Early Learning*, London: Paul Chapman Publications

Tassoni, P. (2002) *Planning for the Foundation Stage: Ideas for Themes and Activities*, Oxford: Heinemann

Tizard, B. & Hughes, M. (2002) *Young Children Learning (2nd edition),* Oxford: Blackwell

3 Best Practice in Pre-school Settings

Pre-school groups need to update regularly so that they are familiar with the latest views on practice in early years care and education. Such developments often reflect the increasing knowledge about child development and child protection, as well as the views of society towards children and their families. The current OFSTED inspections required under the Children Act 1989 also link to what is currently thought to be best practice.

This unit looks at five key areas of practice and is divided into the following sections:

▶ Implementing anti-discriminatory practice in pre-school settings

▶ Providing a safe, secure and stimulating environment that promotes children's early learning

▶ Applying an understanding of children's physical needs to all aspects of their care and education

▶ Policies and procedures in pre-school settings to protect children from abuse

▶ Ways of working in partnership with parents to promote children's learning and development

Implementing anti-discriminatory practice in pre-school settings

The way in which we work with children reflects society's changing views about equality and fairness. Indeed, it could be argued that the early years sector plays a crucial role because children learn about attitudes from a very young age. This section looks at the importance of **anti-discriminatory** practice and considers practical ways in which it should shape practice in the early years sector.

What is anti-discriminatory practice?

It is an accepted view in society and in the early years sector that every child is special and should be given opportunities to fulfil his or her potential. While this is an easy thing to say, it requires significant effort and thought to put into practice. Anti-discriminatory practice means thinking about every aspect of what we do with children and their families and considering whether our actions meet their needs. It also means being aware of our preconceived ideas about groups of people, and being prepared to think about how these ideas may affect our practice. The example below shows how one pre-school began to think about the children's needs in their setting.

CASE STUDY

Staff at Little Gems pre-school thought about some of the activities that were provided for children. They realised that the creative activities they had planned actually reflected their tastes and interests rather than those of the children. Activities such as decorating flowerpots and making necklaces with beads were enjoyed by some children, predominantly girls, but were not appealing to many other children. The staff decided to think more carefully about their planning, and to make sure that creative activities were more varied and reflected the interests of individual children.

1 What skills would children miss out on if they rarely took part in creative activities?

2 Why is it important for children's interests to be considered?

3 What type of creative activities does your setting provide? Do they meet the interests and needs of all the children?

The importance of incorporating anti-discriminatory strategies

It is now recognised that adopting anti-discriminatory strategies is a key way in which we can make society fairer. Traditionally, groups of children have been discriminated against because they were seen as being different in some way, for example, having a disability or a different home background or culture. In some cases, this **discrimination** was overt: parents were simply told that there was no place available for their child. In other cases, the discrimination was less obvious, but the attitudes of staff and unwillingness to adapt or extend activities meant that children were not able to fulfil their potential.

In terms of our society, any discrimination that affects children has long-term effects. Some children may eventually reject the values of the society that has been hostile to them, while other children, whose potential has not been recognised, will fail to contribute. The importance of incorporating anti-discriminatory strategies is reflected in the National Standards that pre-school settings have to comply with in order to be registered.

Thinking 'win–win' in pre-schools

In many ways, creating an atmosphere in which all children and parents feel welcome and everyone knows they are seen as equal, is a real winner! In management-speak, anti-discriminatory practices create a 'win–win' situation.

Better exchange of information

Adopting anti-discriminatory practices encourages the exchange of information between parents and staff.

Stronger relationships

Anti-discriminatory practices mean that everyone feels valued and that their ideas are respected. Parents, staff and volunteers are likely to have stronger relationships and work together more effectively.

Evidence meets the required National Standard 9

Good practice should meet the evidence requirements.

Adopting anti-discriminatory practices

Children achieve and develop life skills

Where anti-discriminatory practices are employed, children are able to achieve and learn at their own rate and level. Unwanted behaviour decreases and children become more thoughtful and respectful of others.

Excellent reputation

Pre-schools that adopt active anti-discriminatory practices quickly develop a strong reputation among parents. This in turn leads to sustainable numbers of children.

Warmer and richer atmosphere

Children are more likely to learn and show responsible behaviour if they see that adults are working well together.

Valuing children and their parents

A major part of anti-discriminatory practice is to consider the 'hidden messages' and values that are part of your setting. Young children are very quick to sense whether they and their families are accepted and cared for. If a child learns that he or his family is not valued, this will affect his sense of worth and behaviour. Settings therefore need to be genuinely welcoming and respectful of all families.

Providing the emotional climate

Children need to feel secure so that they are able to relax sufficiently in order to learn and participate. Young children will need to feel that we care and like them, especially those who are separating from their main carers for the first time. Thus, in addition to key worker systems for our youngest children, we need to think about the way in which we respond to children's behaviour. Excluding a child physically from activities or being punitive can send out the message that the child is neither wanted nor liked. This often leads to further unwanted behaviour, which in turn means that the child misses possible learning opportunities by being excluded.

Motivating children

Most early years practitioners understand that praise and encouragement are key ways in which we can motivate children. However, it is easy to forget that the way in which we plan activities and approach children's behaviour can also affect their desire to learn. Traditionally, children who have not wanted to join in or try out activities have been labelled 'difficult'. Today, the recommended approach is to consider our practice in terms of how we respond to children's needs and interests. This may mean, for example, taking a maths activity over to a sand tray if this is what a child particularly enjoys, or playing games in very small groups to increase participation. Anti-bias practice therefore involves analysing children's responses to situations and thinking about the changes we might make in order that they learn more effectively.

All children have the right to play and learn

Recognising and challenging discriminatory practice

It is not uncommon for pre-school settings to have adopted, over a period, practices that are discriminatory. In many cases, the discrimination is not intended, but is rather the result of thoughtlessness and lack of consideration. The annual outing may cause financial difficulties for some parents, or the making of Mother's Day cards may make a child who lives with a single-parent father feel awkward. Reviewing how best to make these activities inclusive and accessible for all children is therefore important.

Reviewing practice

A good starting point when challenging and recognising discrimination is to look at the current practice of your setting. Many practices are simply handed down from supervisor to supervisor, without necessarily being reviewed.

Session times

Many pre-schools want to serve their local community. The start and end times of sessions may have been set many years ago, when family structures and lifestyles were different. You should consider whether the current session times reflect the needs of parents and their children, or whether they act as a barrier to some families.

Settling-in policies

Settling in can take some time. Consider how flexible your approach is to individual children or whether the pre-school expects all children to follow the same pattern. Anti-discriminatory practice means that individual needs are taken into account and that children are not expected to all be 'the same'.

Accessibility

Accessibility is an issue for many groups of people, including children with mobility needs. Many parents will have younger children in pushchairs; in addition, some parents will use devices to increase their own mobility. Look at how accessible your setting is and consider ways of increasing accessibility. Consult with local voluntary groups as to how best to make your building accessible.

Financial assistance

The ability to pay fees or 'extras' can be an issue for many parents. While pre-schools need to balance their books, consider ways of making payments easier for parents and also whether the 'extras' can be funded in different ways, for example, by applying for grants in the local community or by carrying out fundraising activities. If financial assistance is available for some families, consider how it is offered, and avoid situations in which children are labelled as being from poor families.

Activities

The Foundation Stage and the **SEN Code of Practice** make it clear that activities need to be planned in accordance with children's learning needs. This means looking for activities that can be simplified, extended or adapted to allow each child to participate at his or her own level. We should therefore avoid situations in which groups of children are seen as 'bright' or 'more able'; this segregation is not necessary in the Foundation Stage.

Curriculum planning

Familiarise yourself with the type of activities, themes and play experiences on offer. Consider whether they link to the interests of all children, or will appeal to certain groups of children only.

Managing children's behaviour

There is an increasing trend to regard children's unwanted behaviour as indicative of the fact that their needs are not being met. For example, children who cannot sit still at story time may be showing that they are tired or bored, or that their language development is not sufficient to cope with the type of story. The traditional approach to managing children's behaviour was punitive and exclusive. A child would be sent away from an activity or not allowed to join in activities that were seen as 'treats'. This approach teaches the child that they are not valued and does not address the cause of the unwanted behaviour. Seeing behaviour policies as part of anti-discriminatory practices is therefore important.

Partnership with parents

The way in which pre-schools work with parents can be an indicator of anti-discriminatory practice. Parents or main carers are key people in a child's life; therefore, the way in which we work with them is crucial. A child whose parents are not valued and respected will come to believe that he or she too is not important. Reflecting on the way in which we communicate to parents is therefore essential. Consider whether some parents are 'favourites': do staff spend more time with them? Think about the way in which parents are addressed, in both speech or writing, and whether these communications contain assumptions about their lifestyle, culture and financial background.

It is also important to think about whether feedback from parents is taken seriously, or whether parents who pass comment are considered 'difficult'.

Challenging discrimination

Occasionally, you may overhear remarks or see actions that are not appropriate and are potentially offensive or damaging. While it might be tempting to keep quiet, it is worth understanding that, by doing so, you are condoning discrimination. Challenging discrimination is a skill that in many ways reflects your ability to be assertive. This does not mean being aggressive – in many cases, the person who is acting or speaking inappropriately may not realise that he or she is being discriminatory or offensive. Rather, challenging discrimination means gently suggesting to the person that his or her remarks or actions are not appropriate, and explaining why.

In situations where you suspect that people are knowingly being offensive, consider telling them that you find their subject of conversation distasteful and that, if they continue, you may decide to leave their company or (if appropriate) report what they have said. Consider the two situations below.

CASE STUDY

Situation one

Andrea is listening to a member of staff talking about her recent visit to the emergency department of a hospital with her son. During the conversation, the member of staff uses the term 'coloured doctor'. Andrea realises that the member of staff is not aware that this term is not appropriate. She interrupts the member of staff and gently says, 'I think you mean "black" as otherwise you are insulting the doctor, which would be a shame considering that she helped your son.'

Situation two

A few parents and the supervisor are having a chat about the weather at the start of the session. One of the parents begins to talk about seeing some gypsies at the weekend. The conversation rapidly becomes excited and racist comments are made. The supervisor decides that this conversation is inappropriate and says, 'I am sorry to disagree, but this is a conversation that I find deeply offensive. We are very much committed here to valuing all children and adults, so I must ask that you think about what you are saying.' An embarrassed hush falls and the supervisor brings the conversation back to what the children will be doing in the morning.

1 Why is it important to challenge discriminatory remarks?

2 Why is it important to explain why some comments are not appropriate?

3 Explain why people working with young children must be committed to anti-discriminatory practice.

Anti-discriminatory practice should be comprehensive

Traditionally, some groups of people are more likely to be discriminated against than others. While quite a lot of attention has been given to gender and race discrimination, it is important to realise that anti-discriminatory practice in the pre-school setting must include attention to the following types of discrimination:

- ethnic
- cultural
- religious
- family background
- ability
- gender or sexuality.

The overall aim of anti-discriminatory practice is that every aspect of the pre-school provision becomes inclusive. Groups of children and their parents should not be discriminated against; for example, because their family background is different from that of other children.

Legislation

As well as adopting an anti-discriminatory approach to the work you do, it is worth being aware of existing legislation that aims to protect the rights of adults and children.

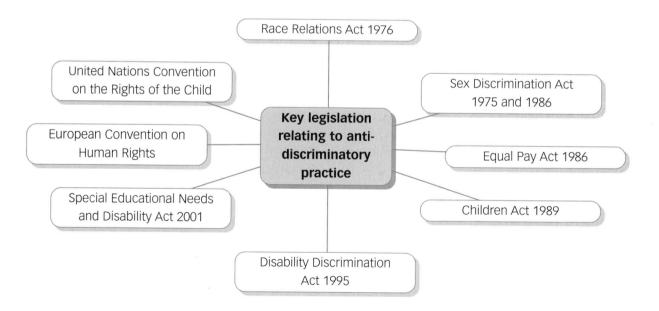

Key legislation relating to anti-discriminatory practice
Race Relations Act 1976

This Act makes it illegal to discriminate on the grounds of race, colour, nationality and ethnic origin in education and training, employment, housing, and the provision of goods and services including entertainment. The Commission for Racial Equality (CRE) was set up to offer advice and to help enforce the Act.

Example of illegal practice under this Act:
It would be illegal for a pre-school setting to refuse a child a place because the family were immigrants.

Sex Discrimination Act 1975 and 1986

These Acts make it illegal to discriminate against someone on the grounds of gender. The law also protects people from sexual harassment. There is also a Commission for Equal Opportunities that provides advice and enforces the Act.

Example of illegal practice under these Acts:
It would be illegal for a pre-school to refuse to interview a man who applied for a position.

Equal Pay Act 1986

This Act makes employers pay equal amounts for work of equal value. The Commission for Equal Opportunities provides guidance and enforces this Act.

Example of illegal practice under this Act:
It would be illegal for a pre-school to pay a man more money than they do a woman who is doing the same work.

Children Act 1989

This is a complex and far-reaching Act, which enshrines many rights for children. It has had a significant impact on the delivery of care in pre-schools. Under this Act, children's rights and needs are seen as paramount. The Act looks at the importance of involving parents and making sure that families, wherever possible, remain united. Under the Act, establishments including pre-schools and crèches have to be inspected.

Since 2001, much work has been carried out by OFSTED. As part of the standards, pre-schools have to show that they promote equality of opportunity and show anti-discriminatory practice for all children in the setting. They also have to show how they identify and respond to children with special needs (Standards 9 and 10).

Disability Discrimination Act 1995

This is the first Act designed to ensure that disabled people are given equal services. It protects individuals against discrimination in several areas, including employment, buying goods and services, and buying or renting property. To allow businesses sufficient time to make reasonable adjustments to their services, the Act is being phased in gradually. When this Act was first passed, a commission was not set up. Subsequent campaigning by groups who represent the interests of disabled people have now been successful in bringing about a commission to enforce the Act.

Special Educational Needs and Disability Act 2001

This Act is divided into two sections. Part one is a reform of the framework of SEN, designed to strengthen the rights of access of parents and children to mainstream education. This reflects the idea of inclusive education in which children are not 'separated' from their peers because of a disability or particular need. Part two of the Act expands the Disability Discrimination Act 1995 to include education, colleges and universities.

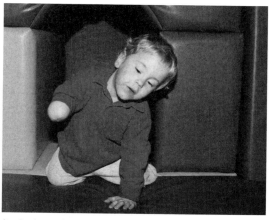

'Inclusive education' also means providing a suitable and safe environment for all children's needs

European Convention on Human Rights

The Human Rights Act came into force in October 2000. It has already made a huge impact on current legislation in this country. It requires courts and tribunals to make judgments using certain articles of the European Convention on Human Rights as a starting point. This Act was not designed specifically to protect children, but they are accorded the same rights as adults. This means that children have a right to dignity, respect and fairness in the way in which they are treated.

United Nations Convention on the Rights of the Child

In addition to the Human Rights Act, the UK is a signatory to the Rights of the Child convention. There are five main strands to this Convention:

1 Reinforces the importance of fundamental human dignity.

2 Highlights and defends the family's role in children's lives.

3 Seeks respect for children.

4 Endorses the principle of non-discrimination.

5 Establishes clear obligations for member countries to ensure that each country's legal framework is in line with the provisions of the Convention.

CASE STUDY

Celie is three and a half years old and is keen to attend the pre-school as her cousin already goes there. The pre-school has a policy that children can only attend when they are clean and dry. The play leader has told Celie's family that she is happy to hold a place for her, but cannot take her until she is out of nappies. Celie's family are disappointed as she has a medical condition which means that she is not yet continent.

1 Explain why Celie is being discriminated against.

2 How might this discrimination affect Celie's learning and development?

3 Identify legislation that might be used to protect Celie's rights.

Policies

Policies are statements that explain a setting's values, procedures and aims. Every setting should have a policy for anti-discriminatory practice or equal opportunities. Pre-school settings that do not have such a policy may not achieve registration, because having a policy is a requirement of Standard 9. Standard 9: Equal Opportunities states that the registered person and staff actively promote equality of opportunity and anti-discriminatory practice. It is important that members of staff read Standard 9 and understand its implications.

As with every aspect of early years practice, the setting's policy should be reviewed and considered regularly. Questions you should ask are:

▶ Does the policy really work?
▶ Does the policy reflect current views and attitudes, for example, with reference to the SEN Code of Practice?

Ideally, you may wish to ask people outside of your setting to comment on your anti-discriminatory practice policy. Sometimes it is easier for an outsider to notice 'gaps' or areas that require further work. As well as having a policy, pre-school settings also need a procedure to follow when there is a breach of policy.

Drawing up a policy

The policy should be relevant to your setting. This means that, while it may be helpful to look at other settings' policies, you should either devise your own policy or customise a sample policy with care. It is essential that the finished policy reflects clearly what is happening in your setting.

There is no single way of drawing up a policy, but it can be helpful to use headings to structure the document. Below is an example of the type of information that could be used to build a policy.

Statement of commitment

▶ What are the aims of the policy?
▶ Who will be responsible for ensuring that the policy is implemented?
▶ How will the policy be reviewed and when will the review take place?

Admissions policy

▶ What is your setting's admissions policy?
▶ How does this reflect the setting's commitment towards equal opportunities?

Respecting children

▶ How do you help children to settle in?
▶ How are each child's needs recognised and met?
▶ How are children actively made to feel welcome and valued?
▶ How are children encouraged to explore their identity and value that of others?
▶ How does the behaviour policy reflect the importance of valuing and respecting children?

Involving parents

▶ How are parents' views about the care of their children respected and acted on?
▶ How are parents positively encouraged to contribute to the pre-school?
▶ How is information exchanged with parents, especially those who do not speak the language of the setting?
▶ How are parents encouraged to provide feedback to the setting?

Resources and activities

▶ How do resources and activities help to promote positive images of culture, religion, diversity and disability?
▶ How are activities adapted to meet the needs of all children?
▶ How do activities and resources contribute to all children's learning?

Staff training and recruitment

▶ How do new staff find out about anti-discriminatory practice policy and other policies in the setting?
▶ What training is provided to keep staff up to date with anti-discriminatory practice?
▶ Who is responsible for monitoring anti-discriminatory practice policy?
▶ How does the setting ensure that staff recruitment is anti-discriminatory?

Challenging attitudes and inappropriate practices

▶ What procedures are in place to ensure that inappropriate attitudes, language or practice are challenged?
▶ What would happen if this occurred?

Reviewing policies

It is usual for most pre-schools to have a variety of policies and procedures. Sometimes these policies are left untouched and become outdated. It is therefore important to review the policies in your setting and check that they reflect current anti-discriminatory practice. For example, you may find that the setting's behaviour policy is not inclusive, or that the policy on working with parents does not emphasise the importance of respecting different lifestyles. It is a good idea for everyone on the staff team to look at the policies and think about whether they reflect the setting's practice. Furthermore, it is important that all staff agree to the policies rather than simply paying 'lip service'.

In addition to thinking about policies that directly affect children, it is important to think about policies that affect staff. Does the procedure for employing staff reflect anti-discriminatory practice?

KEY POINTS

Anti-discriminatory policy: key questions

▶ Do policies reflect the need for pre-school settings to be inclusive?
▶ Is a member of staff responsible for monitoring anti-discriminatory practice?
▶ Are parents aware of the policy?
▶ Are parents and others invited to comment about practices in the pre-school?
▶ How much training has there been on anti-discriminatory practice since the policy was last reviewed?

Links to National Standards

Standard 9 of the National Standards is about ensuring that children are valued and that the setting actively promotes equality of opportunity. Inspectors will look at your setting's policy and the way in which the pre-school is run, including the activities and resources that are available. You will need to show that children's individual needs are identified and met. It is also important to show the ways in which the setting promotes positive images of culture, ethnicity, gender and disability through resources.

Providing a safe, secure and stimulating environment that promotes children's early learning

The environment that we provide for children plays an essential part in the way that children are able to settle in, play and learn. This is recognised by Standards 3, 4, 5, 6 and 7 of the National Standards, which are used by OFSTED to register pre-schools. This section looks at practical ways of providing such an environment and also considers the legislation that covers health and safety.

The effect of the environment of the pre-school setting on children's learning and development

The term 'environment' is broad. It covers layout, furniture and decoration but also the emotional climate that is created. Getting the environment right for children makes a considerable difference. Children who feel comfortable, yet stimulated in the environment are able to settle in and enjoy learning. It also has an impact on parents as they can see that the environment will be a safe and secure one for their children. Interestingly, children also respond to the environment that they are in. Behaviour can be improved in responsive, stimulating environments that have been carefully planned.

Key components of an effective environment for children

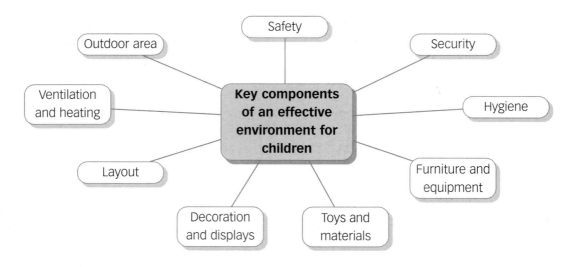

Safety

Safety is of paramount importance when working with children. Parents need to leave their child knowing that he or she is safe. This means that the environment needs to be assessed for risks, and staff need to supervise children consistently.

Security

Security is becoming an increasingly serious issue. Children must be kept secure, either from wandering out or from strangers gaining access.

Hygiene

Good hygiene is about preventing germs from spreading and invading our bodies. Poor hygiene can have devastating results because young children are particularly vulnerable to infections. Food poisoning in a young child can be fatal, while repeated colds can cause ear infections and temporarily affect a child's hearing. Staff therefore need to be aware of how to provide a hygienic environment that is safe for children to play in.

Ventilation and heating

Adequate heating and ventilation helps to meet young children's physical needs. Good ventilation also prevents germs from building up in the air. Interestingly, an overheated room can contribute to children's unwanted behaviour.

Furniture and equipment

Furniture and equipment can play an important part in the daily life of a pre-school. Heavy or poorly designed furniture can mean that the layout of the setting is difficult to change. This can prevent staff and children from carrying out certain activities. For example, a high cupboard will prevent children from being able to put equipment away, while non-adjustable tables might not be comfortable for children to sit at. Another priority is ensuring that sufficient storage exists, since this affects the ease with which children can tidy up and access activities. Children who do not have the opportunity to select equipment and tidy up will not be developing self-reliance and independence.

Layout

The way in which space is used in a pre-school can have a significant effect on how adults and children operate within it. Some layouts encourage children to run between activities, while others prevent staff from supervising children adequately. The setting's layout can also affect how many children are able to access an activity, and thus reduce its appeal. For example, many children enjoy playing in an area that is slightly screened off so that they can engage in role-play more effectively. Layout is also important in avoiding accidents.

GOOD PRACTICE ✓ Look out for and avoid creating layouts that might encourage children to move at speed in confined areas, for example, a long straight pathway from one end of the room to another.

Outdoor area

It is very easy to focus on the indoor environment and forget that children need to spend time outdoors. Being outdoors can help children's circulation, physical movement and general well-being. Where possible, play activities should be provided outdoors, as well as the more traditional outdoor equipment such as tricycles, slides and pushchairs.

Toys and materials

The ability of children to concentrate and engage in play is partially linked to the materials and toys with which they are provided. Toys and materials need to be age and stage appropriate and linked to children's interests. This means providing a range of toys and materials that enable children to learn a variety of skills and also enhance aspects of their development.

It is important that sufficient toys and materials are available to allow several children to engage in the same type of play should they wish. As toys and materials are significant costs in the running of a setting, it is important that decisions about which ones to buy are carefully evaluated, and that those that are bought are used well.

> **A QUICK THINK!**
>
> *Think about a pre-school environment that you have visited or in which you have worked.*
>
> ▶ *To what extent is it a welcoming environment for children?*
> ▶ *How are parents made to feel welcome?*
> ▶ *What changes might you make in order to improve the environment?*

GOOD PRACTICE ✓

Using toys and materials

▶ Look out for safety marks on toys and always read the instructions carefully.
▶ When using second-hand toys, it is essential that they are checked very carefully for wear and tear and cleanliness. Many settings avoid using second-hand toys with moving parts, such as tricycles.

The Lion, CE and Kite marks are all indications of approved products

Decoration and displays

The actual look of a setting can make a huge difference to the way in which children come to settle and behave. Children respond to seeing attractive displays, especially of their own work: it helps them to feel ownership.
If children are encouraged to contribute to the care of displays, it can make them feel responsible.

Ensuring that the environment meets the needs of children at different stages of development

As children grow and develop, so their needs change. This needs to be reflected in the pre-school environment.

Identifying the needs of the under-threes

Maintaining safety and hygiene is a priority: young children do not have a sense of danger and, at the same time, they are curious. Toddlers in particular can be determined to explore. It is therefore important to be aware of the physical stages of development of each child, and to consider how this will affect the child's safety.

▶ Children who are attempting to walk need to have stable furniture to pull up against, while children who are mobile might attempt to stand on furniture.

▶ Young children also have physical needs that need to be catered for effectively. Nappy-changing areas must be safe and hygienic, but also pleasant and welcoming for the child.

▶ Thought should be given to where children will eat and how the layout of the eating area will encourage them to enjoy the experience.

The role of safety equipment

For children under three years of age there is a need to provide safety equipment, especially to keep mobile babies and toddlers safe. Having said this, however, safety equipment is not a substitute for good supervision and adults must not be lulled into a false sense of security.

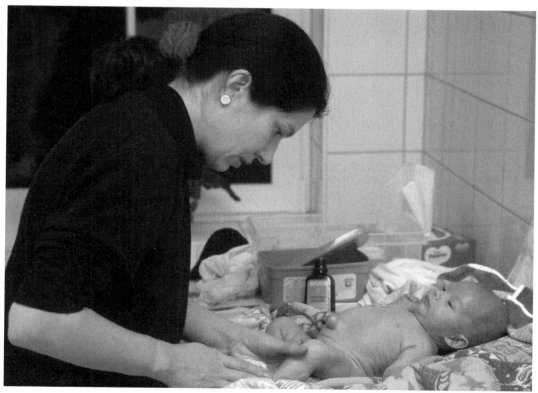

Is your nappy changing area clean and hygienic?

Type of equipment	Purpose	Precautions
Reins and harnesses	These are required for outings and for babies and toddlers in high chairs.	Care must be taken that these fit snugly, but not too tightly. Staff should always position a harness so that it can easily be undone if the child chokes.
Safety gates	These prevent children from moving into areas that might be hazardous, for example, stairs and kitchens.	Look out for gates that are easily opened by adults. Safety gates may be needed in rooms with older children.
Plastic corners	These are used to prevent toddlers from walking into the corners of furniture.	
Plastic plug covers	These are used to prevent children putting their fingers into live electric sockets.	Plug covers are also needed to protect older children.
Latches and window locks	Latches prevent children from having access to cupboards and drawers that may have dangerous contents. Window latches prevent children from falling out.	Some latches are easier to use than others.
Fire guards and radiator covers	These prevent children from touching hot radiators or gas appliances.	Make sure these are securely in place.

Types of safety equipment for children under three years of age

Identifying the needs of children in the Foundation Stage

Health and safety remains a key issue in creating an environment for children in the Foundation Stage because children do not magically become aware of safety when they reach three years old. Therefore, some safety equipment may still be required to keep older children safe, for example, plug covers and safety gates. In addition, the provision layout needs to be created with supervision in mind, although this should become increasingly discreet as children mature. Children in the Foundation Stage also need to enjoy independence, make choices and create their own play situations. Thus, many pre-schools create areas of provision within their settings to allow children to enjoy playing freely.

Current legislation linked to pre-school settings

The environments that pre-schools, nurseries and childminders provide are regulated to ensure that all children are safe and receive a good standard of care. The current regulations are linked to the Children Act 1989. This Act provides for the registration of all childcare providers who care for children for longer than two hours at a time.

The National Standards

Since September 2001, the Early Years directorate at OFSTED has taken on this inspection role. The inspection takes place each year and providers are currently inspected against the set of **National Standards**, of which there are 14. Collectively, the standards cover all aspects of children's care, including safety, food and drink, and child protection. Below is a chart showing the National Standards, which includes an OFTSED descriptor of each standard.

National Standard	Title	Descriptor
Standard 1	Suitable Person	Adults providing day care, looking after or having unsupervised access to children, are suitable to do so.
Standard 2	Organisation	The registered person meets required adult:child ratios, ensures that training and qualification requirements are met, and organises space and resources to meet the children's needs effectively.
Standard 3	Care, Learning and Play	The registered person meets children's individual needs and promotes their welfare. The registered person plans and provides activities and play opportunities to develop children's emotional, physical, social and intellectual capabilities.
Standard 4	Physical Environment	The premises are safe, secure and suitable for their purpose. They provide adequate space in an appropriate location, are welcoming to children, and offer access to the necessary facilities for a range of activities in order to promote children's development.
Standard 5	Equipment	Furniture, equipment and toys are provided that are appropriate for their purpose and help to create an accessible and stimulating environment. They are of suitable design and condition, are well maintained and conform to safety standards.
Standard 6	Safety	The registered person takes positive steps to promote safety within the setting and on outings and ensures proper precautions are taken to prevent accidents.
Standard 7	Health	The registered person promotes the good health of children, takes positive steps to prevent the spread of infection and adopts appropriate measures when children are ill.
Standard 8	Food and Drink	Children are provided with regular drinks and food in adequate quantities for their needs. Food and drink is properly prepared, nutritious and complies with dietary and religious requirements.
Standard 9	Equal Opportunities	The registered person and staff actively promote equality of opportunity and anti-discriminatory practice for all children.
Standard 10	Special Needs	The registered person is aware that some children may have special needs and is proactive in ensuring that appropriate action can be taken when such a child is identified or admitted to the provision. Steps are taken to promote the welfare and development of the child within the setting in partnership with the parents and other relevant parties.

National Standard	Title	Descriptor
Standard 11	Behaviour	Adults caring for children in the provision are able to manage a wide range of children's behaviour in a way that promotes their welfare and development.
Standard 12	Working in Partnership with Parents and Carers	The registered person and staff work in partnership with parents to meet the needs of the children, both individually and as a group. Information is shared.
Standard 13	Child Protection	The registered person complies with local child protection procedures approved by the Area Child Protection Committee and ensures that all adults working and looking after children in the provision are able to put the procedures into practice.
Standard 14	Documentation	Records, policies and procedures that are required for the efficient and safe management of the provision and to promote the welfare, care and learning of children, are maintained. Records about individual children are shared with the child's parent.

The National Standards

Health and safety legislation

In addition to the National Standards, there exists legislation about health and safety. There are two key pieces of legislation that affect health and safety in early years settings:

▶ the Health and Safety Act 1974
▶ the Children Act 1989.

These Acts are designed to enable further legislation to be passed to update their provisions; these updates take the form of regulations. One example is the 1997 Fire Precautions (workplace) Regulations, which made it compulsory for workplaces to have 'running men' symbols to help people see where they should go in the event of a fire. The changing nature of health and safety means that pre-schools must stay up to date with current regulations because ignorance of regulations is not considered a defence in law.

Health and Safety Act 1974

This Act was designed to protect employees, so many of its provisions apply to workplaces in which there are five or more members of staff. The Act gives duties to both employees and employers.

Duties of employees

The Act is clear that employees must follow the setting's health and safety procedures and use the health and safety equipment provided. Employees should not put others at risk by their actions, for example, by failing to report a faulty plug when there is a procedure to do so.

Duties of employers

The Act places significant duties on employers. Employers have a duty of care towards their employees and must take every reasonable step to consider their health and safety and to minimise risks. This means providing adequate training and protection, and carrying out risk assessments. Under this Act, settings with five or more employees must have a health and safety policy that explains how risks are to be minimised. Most pre-schools appoint a senior member of staff to be responsible for health and safety.

Regulation title	Description
Control of Substances Hazardous to Health Regulations (COSHH) 1994	These regulations look at the storage and use of chemicals and other hazardous materials. In pre-school settings, this might include cleaning products and the disposal of nappies. The regulations require settings to assess the risks and then write a procedure for managing the risks, for example, locking bleach in a cupboard and providing gloves.
Reporting of Injuries, Diseases and Dangerous Occurrences (RIDDOR) 1995	Workplaces must provide an accident report book for their employees (the Children Act 1989 regulations require an accident book for noting down injuries to children). Any injuries to an employee that mean that he or she cannot work for three or more days must be reported to the Health and Safety Executive.
Fire Precautions (workplace) Regulations 1997	Workplaces have to show how they would evacuate the building and carry out practices. Signs showing what to do in the event of a fire must be placed in every room. (Note that the Children Act 1989 also requires settings to have an evacuation procedure.)
Health and Safety (First Aid) Regulations 1981	Every workplace must have a first aid box and appoint at least one trained first aider to be responsible in the event of an accident. The contents of the first aid box are left to the discretion of the workplace. (Note that the Chidren Act 1989 requires that any medication given to children is recorded.)

Significant regulations under the 1974 Health and Safety Act

Children Act 1989

This Act is designed to protect children and to give them legal rights. It is a wide-ranging piece of legislation because the idea was to combine many existing pieces of legislation into one Act. As part of the Act, people who care for children, such as childminders, and settings caring for children need to be inspected. OFSTED has carried out this inspection role since September 2001.

Regulations that detail the standards of care for children come under the Children Act and include several relating to the health, safety and welfare of children. These regulations need to be dovetailed into your pre-school's compliance with the 1974 Health and Safety Act. Below is a chart showing some of the key regulations that you will need to comply with and that OFSTED is likely to check during their visit. Note that simply following these regulations alone is not sufficient to meet the requirements of an inspection.

Links to National Standards	What you need to do
Suitable person	OFSTED must be informed about people who may come into contact with the children, such as staff, volunteers and people who live on the premises.
Organisation	You must have procedures in place if a child is lost or a parent fails to collect his or her child. You must keep a record of the names and details of anyone who will be in regular contact with the children.
Physical environment	OFSTED must be informed if any changes are made to the premises or the way in which they are used.
Safety	You must have a policy in place which shows the procedure in the event of a fire.
Health	A record has to be kept of all medicines administered to children. A signed record of accidents must be kept in the setting. Serious accidents that result in injuries or death to children must be reported to OFSTED. You must report all notifiable infectious diseases to OFSTED.
Working in Partnership with Parents and Carers	You must keep records of the name, address and date of birth of each child, and the name, address and telephone number of a parent. You must have a complaints policy for parents to use.
Child Protection	A policy must be in place that shows how children are to be protected from abuse and the procedure to be followed in the event that abuse is suspected.
Documentation	Records that link to the regulations must be kept for at least two years following the last entry. OFSTED must be informed of significant changes or events, for example, members of staff leaving, a change of use of premises, longer opening hours, etc. Records as required by the National Standards must be kept on the premises. (See the National Standards for the comprehensive list.)

Examples of regulations linked to health and safety under the Children Act 1989

POINT OF INTEREST

Finding out information about current health and safety regulations

You can find out more about health and safety by contacting the Health and Safety Executive. This is a government agency that advises on health and safety and has the power to investigate and bring prosecutions against employers. They have a helpline and publish information leaflets. Contact www.hse.gov.uk or telephone on 08701 545500.

You can also find out more about accident prevention by contacting the Royal Society for the Prevention of Accidents (ROSPA) at www.rospa.org.uk

How written policies can help to ensure the safety of children

While policies in themselves do not keep children safe, they do help staff and volunteers to understand their role. Pre-school settings need to have up-to-date health and safety policies. Most pre-school settings designate one member of staff to be responsible for checking that the policies are current and are being followed. As legislation governing health and safety and recommendations can change, it is important that the designated person receives regular training and has sufficient time to review new documents.

Implementing and monitoring a health and safety policy

Health and safety is a complex area and covers many facets of our work with children. Below is a list of some key questions that need to be addressed as part of a health and safety policy.

KEY POINTS

Health and safety policy: a quick checklist

▶ Is time put aside in staff meetings for health and safety to be discussed?
▶ Are new members of staff given the health and safety policy and is time spent discussing its implications with them?
▶ Does everyone working in the setting understand how to report health and safety incidents?
▶ Are members of staff aware of procedures to deal with body products such as soiled clothes and blood?
▶ Are staff aware of evacuation procedures?

Induction of new staff members and volunteers

As with other policies such as child protection, the health and safety policy of your setting needs to be shared with new members of the team. It is a good idea for the person responsible for health and safety to spend time explaining procedures and, if necessary, show a new member any particular systems that are in place. If you are responsible for doing this, try not to 'overload' new members of staff with information. Provide them with written information as well as verbal information, so that they can spend time taking it in later. Most settings ask that new members of the team sign to say that they have read the setting's policy and agree to abide by its terms.

How to implement and review procedures for handling emergencies and first aid

Procedures for emergencies

All staff should understand what to do in an emergency. This is not only a requirement for registration; it also make common sense. Regular fire drills and evacuation **procedures** should be practised so that both staff and children become familiar with them.

The responsibility for organising practices should lie with a designated member of staff. This is usually the person who has responsibility for health and safety within the setting. Ideally, some practices should be carried out without warning, at different times of the day and with the assumption that fire has broken out in different places. This allows procedures to be tested in realistic conditions, and also ensures that part-time members of staff are involved. A record of each practice should be kept, because it may be scrutinised on inspection.

Once a practice is finished, staff should be encouraged to give **feedback**. Such feedback can be invaluable: problems can be ironed out or suggestions for improvement considered. Such comments and notes should be added to the practice records. New members of staff should also be given training in evacuation procedures, and it is usual for them to sign to show that this information has been given.

KEY POINTS

Emergency evacuation

▶ Is one member of staff designated for fire safety?
▶ Are frequent practices carried out?
▶ Are fire alarms and fire safety equipment regularly checked and recorded?
▶ Are new members of staff aware of the procedures for evacuation?
▶ Are notices and signs relating to evacuation clearly displayed?
▶ Who is responsible for contacting emergency services?
▶ How would emergency services be contacted?
▶ Is there regular liaison with fire prevention officers?

Reviewing evacuation procedures

▶ How were parents/visitors alerted to the fire?
▶ What was the overall evacuation time?
▶ Did everyone evacuate? If not, why was this?
▶ Were any problems encountered, for example, blocked or locked exits?
▶ Were registers taken and were they accurate?
▶ Did everyone meet at the appointed location?
▶ Was the location of the evacuation point appropriate?

CASE STUDY

Caroline is health and safety officer for the Busy Bees pre-school. She has decided to call a fire practise. She deliberately does not tell anyone except the supervisor so that she can find out how well the procedures are working. Afterwards, two members of staff are quite dismissive of the practise. They say it is a waste of time.

1 Explain the importance of regular fire practises.

2 Give two reasons why staff should not always know that a fire practise is going to happen.

Procedures for first aid

While serious accidents are, thankfully, rare in pre-school settings, staff must know the procedure for handling accidents whether serious or minor. It is a requirement that each setting has a designated person for first aid, although ideally everyone in the setting should at least have a basic first aid qualification. It is also useful to keep a record of when staff attended training, since first aid qualifications need to be regularly renewed.

It is a requirement that records are kept of any injury a child sustains in the setting, regardless of how superficial. In addition, an accident record book is required for staff and other adults. It is a good idea to look regularly at where and how accidents are taking place because the setting's layout or a certain piece of equipment may prove to be the source of a problem.

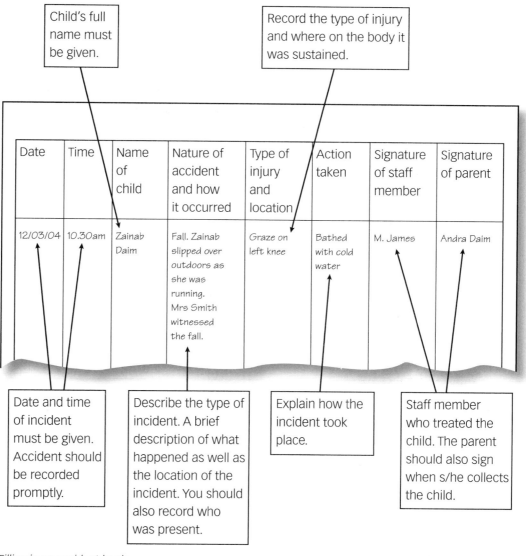

Child's full name must be given.

Record the type of injury and where on the body it was sustained.

Date	Time	Name of child	Nature of accident and how it occurred	Type of injury and location	Action taken	Signature of staff member	Signature of parent
12/03/04	10.30am	Zainab Daim	Fall. Zainab slipped over outdoors as she was running. Mrs Smith witnessed the fall.	Graze on left knee	Bathed with cold water	M. James	Andra Daim

Date and time of incident must be given. Accident should be recorded promptly.

Describe the type of incident. A brief description of what happened as well as the location of the incident. You should also record who was present.

Explain how the incident took place.

Staff member who treated the child. The parent should also sign when s/he collects the child.

Filling in an accident book

Implementing first aid procedures

▶ Is a member of staff designated for first aid?

▶ Are there signs showing where first aid kits are to be found?

▶ Do all members of staff know where the first aid kits are situated?

▶ Are first aid kits checked regularly?

▶ Are first aid kits out of reach of children but accessible for adults?

▶ Do staff understand the importance of filling in the accident book?

Reviewing first aid procedures

▶ Is the accident book filled out promptly and signed each time?

▶ Are emergency contact details kept up to date?

▶ Does a 'spotcheck' of the first aid kit reveal any deficiencies?

▶ Are procedures for first aid emergencies displayed?

▶ Are first aid qualifications still valid?

▶ Do staff wear protective gloves and handle waste products safely?

How to maintain a hygienic environment

Good hygiene is essential in early years settings. Young children are more vulnerable to infections because their immune system is still developing. Repeated illness in children can affect their overall development since they miss out on play and activities. Children in groups are particularly vulnerable to food poisoning, colds and other infections because bacteria and germs can spread easily. Good hygiene is about preventing the possible spread of infection. This is becoming particularly important as many strains of bacteria are now becoming immune to antibiotics.

It is thought that, given the right conditions, a single bacterium can produce a colony of 250,000 in six hours.

Understanding how germs are spread

A host of organisms can infect the human body. Major groups are bacteria, viruses, fungi and parasites, such as worms and nits. Understanding how these organisms infect us can be helpful when thinking about prevention.

Inhalation

Some germs are airborne and we breathe them in, for example, colds and influenza.

Inoculation

Some germs infect us because they enter through the skin via cuts, grazes and other wounds.

Ingestion

Some bacteria, viruses and parasites, such as threadworms, infect us when we swallow them. This is an easy way for germs to enter babies and young children, who frequently put their hands in their mouths. Remember that babies explore objects, such as toys, by putting them in their mouth.

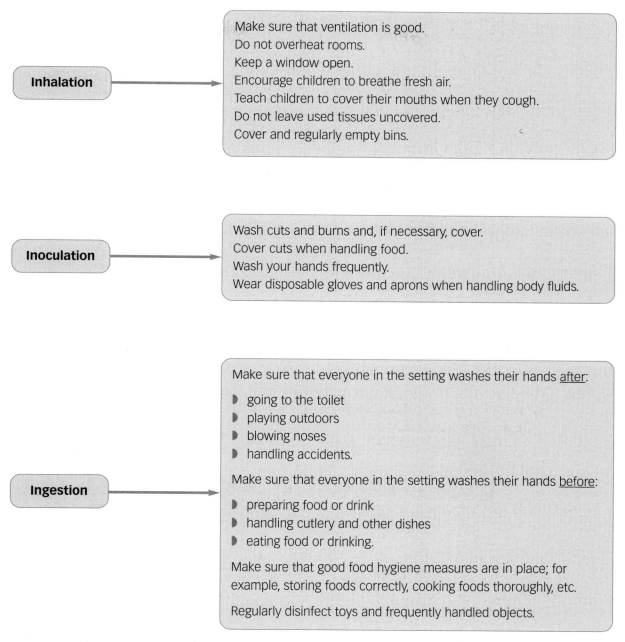

Inhalation

Make sure that ventilation is good.
Do not overheat rooms.
Keep a window open.
Encourage children to breathe fresh air.
Teach children to cover their mouths when they cough.
Do not leave used tissues uncovered.
Cover and regularly empty bins.

Inoculation

Wash cuts and burns and, if necessary, cover.
Cover cuts when handling food.
Wash your hands frequently.
Wear disposable gloves and aprons when handling body fluids.

Ingestion

Make sure that everyone in the setting washes their hands <u>after</u>:

▶ going to the toilet
▶ playing outdoors
▶ blowing noses
▶ handling accidents.

Make sure that everyone in the setting washes their hands <u>before</u>:

▶ preparing food or drink
▶ handling cutlery and other dishes
▶ eating food or drinking.

Make sure that good food hygiene measures are in place; for example, storing foods correctly, cooking foods thoroughly, etc.

Regularly disinfect toys and frequently handled objects.

Measures to prevent the spread of infection

Maintaining cleanliness

You will need to have a regular routine of cleaning in order to maintain a high standard of cleanliness in the setting. It is important that staff understand their responsibilities in relation to cleaning. You will also need to make sure that all staff who prepare food have had training, for example, a basic food hygiene certificate.

Using cleaning products

It is not advisable to use cleaning products when children are around. Some cleaning products, especially aerosols and sprays, can trigger breathing difficulties in children with asthma. There is also the danger that products left unattended may be swallowed or spilt.

When using cleaning products, it is essential to read the instructions on the packaging because some products must be used with gloves. Take care to ensure that different cleaning products are not mixed because some products can produce strong chemical reactions when combined.

Area/item	Method
Hard floors	Wash with disinfectant every day and during the day if there are spills. Floors in wash areas and kitchens need particular attention.
Carpeted areas	These should be thoroughly vacuumed and arrangements made for them to be shampooed regularly.
Toilets, hand basins, sinks	Bacteria favour damp conditions to multiply and so these areas need to be cleaned at least once a day to prevent the spread of infection. Attention should be paid to handles on toilets and doors in these areas.
Door handles	Frequently used door handles should be wiped each day with disinfectant.
Tables	Tables should be wiped over at the end of each activity with disinfectant. If they are used to serve food, they should be cleaned at the beginning and the end of the meal. The legs of the table should also be given attention.
Chairs	The backs and sides of chairs are often handled and if they are used at food tables can become dirty. Chairs should therefore be wiped over frequently.
Bins	Bins should be emptied regularly and covered over. Separate bins are needed for waste paper and for soiled waste materials. Waste materials such as nappies should be put in a bag and then put into a covered bin. This bin should be out of reach of children.
Feeding equipment	Beakers, plates, cutlery – anything used to serve food – must be cleaned thoroughly. Staff should wash their mugs properly as dirty mugs are a common cause of infection in staff rooms.
Toys and frequently handled equipment	Wipe down with disinfectant, rinse if necessary. Pay particular attention to objects such as pencils if children suck the ends, and toys that babies put in their mouths.
Cuddly toys, bedding and soft furnishings such as cushions	Surprisingly high levels of bacteria can build up on fabrics. This means that cuddly toys, bedding and cushion covers, etc. need to be washed regularly – at least weekly. Toys that are not easy to clean should be discarded.
Outdoor area	Check that animals, including birds, have not fouled. Make sure that equipment is clean and wipe it if necessary. Cover sandpits to avoid parasitic infection and always check for fouling before use. Remove any litter. Wear disposable gloves while cleaning outdoors.

Routine cleaning

CASE STUDY

Emma is working in the kitchen preparing children's food. She accidentally knocks a tray of food onto the floor. She realises that this could mean that the children will not get their lunch on time. As no one is around, she decides to scrape the food up and camouflage it with some grated cheese.

1 Why does this example show poor practice?

2 What are the risks to the children?

3 Suggest what Emma should have done instead.

How to equip and set out a physical environment that supports children's learning and development

The layout that we provide for children will have a significant impact on their behaviour and learning. It is therefore very important to consider the environment and how it meets children's needs.

Meeting the needs of the under-threes

The very young child needs to feel secure, and this should be a priority when looking at the physical arrangement of rooms. Children under three years of age need the reassuring presence of an adult nearby, and will often want to 'check in' while playing. This is why key worker systems are very much needed when working with young children (see page 33), and why creating a homely environment in which children can readily see adults is important.

If young children are spending significant amounts of time in a setting, it is essential that they do not spend all of their time in one room. Like adults, children need a change of environment. This may mean that children spend plenty of time outdoors or in places in which they can move freely, for example, to enable them to use trolleys, sit-and-rides, and tricycles.

KEY POINTS **The play environment for under-threes**

- Create some small spaces in which children can feel secure.
- Look for ways of helping children to see adults.
- Provide mobiles, mirrors and music for young children.
- Make sure that equipment and toys are age appropriate.
- Create storage areas that allow children to access toys.
- Make sure that nappy-changing areas are attractive and hygienic.
- Try to look at the layout from the child's point of view (lie down and notice what they see).
- Make sure that children have access to a range of play types during the session, for example, heuristic play, play with sensory materials and imaginative play.

Is the equipment age appropriate?

Meeting the needs of Foundation Stage children

The need for security remains throughout children's early years. However, children will increasingly need opportunities to play in a variety of ways to allow them to develop a wide range of skills and become independent. Most pre-schools therefore create different areas of provision for Foundation Stage children so that they can play with different materials. This is usually a helpful approach, but care needs to be taken that play does not become too 'clinical' and that children who want to combine play materials are not thwarted, for example, making 'dough' cakes and taking them into the home corner.

Thought must also be given to meeting the needs of children who are not yet three years old. Some pre-schools manage this by creating a 'safe haven' whereby the youngest children can play in a smaller area but still have the freedom to go and explore with the older children if they wish.

Small-world play

Small-world play includes animals and everyday objects, such as cars and dinosaurs, as well as play people and doll's houses. Small-world play can be set out on the floor or on a low table. It is useful if children know where they can find additional pieces, characters or bricks to enhance their play. It is also helpful to leave the storage container nearby so that children can tidy up for themselves at the end of the session.

GOOD PRACTICE ✓

Small-world play

- Make sure that small-world sets are kept clean.
- Encourage children to tidy up at the end of the session.
- Check that there are sufficient pieces for the number of children who want to play.
- If small-world play is put on the floor, make sure that it is not in an area in which other children may inadvertently trample on it.

Sand and water

Sand and water are 'core activities' in early years settings. Look out for sand and water trays that have large wheels so they can be moved easily. Consider providing sand and water play in small containers, such as washing-up bowls, to allow individual children to play on a small scale.

You can use small household containers in sand and water play

Sand and water play

 ▶ Position the water tray near a source of water.
 ▶ Provide cloths nearby so that children can wipe up spills for themselves.
 ▶ Provide a dustpan and brush for sweeping up sand on the floor.
 ▶ Keep separate toys for sand as they can become scratched.
 ▶ Make sure that aprons are kept nearby so that children can access them easily.
 ▶ Position sand and water play so that staff can easily supervise it.
 ▶ Provide small-world toys for use in the sand and water tray.

Dough, Plasticine and other malleable materials

Play with malleable materials helps children's physical skills, but also provides them with props for imaginative play. Consider how children can be encouraged to combine these play types.

Dough, Plasticine and other malleable materials

 ▶ Position this type of play on a table.
 ▶ If chairs are provided, make sure they are high enough to allow children to see what they are doing.
 ▶ Provide resources that encourage children to make 'food' and other imaginative play props.
 ▶ Put out a selection of tools including scissors for children in the Foundation Stage.

Construction play

Construction play can include bricks, train sets and other equipment that encourages children to interlink, connect and join materials.

Construction play

 ▶ Make sure that there is sufficient equipment because children can have strong preferences.
 ▶ Consider where children most enjoy playing with the equipment, for example, on the floor or a low table.
 ▶ Ensure that there is sufficient space because this type of play can 'expand'.
 ▶ Provide small-world figures to enable children to combine this type of play with small-world play if they choose.
 ▶ Put storage containers nearby so that children can add to their play or tidy away when they have finished.

Quiet area

Most pre-schools have some form of quiet area for children. It is generally used for books, stories and listening to tapes, though some pre-schools use the quiet area for floor puzzles.

Quiet area

▶ Make sure that books are accessible.
▶ Check that books are attractive and have positive non-stereotypical images.
▶ Provide a range of books including factual books.
▶ Make sure that the area is comfortable, for example, carpeted with cushions or comfortable chairs.

Role-play areas

Role-play areas encourage children to develop language and social skills, and this helps them to feel empowered. It also helps them to learn more about their world.

Ideally, it is worth having two role-play areas in a setting. This is because it allows for the existence of both a permanent 'home' corner and a changeable 'themed' corner. Children can then be encouraged to move from their 'home' to another place in their play, for example, going to the shops or the doctor's surgery.

Role-play areas

▶ Make sure that children are involved in choosing toys and props for role-play areas.
▶ Look out for 'real life' props that children can handle and use.
▶ Make sure that home corners reflect children's own homes.
▶ Position role-play areas so that children can go in and out of them without disrupting other activities.
▶ Try to find places in which to hang dressing-up clothes.

Painting and creative area

Children enjoy using paint, collage and creating models. It is important that children are able to access tools and resources easily so that they can make their own choices.

Allow children to make their own choice of resources easily

Painting and creative areas

▶ Check that this area is positioned near to a sink.

▶ Make sure that aprons are provided and that children can access them independently.

▶ Provide a good range of tools, paper and other materials.

▶ Consider providing palettes rather than pots of paint; they allow children to learn to mix colours for themselves.

▶ Provide opportunities for children to paint on a large scale by creating a painting wall.

Outdoors

Outdoor provision has sometimes been seen as an 'add on', but it is now increasingly used to help children learn as well as enjoy physical play.

Outdoor areas

▶ Make sure that equipment such as sit-and-rides, climbing frames, tricycles and slides are weight bearing.

▶ Consider providing items that encourage role-play outdoors, for example, pushchairs, umbrellas and fabric to make dens.

▶ Aim to provide messy play, for example, play with leaves, mud, sand and water.

▶ Look carefully at the layout of outdoor areas to ensure that good supervision can be maintained.

Making the layout inclusive

Inclusion is about ensuring that no children are unable to access opportunities because of a disability or special need. A child should not have to watch others from a distance because he or she cannot join in, nor be excluded from a game because he or she is not the same 'level' as other children. Inclusion thus means identifying the particular needs of the children in your setting and making the appropriate adjustments. It is vital here to stress the individual nature of these adjustments; for example, a child with sight problems will have very different practical needs from a child with autistic spectrum disorder. It is also important to understand the range of adjustments that might be needed. Some children will require equipment or changes to the location of activities, while others may need greater adult input. A good starting point is always the child's parents: they often know from first-hand experience what interests their child, and will probably have developed some strategies to help him or her.

Behaviour and layout

In terms of children's behaviour, it is always worth observing how children use their environment. Layouts that are very open can create a noisy environment, which some children may find hard to cope with. Similarly, behaviour that is deemed unwanted is sometimes linked to a shortage of interesting activities. In such situations, children are constantly on the move because they have not found anything that particularly engages them.

Toys and equipment need to be accessible for children

In order to encourage children's confidence and independence, it is important to make toys and equipment accessible for children. This encourages them to be self-reliant and expand their play. It can therefore be helpful for some toys and equipment to be located near the area of play, for example, a dustpan and brush near to the sand area or boxes of bricks near to the construction area.

How to involve parents in the setting's safety procedures

It is important to involve parents in the safety procedures of your setting. In this way, potentially worrying incidents can be avoided. It is also reassuring for parents to know what systems are in place. Ideally, parents need to be informed about the setting's safety procedures during admission and settling-in procedures. It is often worth taking the time to explain to parents the importance of your safety procedures: many parents do not realise that the law requires that attendance registers, contact details and other records are kept.

Children's details

Parents need to provide sufficient details about their child so that we can act appropriately in the event of an emergency or routine problem. Details should include:

▶ Contact details of parents – their home address and work contact numbers. It can also be helpful if parents identify who should be contacted first in the event of an emergency.
▶ Medical information – this should include the contact details of a child's doctor as well as any known allergies or pre-existing medical conditions.
▶ Other information – this might include information about meeting the child's care needs, for example, diet and skin care, and parental preferences.
▶ Collection arrangements – the details of who will usually collect the child.

Keeping information up to date

It is essential that children's information is up to date because these records form part of the regulations of the Children Act 1989. It is therefore a good idea to ask parents each year to look at the information they have given and check it is correct. Mobile phone numbers or a parent's place of work may have changed. Occasionally, it is worthwhile including a reminder in a newsletter or placing a sign in the entrance area.

Registration

Registration is an essential part of keeping children safe. It is important that we know how many children are in the setting at any one time in case there is a fire. It is also a requirement of the National Standards that a daily record is kept showing the hours that children have attended. It can therefore be helpful to have one member of staff available to talk to parents near the entrance. This means that a careful eye can be kept on who has arrived and whether gates or doors are being closed. In addition, having a member of staff available to greet parents and children can be a lovely way of getting to know parents, while also keeping an eye out for children who may need a little help with settling. Some pre-schools have a system whereby parents 'sign' in their children as they arrive, while others have a system in which parents find the name card for their child and encourage the child to post it in a box. It is useful to create a registration area that is large enough because several parents may arrive at once.

Procedures for collecting children

Parents and main carers also need to understand the procedures for collecting children. Simply taking a child can create all kind of difficulties, so parents need to understand that a procedure is in place for the safety of their own child and that of other children. Most settings have a system whereby parents come into the hall or room at the end of the session and personally collect their child. This can work well because it avoids situations in which children are hanging around near an entrance. It also means that parents can have a quick word with staff, which can help to build good relations. However, bringing parents into a room to collect their children can be hectic, so it is useful to have a member of staff supervise the entrance and say goodbye to children and parents as they leave.

Arrangements as to who collects the child

At the end of each session, it is essential that the right child goes home with the right person. Most pre-schools ask parents on the admission form to write down the key person or people who are authorised to collect their child at the end of a session. This can be extremely important information, especially when there are child protection issues or court orders. Parents need to know that they <u>must inform the setting</u> if they wish their child to be collected by someone else. Some settings produce simple slips that parents can complete if they wish their child to be collected by someone else. This is helpful as it provides a record for staff at the end of the session. In situations where it is unclear who should be collecting a child, a clear procedure should be followed. This procedure should be written down, as is required for compliance with the Children Act 1989 regulations.

Signing out before the end of a session

As well as having a system of registration when children arrive, it is important to have a system for signing out children who leave before the end of a session. This means that if an evacuation were necessary, time would not be wasted in looking for a child who had already left. Ideally, information about who has signed out should be recorded alongside the register so that the information is together.

Visitors' book

Parents who are staying to help or visitors, including those on official business such as early years advisers, should be signed in and out of the premises. Again, this is important in the eventuality that an evacuation of the building is required. Visitors should also be given a badge identifying their status. This should help to prevent a situation in which, for example, a visitor attempts to take a child and in doing so is unchallenged by another adult.

Supervision of visitors and other adults in the setting

It is essential that all visitors including tradespeople, such as builders, are supervised when they are in the building and not allowed to have unsupervised contact with children. This should include parent helpers and volunteers unless they have been police checked. This may seem a drastic measure, but there have been incidents in which children have been abused by adults in the setting. While young children may have some understanding of not talking to strangers, they will not necessarily understand that a person who has come to fix the floor or help serve snacks is still a 'stranger'. To save potential embarrassment, it is therefore important that a sign or a notice is clearly displayed at the entrance which states that this is the setting's policy.

Applying an understanding of children's physical needs to all aspects of their care and education

Children's physical needs in relation to their overall development

Children's physical needs have to be met so that they can learn and settle well. Children who are tired, hungry or dirty will not be able to access learning effectively. This means that as part of the overall organisation of the pre-school, we need to identify children's physical needs and check that they are being met. As physical care is a sensitive area, we must also check with parents as to how they wish their child to be cared for.

Developing routines that meet children's needs

The routine of the setting can be very important in meeting children's physical needs. Rigid routines that require all children to do the same thing at the same time, such as queuing to use the toilet or having snack time together, are not recommended. The danger with a 'mass production' approach to caring for children is that we will not be able to accommodate a child's individual needs. For example, a child may have a strong bladder or may have had a very early breakfast and be hungrier earlier in the morning. The National Standards also make it clear that we should be respectful of children's dignity; being forced to go to the toilet because it is the routine of the setting does not demonstrate this.

In order to create a flexible routine, a pre-school may need to look carefully at the way its staff are deployed and the layout of the setting. For example, it is good practice to have a self-service approach to snack time. This means setting aside a table from which children can help themselves to a drink and a healthy snack at any time during the morning. Key worker groups can be helpful in creating routines, because the key worker should have a good understanding of the needs of the individual children in his or her group. Having a small group together for a story or lunch can help children to feel part of a community; it also allows staff to tailor their approach according to individual children.

Nutrient	Benefits to the body	Example of foods
Fats	Energy Also needed for the body to absorb vitamins A and D	Butter, olive oil, margarine, vegetable oils, as well as present in meat, fish and dairy products
Carbohydrates	Energy	Bread, pasta, flour, potatoes, sweet potatoes, plantains and bananas, vegetables
Proteins	Energy Growth and repair	There are two types of proteins. Proteins that are found in meat, fish, soya and dairy products can be absorbed by themselves by the body, while proteins found in vegetable products such as peas, beans, lentils, need to be eaten in combination with other food so that the body can take in the protein – e.g. beans on toast, lentil and barley soup
Mineral elements	There are many minerals needed in a balanced diet. The role of some has not yet been fully identified	Traces of mineral elements are found in many vegetables, particularly if eaten with skins
Iron	Helps blood to carry oxygen	Red meat, broccoli, spinach, plain chocolate, egg yolk
Calcium and phosphorus	Used for maintaining and repairing bones and teeth	Milk, cheese, yoghurt and other dairy products. They are also added to white flour
Fluoride	Used for maintaining and forming teeth and bones	Sea fish, added into some water, also often taken in by the body through toothpaste
Vitamins	Many diseases are caused by lack of vitamins, even though the amounts needed by the body are very small	
Vitamin A	Healthy skin, growth and development. Needed for maintaining good vision	Fat-soluble – found in fats – dairy products, cheese, margarine, apricots, fatty fish
Vitamin B group	Growth and development, appetite, helps release energy from other foods, good for the nervous system	Bread, flour, meat, yeast, pasta, rice, noodles – added to some breakfast cereals
Vitamin C (fragile – easily destroyed by cooking processes)	Needed for forming bones, teeth and blood vessels, needed for skin	Fresh fruits and greens – e.g. oranges, kiwis, potatoes, blackcurrants, cabbage
Vitamin D	Needed for bones and teeth	Dairy products – e.g. milk, cheese, yoghurts, and fish, added into margarine
Vitamin E	Not completely understood but links to fertility, protection from cancers and heart disease	Vegetable oils, green leafy vegetables, milk, nuts
Vitamin K	Helps blood to clot	Green vegetables – e.g. spinach, broccoli, peas

How to provide for children's dietary needs

Food and drink are essential in meeting children's physical needs. Food is required to give energy and help the body grow, while water is required to maintain the body's vital organs. Children who are hungry or thirsty will find it harder to concentrate and participate in the activities of your pre-school. The importance of food and drink is reflected in Standard 8 of the National Standards (see below). While pre-schools cannot be completely responsible for children's diets, we do have a duty to ensure that the food and drink that we serve them are healthy and nutritious. This is currently a 'hot' issue because it is reported that a significant proportion of young children are overweight.

> *Children are provided with regular drinks and food in adequate quantities for their needs. Food and drink are properly prepared, nutritious and comply with dietary and religious requirements.*

Standard 8, National Standards

A balanced diet

Eating healthily is always a question of balance. It is not just a question of dividing foods into 'bad' and 'good' because too much of any one type of food is likely to cause problems. This is because foods are composed of nutrients and the body needs a range of foods in order to get the correct mix of nutrients.

Each nutrient has a specific role to play in the body. There are five nutrient groups in total; meals that are nutritious will contain nutrients from all five groups.

Children's dietary requirements

Children's dietary requirements are not quite the same as those for adults. Firstly, this is because children are developing their tastes. We should therefore be careful not to give them the taste for high fat, salty or sugary foods. We also need to be aware that in relation to their body weight, children actually need proportionally more energy than adults do. This is because children are growing and are generally more active. As a child's stomach capacity is less than that of an adult, children should be given foods that are nutrient dense. For children under three years of age, this includes full-fat milk. It also means that low-fat diets, which may be safe for adults, should not be followed unless medical advice is sought.

Providing nutritious snacks and foods

To ensure that children are getting sufficient nutrients, we should consider the nutrients that are in different types of food when planning menus or snacks. We should also consider the way in which the food is prepared because part of the food's goodness, for example, vitamins, can be lost during the cooking process. Generally, to retain the maximum amount of vitamins it is a good idea to serve fresh fruit raw and vegetables lightly steamed.

	Day 1	Day 2	Day 3	Day 4	Day 5
Mid-morning	Diluted orange juice Banana	Water Grapes	Milk Cheese straws	Milk Raisins	Water Satsuma
Lunch	Pitta filled with tuna and sweetcorn Fresh lychees Water	Turkey curry with rice Yoghurt Water	Macaroni cheese Broccoli Ice cream and fresh fruit Water	Shepherd's pie Carrots and peas Blackcurrant fool Water	Trinidad fruit stew (made with plantains) Banana and custard Water

When planning a menu for children, it is worth thinking about how easy the food is for children to manage. Look out for foods that do not require endless chewing and think about the ease with which children can feed themselves.

Using children's appetites as portion guides

Children themselves are generally good indicators of how much they can eat. Children who are very hungry are sometimes about to have a growth spurt, while children who are fighting infections may be off their food. This means that wherever possible children should be encouraged to serve themselves; providing that a good range of food is available, they should get the nutrients they need. If puddings or desserts are served, it is important that these are as nutritionally sound as other parts of the meal, for example, yoghurt and fresh fruit. It is not a good idea to 'label' these as treats otherwise children will learn the hidden message that the main course is a chore.

POINT OF INTEREST

Five-a-day campaign

The importance of fruit and vegetables in increasingly recognised. It is suggested that children and adults should aim to eat five portions of fruit and vegetables a day. This means that instead of biscuits, many pre-schools provide fresh fruit and vegetables, for example, carrot sticks.

Look out for the five-a-day campaign and find out whether your pre-school may be entitled to free fruit.

Foods to avoid

▶ Salt

Children should not be given salty foods, such as crisps, or have salt added to their food. Too much salt can affect the kidneys and lead to long-term health problems.

▶ Raw or partially cooked eggs

Eggs are perfectly safe provided that they are completely cooked. Eggs that are only partially cooked, for example, boiled eggs with runny yolks, should be avoided because there is a risk of food poisoning.

▶ Foods that are high in fats and low in other nutrients
While young children do need fat in their diets, it is important that they do not acquire a taste for high-fat processed foods, such as chips, pies and crisps. Learning to like such foods simply stores up problems for later in life because they are low in other nutrients. Cheese, milk and yoghurts, which do contain fat, are considered to be good for children.

▶ Sugar
We should avoid encouraging children to develop a 'sweet tooth'. While it is good to provide children with foods that are naturally sweet, such as melons or pineapples, it is not a good idea to include too many foods with added sugar. Too much sugar in a child's diet can cause obesity and dental decay. It also stores up problems for the future because children will find it harder to enjoy fresh fruit and drinks that are plain. It is for this reason that many dietitians do not recommend giving children foods that contain artificial sweeteners: while they do not contain any calories or sugar, they do teach children to enjoy sweet tastes.

Children enjoy making their own sandwiches

Ideas for healthy snacks

You should aim to provide children with snacks that are nutritious and easy for them to eat. It is good practice to involve children in the preparation of snacks, an activity which can be planned and prove rewarding for all involved.

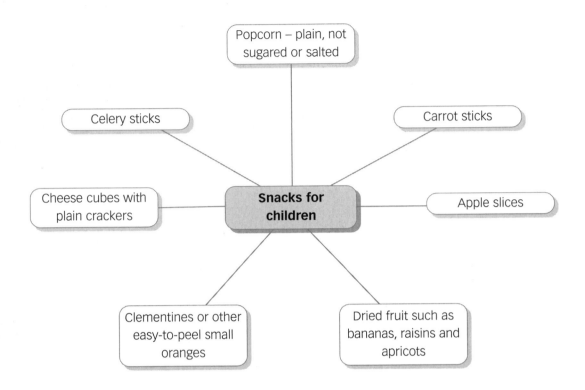

Attitudes towards food

Children learn about food partly from the adults around them. Therefore, if we want children to enjoy their food and eventually choose foods that are good for them, they need to see us eating healthily. This means that adults should try to sit with children at snack and meal times. It is also important to avoid comments that may teach children to dislike certain foods or to become worried about their body shape.

POINT OF INTEREST

Finishing everything up

Many dietitians feel that children should not be 'pushed' into finishing everything on their plate. While gentle encouragement to eat is fine, children should not be made to sit at a table or refused other foods as a punishment. The idea is that children who are taught to finish everything even when they are not hungry, may later find it harder to control their eating habits because they have learnt not to follow their appetites.

Religious and cultural dietary needs

For some families, food plays an important role in their culture, religion or social beliefs. A good example of this is the increasing trend for some families to eat only meat and poultry that has been reared ethically, or to insist that fruit and vegetables are organically grown. Such beliefs have to be respected and we will therefore need parents to specify how best to meet their child's dietary requirements. The chart below shows some of the common food restrictions.

Food	Muslim	Jew	Sikh	Hindu (mainly vegetarian)	Rastafarian (mainly vegetarian although take milk products)	Vegetarians	Vegans
Lamb	Halal	Kosher	Yes	Some	Some	No	No
Pork	No	No	Rarely	Rarely	No	No	No
Beef	Halal	Kosher	No	No	Some	No	No
Chicken	Halal	Kosher	Some	Some	Some	No	No
Cheese	Some	Not with meat	Some	Some	Yes	Yes	No
Milk/yoghurt	Not with rennet	Not with meat	Yes	Not with rennet	Yes	Yes	Soya and other substitutes
Eggs	Yes	No blood spots	Yes	Some	Yes	Yes	No
Fish	Halal	With fins, scales and backbones	Some	With fins and scales	Yes	Some	No
Shellfish	Halal	No	Some	Some	No	Some	No
Cocoa/tea/coffee	Yes	Yes	Yes	Yes	Yes	Yes	Yes
Fast periods	Ramadan	Yom Kippur					

Food allergies

Some children can be **allergic** to certain foods, and in extreme cases an allergic reaction can be fatal. This means that care needs to be taken when preparing and serving food to ensure that children do not eat foods that trigger a reaction. You should also check the ingredient label on purchased food products before giving them to children. If in doubt about any food, always check and err on the side of caution. Parents tend to have up-to-date advice and some may prefer to bring in their own snacks and foods to avoid any confusion. Your pre-school should have a procedure in place that helps staff to identify those children who have specific dietary requirements, and this may be checked at inspection.

Below is a chart of some of the more common food allergies. This is not a comprehensive list and therefore it is vital that information is exchanged with parents.

Food	Reaction and recommendation
Nuts	Some children have violent reactions to nuts and products that contain nuts, such as marzipan. The advice is to avoid giving nuts, including peanut butter, to all children below the age of five years.
Gluten	Gluten is found in wheat and other flours. Products such as bread, biscuits and pizzas are not suitable for children with this allergy.
Lactose	Some children are unable to digest lactose found in dairy products. Foods such as milk, yoghurt and cheese are not suitable for children with this allergy. Parents should be asked about substitute foods.
Chemicals and preservatives	Some children have strong reactions to preservatives and colourings found in manufactured foods.

Some common food allergies

Diabetes mellitus

Diabetes is a medical condition in which the body has difficulty regulating the amount of sugar in the blood. If a child in your setting has diabetes, it is essential for all staff to follow the child's diet and eating patterns. Going without food or drink for a period, or being given foods that are high in carbohydrates and sugars, can have severe effects on the child. Usually, parents are able to give advice as to when and what their child should be eating. It is usual to find that children with diabetes require frequent snacks so that their blood sugar levels can remain stable.

GOOD PRACTICE

Children's diet and eating habits
- Do staff sit and eat with children?
- Are children encouraged to serve themselves?
- Are staff aware of the specific dietary needs and allergies of children?
- Is food chosen which is nutritious?
- Are children able to follow their own appetites?

CASE STUDY

Sandy, the supervisor, has launched herself on yet another diet. Her target is to lose a stone in a month. She is not eating any carbohydrates and is restricting herself to a drink at lunchtime. At lunch, she sits with the children and talks to them. One of the children asks her where her lunch is. Sandy says that eating too much has made her fat.

1 In what way is Sandy acting as a role model for children?

2 What are the dangers of young children learning about dieting?

3 What messages should young children learn about food?

Drinks for children

Water

Water is essential for life as it helps to keep the body healthy. Young children need sufficient water because it helps to regulate their body temperature and keep vital organs working effectively. The amount of water that children drink therefore needs to be monitored. This is especially so in hot weather because children can become quite poorly when dehydrated.

Other drinks

The best drinks for children's nutrition and health are water and milk because they do not contain sugar or acidic substances. Other drinks, such as juice, squash and flavoured water, can cause dental decay over time if children drink them frequently. In the case of juices, the sugar or acid remain on the teeth and combine with the mouth's saliva to cause plaque, which erodes the enamel. If these drinks are offered, children should be encouraged to finish them quickly so that the teeth are exposed for a shorter length of time to the sugar and acids. Problems occur when children use beakers and constantly sip small amounts of drink over a period. This results in the child's teeth repeatedly being coated with sugar or acid, which allows the plaque to remain on the teeth for longer.

GOOD PRACTICE

Children's drinks

▶ Is water freely available?

▶ Are children helped to serve themselves?

▶ Do staff check that younger children are drinking, especially in hot weather?

▶ Are beakers, cups or bottles provided that are stage and age appropriate?

▶ Are staff aware that some drinks can have a detrimental effect on children's teeth?

Responding to accidents and signs of illness

While every effort should be made to prevent accidents, it is also important that everyone knows what to do if a child has an accident. This section looks at how to respond to an accident. While this information might be helpful, it is not a replacement for attending a basic first aid course. Such courses will give you practical experience of how to administer first aid correctly. In addition, techniques for first aid do change, so you should always take refresher courses.

Responding to an accident

It is important to respond to every accident with care. What might seem a simple bump to the head might later result in concussion. If you are the nearest adult when an accident occurs, you should remain calm and take the following steps.

1 Keep calm
- This reassures children and helps them to follow your instructions.
- It prevents further accidents.
- It allows you to assess the situation more accurately and make the right decisions.

2 Look out for any further dangers
- What was the cause of the accident? Is this still a danger?
- Do other children need to be evacuated?
- Does the casualty need to be removed to prevent further injury?

3 Assess the extent of the injury
- Is the child breathing, talking?
- Can you see bleeding?
- Is the child in great pain?

4 Decide on the type of help required (see tables on major and minor injuries)
- Is emergency help required?
- Is a first aider's assistance required?

5 Summon help
- Is it safe to ask one of the other children to get help?
- Can help be summoned by calling out?
- Is there a telephone or other means of getting help?

Responding to an accident

When to contact emergency services

Emergency services should <u>always</u> be contacted if any of the following apply:

- the child has stopped breathing
- you cannot find a pulse
- the child has difficulty in breathing or the skin and lips are turning blue
- the child is vomiting blood
- the child is unconscious or not responding
- the child is bleeding profusely.

General points

- Call or shout for help.
- Stop any treatment and follow **ABC*** if a child stops breathing.
  *Check **A**irways for obstructions
  Look out to see if child is
  Breathing
  Take a pulse to see if blood
  is **C**irculating
- Do not give food or drink to children who have had a major accident.
- Remain calm and reassuring.

Poisoning

(Children may not look well, begin vomiting or you may see what has been taken.)

- Ask the child what he or she has eaten or drunk if this is possible.
- Watch for signs of losing consciousness.
- Do not make the child vomit or give any drinks.
- Take the suspected poison with you to the hospital so that they can give the appropriate treatment.

Cuts and wounds

- Direct pressure needs to be applied to the wound with a clean pad. If it is a large wound, try to press the edges together.
- Do not remove anything from a deep wound as you may cause more bleeding.
- Tie a bandage around the pad – firmly but not too tightly.
- If blood comes through, apply another pad and bandage over the top.
- Keep applying pressure for about 15 minutes.
- Lay the child down and raise the injured part so that it is higher than the heart.

Fractures, dislocations and sprains

- It is not always easy to spot that a child has a fracture, but signs may include:
  - loss of movement and power
  - swelling
  - awkward angle of limb.
- Keep the child still and get a first aider to come and help you.
- If a leg is thought to be broken, tie bandages around both legs above and below the fracture to keep the leg still.
- Use a scarf or bandage to make a sling to keep an arm still.

Choking

- Hold the child so that his/her head is downwards. This can be over your knees.
- Slap firmly five times between the shoulder blades.
- Repeat if necessary.

Burns and scalds

- Cool down the affected area immediately using cold water or any harmless liquid – milk – if you are not near water.
- Do this for at least 10 minutes.
- Keep talking to the child and explain what you are doing.
- Do not remove clothes that have stuck to the skin or put on creams of any kind.
- Cover the area with a clean cloth – e.g. a teacloth (do not use anything fluffy like a towel).

First aid

It is essential not to waste time before contacting an ambulance if a child's condition causes concern. It is always better to err on the side of caution than wait to see if the child's condition improves. If you decide that emergency services need to be called, make sure that either you do this or another responsible adult does – sometimes in the confusion of an accident everyone thinks that someone else has made the call. While waiting for the emergency services to arrive, you should try to get the help of a trained first aider.

Information that the emergency services will need

Keeping calm is essential when contacting the emergency operators. In order to dispatch help they need clear information and will therefore run through a series of questions. The type of information required includes:

- type of emergency help required
- your name
- location of where you are telephoning from
- location of incident and any landmarks
- cause of the accident
- symptoms and signs of injury
- age of the child.

Before or once the emergency help has arrived, you should refer to the child's admission details and emergency contact details. This is important as the child might be allergic to some medicines or the child's doctor may need to be contacted.

Resuscitation

Resuscitation should be carried out <u>only</u> if you have been trained to do so. If you have not, summon a first aider immediately.

Dealing with minor injuries

Fortunately, most pre-school staff will only ever tend to minor injuries. When children have had a knock, bump or graze, it is good practice for them to be seen by the first aider in the setting. This is important as children will need to be assessed carefully. The accident book should be filled in and signed, regardless of whether any treatment was necessary. You should also ensure that parents are informed of the accident and ask them to countersign the accident book. This is vital because it is one of the regulations of the Children Act 1989.

Responding to illness in children

Children's high metabolism means that they can quickly go down with an illness, so they may become poorly while in our care. It is important that we are vigilant because children want to be with their parents when unwell and we also need to avoid the spread of infection. A quick response is especially important because some infections, for example, meningitis, can quickly take hold of a child and getting prompt medical attention can save lives.

Injury	Treatment	Check for
Bump to the head – e.g. falling over or running into another child	Apply cotton wool squeezed in cold water. If the bump is bad, apply wrapped crushed ice.	Drowsiness, vomiting or headaches – these could indicate concussion.
Nose bleed	Tip the head forward. Pinch the soft part of the nose just below the bridge. Wrapped crushed ice can be put on to the nose if needed.	Seek medical attention if the bleeding continues for more than half an hour or if it is mixed with clear fluid.
Grazed skin	Rinse the wound with clean water. Allow to heal in the air.	
Bruises and trapped fingers	Apply cotton wool squeezed in cold water or wrapped crushed ice.	Run a hand gently over the limb to check that nothing feels lumpy which might be a sign of a fracture.
Vomiting	Do not leave the child. Reassure him/her. Offer a sip of water to take away the sour taste.	If vomiting occurs after a bump to the head, medical attention is needed as this is a sign of concussion.
Insect stings	Reassure the child. Try to remove the sting by scraping it out with a finger nail. Do not squeeze the sting. Use a wrapped ice pack to reduce the swelling.	Urgent medical help is needed if the sting is in the mouth or if the child starts to look ill. Some children are allergic to stings.

Treating minor injuries

The better that we know a child, the easier it is for us to identify quickly that he or she is feeling poorly. Signs that a child may not be well include:

▶ lack of appetite
▶ poor skin – colour pale or greyish
▶ rings around the eyes
▶ fretfulness
▶ tiredness
▶ difficulty in participating and concentrating
▶ requests for a comforter or needing the reassurance of an adult
▶ vomiting
▶ headache
▶ flushed cheeks
▶ wetting or soiling.

Avoiding the spread of infection

If children are feeling poorly, it is important that we take steps to minimise the risks of spreading infection to others. This means that we should take the child away from other children while waiting for the parents to collect him or her. It is therefore a good idea for settings to consider having in their layout an area in which poorly children can wait. Some children will want to lie down, while others will be happy just to stay in the company of a familiar and reassuring adult. If toys or other equipment are used to entertain the child while he or she is waiting, it will be important for these to be washed once the child has left.

The table on pages 180–1 show common childhood illnesses and how to treat them.

Providing reassurance and comfort

All children will need reassurance and comfort if they have had an accident or are feeling unwell. They will also look to us to remain calm and will often react according to the cues that we give them. Talking in a calm way and reassuring the child will be hugely helpful, as will giving the child a cuddle and letting him or her know that he or she is safe. It is also a good idea to talk to the child about what is happening, because not understanding can be very frightening.

It is normal for children to want to be with their parents when they are feeling unwell or after an accident; some children can feel unsettled after a slight bump. Contacting parents if a child is unwell or has had an accident is important because the parents and child may not trust us in the future if we do not.

Meeting children's needs for rest and sleep

Sleep has a vital function in keeping both adults and children healthy. It is not known why we need so much sleep, but it appears that sleep allows the brain to process information and the body to repair and grow cells. Sleep is particularly essential for children. While recommendations vary as to how much sleep young children need, on average most children until the age of five years will need around twelve hours sleep a day, with babies and toddlers needing more. This sleep will not necessarily be taken in one single block because some young children need naps during the day. In addition to having periods of sleep, children also need time to rest during the day.

What happens when children do not get sufficient sleep?

Children who do not get sufficient sleep are vulnerable to infections. In addition, they may not grow properly and will find it harder to concentrate and control their behaviour. Sleep is particularly needed when children are fighting an infection; it is an important weapon in nature's armoury.

Common childhood illnesses

Illness	Incubation	Signs and symptoms	Treatment	Complications
Common cold	1–3 days	Running or blocked-up nose, sneezing, headache, tiredness, temperature.	Keep up fluid intake. Rest and sleep.	Ear infection, bronchitis.
Chicken pox (Varicella)	10–14 days	Groups of red spots with raised white centres that become itchy on trunk and limbs. Slight fever.	Calamine lotion to relieve itchiness. Nails could be cut short to prevent scratching.	Scars caused by spots becoming infected.
Ear infection		Pains – e.g. earache, headache; persistent or intermittent vomiting.	Seek medical attention. Antibiotics, paracetamol.	Hearing loss – temporary (sometimes permanent where children have repeated infections).
Food poisoning	$\frac{1}{2}$–36 hours	Diarrhoea, vomiting.	Fluids only for 24 hours. Seek medical assistance after 24 hours.	Weight loss, dehydration and, in severe cases, death.
Gastroenteritis (inflammation of the stomach lining)	Cause bacteria: 7–14 days Cause virus: $\frac{1}{2}$ –36 hours	Nausea, diarrhoea, vomiting.	Keep up fluid intake. Seek medical advice if symptoms are severe.	Weight loss, dehydration and, in severe cases, death.
German measles (Rubella)	14–21 days	Mild symptoms including a pink rash on head, spreads to trunk and limbs, sore throat and slight fever.	Rest if needed.	No complications, but this disease can cause serious problems for unborn babies if a pregnant woman is infected. Children are at their most infectious a few days before symptoms show until one day after the symptoms disappear.

Illness	Incubation	Signs and symptoms	Treatment	Complications
Measles	8–14 days Koplik's spots appear in the mouth on inner cheek. These are bluish-white spots that appear before the main rash.	At first: fever, runny eyes, sore throat and cough. Red rash (often blotchy) appears, often starting from the head and spreading downwards.	Rest, plenty of fluids and paracetamol if needed to treat fever.	Ear and chest infections and, in rare cases, encephalitis (inflammation of the fluid around the brain).
Meningitis, viral and bacterial	2–14 days variable	Fever, severe headache, nausea, stiff neck and blotchy skin rash that can look like bruising, drowsiness and dislike of light. Babies may arch back and their cry is high-pitched. Symptoms develop rapidly.	Urgent and immediate medical attention. Antibiotics and observation.	Deafness, brain damage and death.
Mumps	14–21 days	Fever, headache, difficulty in swallowing with swollen face and glands in the neck.	Keep up fluid intake, rest, paracetamol for pain relief if necessary.	Meningitis orchitis (inflammation of the testes in young men).
Tonsillitis		Very sore throat, fever, earache, headache and pain on swallowing.	Antibiotics and rest.	Ear infection – temporary, deafness (rare).
Whooping cough (Pertussis)	7–21 days	Spurts of violent coughing with child taking in a deep breath – 'whoop' sound made, vomiting.	Antibiotics in early stages, rest, reassurance and food after coughing attacks.	Nosebleeds, pneumonia, brain damage.

Recognising that children are tired

Children do not always realise that they are tired. This means that we must keep an eye out for signs that a child needs to rest or have a nap (see below).

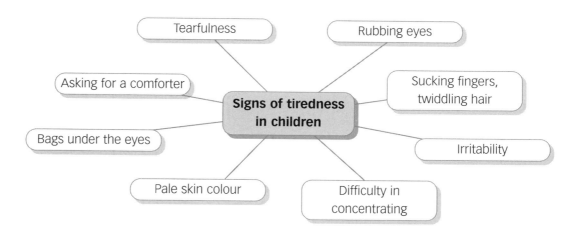

Tearfulness

Rubbing eyes

Asking for a comforter

Signs of tiredness in children

Sucking fingers, twiddling hair

Bags under the eyes

Irritability

Pale skin colour

Difficulty in concentrating

Helping children to sleep

Children cannot fall asleep unless they are sufficiently relaxed. This means that we need to create environments in which children feel secure, and look at ways to help them wind down and relax. You may need to ask parents how they settle their child down for naps and whether the child needs a comforter.

In addition to helping children to relax, it is also important to check that children's other physical needs have been met. Children will sleep better when they are not hungry or thirsty and do not need a nappy change or to go to the toilet. Most pre-schools therefore create a routine for children so that these needs can be met before taking a nap.

Making sure that the environment is comfortable
Children need comfortable, quiet and relaxed rooms in which to fall asleep; they should be clean, attractive and well ventilated. Most pre-schools set aside an area or room in which children can fall asleep. Noisy environments distract children and make it harder for them to relax and wind down. It is useful to develop some sort of a

A comfortable spot to relax in!

pattern. This may include children having the same mattress or cot each time and, ideally, the same person responsible for settling the children down. This is useful because the person will then get to know the children well.

Helping children to wake up

While some children wake up easily after a nap, some children feel quite groggy and unsettled. Learning about the individual child is essential here. Children who feel groggy may need plenty of cuddles and time to wake up fully. Rushing a child to join an activity will only make him or her feel disorientated and insecure, and may make him or her fearful of falling asleep in the setting again.

It is also important to offer children a drink to prevent them from becoming dehydrated. The body loses water during sleep and this should be replaced on waking.

Helping children to rest

Young children enjoy being active, but they also need time to rest and relax. While adults tend to sense that they are becoming tired, children will often suddenly flag. This sudden drop in energy may reveal itself as a lack of concentration or in the child's behaviour. Tired children find it hard to be patient. We may also find that children who are accustomed to having a nap at home cannot settle but are still tired. We therefore need to find ways of helping children to rest. Look at the routine of the setting to make sure that children have varied levels of activity. When choosing activities to help children rest, remember that different children prefer different activities. Children will be unable to rest if they dislike what is being offered.

Listening to a story in a small group or individually with an adult

Watching a video

Activities that can help children to rest

Looking at books in a quiet corner

Playing with small-world toys on a floor

Doing jigsaw puzzles

Informing parents about their child's sleep patterns

It is good practice to tell parents how much sleep or rest their child has had. This is important because sometimes a child who has slept more than usual may be fighting an infection, or it may explain the behaviour of a child who has missed his or her usual nap.

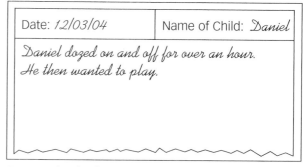

Date: *12/03/04*   Name of Child: *Daniel*

Daniel dozed on and off for over an hour. He then wanted to play.

An example of a sleep slip

Providing for young children's personal hygiene needs

Young children rely on adults to meet their personal hygiene needs. This requires a sensitive approach. It is good practice for a children's key worker to be responsible for carrying out tasks such as nappy changes and washing. As children's physical skills develop, we should encourage children to help themselves as much as possible. The aim of our work should be to encourage children to become as independent as possible.

Nappy-changing

While some children are out of nappies as early as 18 months, most children need a lot longer: some children may continue to use nappies when they have turned three years old. Pressurising children into toilet training before they are ready simply does not work in the long term. In pre-schools that take children in nappies, it is essential to create an area in which nappy changes can take place hygienically and discreetly.

GOOD PRACTICE ✓

Nappy-changing

- Make sure that the items you need are to hand.
- Encourage children to do as much as they can in preparation for the nappy change, for example, finding the clean nappy and helping to undress.
- Talk to the child during the change.
- Encourage the child to wash his or her hands afterwards.

Helping children to move out of nappies

Children can be toilet trained only when they are physically ready for it and also motivated to learn. There is no magic age: some children are ready quite early on and others require longer.

Signs that a child may be ready for toilet training include:

▶ becoming aware that he or she has soiled or wet his or her nappy
▶ the nappy is dry for long periods
▶ a growing interest in toilets and potties
▶ sufficient language to express the need to go to the toilet.

In addition, a child's body must be sufficiently mature. This takes longer for some children than for others.

POINT OF INTEREST

Observing a child's co-ordination

In some countries, early years practitioners look at whether the child's co-ordination is sufficiently developed by watching how the child walks up steps. Children who are able to use alternate feet as opposed to putting one foot on a step and then another are thought to be physically ready for toilet training.

Working with parents

How and when toilet training takes place will need to be agreed with the child's parents. The key is to ensure that the child is relaxed and ready; a favourite potty from home may be required. Regular exchanges of information are also necessary so that parents and practitioners can assess whether the toilet training process is working.

Once it has been agreed to begin toilet training, it is important not to pressurise the child. Telling a child that he is 'a big boy now' may backfire if you discover after a few days that he is not actually ready; this situation may knock the child's confidence. A low-key approach is therefore worthwhile: simply show the child where the potty is and give the odd reminder. If the child is ready to use a potty, there will be few accidents. Forcing a child to stay on a potty is not usually effective because it stresses the child. This can cause the muscles involved in passing urine or motions to fail to relax sufficiently to allow anything to happen.

GOOD PRACTICE

Toilet training

▶ Check that the child is physically ready and motivated.
▶ Avoid pressurising the child.
▶ Give the child the odd reminder.
▶ Make sure that the potty is nearby.
▶ Make sure that the child's clothes are easy for him or her to remove.

Coping with accidents

Many young children wet or soil themselves at one point or another. Sometimes this is because they are fighting an infection; at other times, it may simply be because they were too preoccupied to notice their body's signals. Whatever the reason, it is essential that we react in a warm and calm way. This prevents situations in which children who have had an accident are too frightened or embarrassed to tell us.

After an accident, control should be given back to the child wherever possible. Encourage the child to do as much of the changing and washing as possible because it will help the child to feel independent. It is also important that we are sympathetic and reassure the child that many children have accidents. We can also ask children if they would like us to remind them to pop to the toilet next time. Where children are having regular accidents, it is important to talk to the child's parents. This is because there are many reasons why children may have a toileting accident, including bladder infections, stress and illness.

When dealing with children's accidents, it is recommended that you wear disposable gloves to avoid contracting any infections.

GOOD PRACTICE

Dealing with accidents
- Reassure the child.
- Take the child to a discreet place where he or she can change easily.
- Have a bag of spare clothes, and make sure that they are attractive.
- Encourage the child to choose the clothes into which he or she will change.
- Provide a towel and cloth so that the child can wash.
- Encourage the child to do as much of the changing as possible.
- Rinse through clothing and pop it in a discreet bag.
- Discreetly clean any equipment, chairs or items that the child was using at the time of the accident.
- Inform the child's parents at the end of the session.

Taking children to the toilet

It is essential that children can go to the toilet when they need to. Children will find it hard to wait if they need to go because their bodies are still developing. Ideally, children should be encouraged to have free access to the toilets. However, if this is not possible because of the layout of the building, children should be escorted there.

National Standards

The National Standards (Standard 4) require that you think about the ways in which escorting children to the toilet will affect your staff:children ratios. You also need to consider how to manage situations in which children encounter other people.

It is also a requirement that the child's need for dignity and privacy is respected. This means that a toilet door should be closed if a child wants it to be closed. The requirement to treat children with dignity also means that it is not good practice to force children to go to the toilet.

GOOD PRACTICE

Taking children to the toilet

▶ Make sure that the toilets are clean and attractive.
▶ Ask children if they wish to have the door closed.
▶ Reassure children that you are on hand should they need assistance.
▶ Encourage children to do as much as they can for themselves.
▶ Wash your hands too!

Hand washing

Hand washing is a key way in which we can reduce the spread of infection. Children need to be taught how to wash their hands using soap and warm water (the temperature should be at least 63 degrees Celsius to kill germs). Children should also learn how to dry their hands thoroughly because warm, wet hands spread germs. It is important that children see adults washing their hands so that they can model their behaviour. You should therefore be seen washing your hands before you eat or after a messy activity.

When	Why
Before cooking **Before eating and drinking**	This prevents bacteria and threadworms from being swallowed and spread. Washing hands before cooking and eating foods helps to reduce the possible risks of food poisoning.
After using the toilet	This prevents bacteria from spreading to other children.
After playing outdoors	Bacteria and invisible parasites from animal faeces can be picked up while playing outdoors. Children should be encouraged to wash their hands.
After activities that are sticky or messy	This helps children to become accustomed to having clean hands. It also prevents children from wiping their hands on their clothes.
After touching animals	Animals can carry infections, so children should learn to wash their hands after touching animals.

Hand-washing facts

Making hand washing fun

Children are more likely to learn to wash their hands if the experience of hand washing is enjoyable for them. Look out for soaps that are attractive and allow plenty of time for children to enjoy the sensation of running water and soap. Praise children who remember to wash their hands. You may like to develop a hand-washing rhyme or song for your setting.

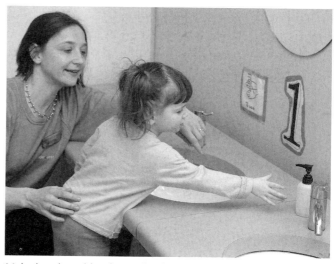
Make hand-washing fun and enjoyable

Nose blowing

Nose blowing may not seem very important, but it is crucial in terms of preventing painful ear infections and cross-infection in general.

Young children have great difficulty in blowing their nose. They therefore need first to be taught to wipe their nose. As wiping is not as effective as blowing, children may need to wipe their nose frequently. Once a young child can wipe his or her nose, we can encourage him or her to have a go at nose blowing. Some children find this a little frightening and we may need to reassure them.

As with hand washing, nose blowing needs to be made as fun and interesting as possible. Consider having attractive tissues and praise children when they fetch a tissue for themselves. It is also worth carrying a packet of tissues with you so that you have some constantly to hand. Tissues should be disposed of immediately, preferably in a bin with a lid. It is also good practice to wash your hands after nose blowing.

Working in partnership with parents

Ask any parent about the way in which they meet their child's physical needs and you will find significant variation in the answers you receive. Some of these differences are linked to cultural and religious practices, while others are the result of medical advice or personal preference. Some parents may have strong feelings about certain products or brands, which they boycott for social reasons. This is why working in partnership with parents to find out about children's particular needs is part of the National Standards.

As a practitioner, it is essential that you do not assume that your way of meeting children's needs is the most appropriate for all children. You should also avoid 'second guessing' what you think parents will want based on a general knowledge about groups of people; for example, some vegetarians are happy for their children to eat fish.

The best way to ensure that parents' wishes are respected is to ask parents directly about how they usually care for their child, and whether their child has any particular requirements. It is also worth showing parents what normally happens in the pre-school because this gives parents the opportunity to flag up their child's particular needs.

Key questions to ask parents

Food and drink
- Are there any foods that your child should not be given, for example, nuts, pork or brands of food?
- Do you have any requirements about the way in which food should be prepared or served?
- What type of drinks can your child have?

Personal hygiene
- Are there any special products or equipment that you wish to be used, for example, when your child washes his/her hands or uses the toilet?
- Are there any procedures that you wish us to follow when your child goes to the toilet or has a nappy change?
- Are there any particular signs that indicate that your child needs the toilet?

Rest and sleep
- What are the signs that your child is tired?
- Does your child need a comforter or other item to help him/her sleep?
- Do you have any preferences about where and when your child rests and sleeps?
- How long does your child usually have for a nap?
- Does your child find it hard to wake up after a nap?

CASE STUDY

Shirley is a pre-school supervisor. She has three children of her own and now has five grandchildren. She believes that children should eat whatever is on their plate and is very suspicious of vegetarian diets. She is also a great believer in using petroleum jelly when nappy changing.

Recently, Shirley was very disappointed to discover that a member of staff had been asked by a parent not to serve his child baked beans. The parent had been concerned that baked beans are high in sugar and, in any case, his child doesn't really enjoy them. Shirley feels that all children should be treated the same and, therefore, if baked beans are good enough for one child, they are good enough for all children.

1 How might Shirley's attitudes create a barrier to good communication?

2 Explain why parents' wishes for their child need to be respected.

3 State three ways in which staff can find out more about parents' preferences for their child.

Policies and procedures in pre-school settings to protect children from abuse

It is a sad fact that some children are abused by adults. Sadder still, are the cases in the past where professionals have failed to act on the signs that children are being abused, even when children try to tell them. In some cases, this has been the result of ignorance, whilst in others, children have been let down because of a lack of procedures. Today, child protection is taken very seriously and this is reflected in the National Standards (Standard 13) and the Children Act 1989.

Recognising possible abuse

Checking the stereotypes

Stereotypes about child abuse can prevent professionals from identifying a problem and can lead to false assumptions. Research on child abuse shows that the following stereotypes are common, but are inaccurate.

Stereotype 1: strangers abuse children

Many people believe that child abuse is carried out by strangers. Surprisingly, this not borne out by the statistics on child abuse: the majority of abusers are people known to the child. Abusers may be family members, friends or even adults working with children. Cases in which strangers abduct and abuse children do occur, but these represent only a small number of abuse cases.

Stereotype 2: abuse occurs in poor families

This stereotype is dangerous because it can mean that children from more affluent families are not thought to be at risk of abuse. Sometimes children from wealthy families who have been abused are not believed because of this stereotype.

Stereotype 3: abuse occurs in single-parent families

Plenty of stereotypes abound about single-parent families. Because child abuse occurs across the social and income spectrum, it is unfair to assume that children from single-parent families will be abused. Focusing on single-parent families can mean that other children who at risk of abuse are not identified.

Stereotype 4: only men abuse children

While statistically, more men sexually abuse children than women do, this does not mean that women do not sexually abuse children. Stereotypes about women as nurturing and 'safe' can mean that children who have been sexually abused by women are not believed.

Types and definitions of abuse

Abuse is often categorised into four types:

- physical abuse
- emotional abuse
- sexual abuse
- neglect.

Many children will suffer more than one type of abuse, and all types of abuse can have long-term effects. Some children will learn from being abused to become abusers, while others will find it hard to trust others. Children can also fail to achieve their academic potential because being relaxed, comfortable and secure are important prerequisites for learning.

Physical abuse

Physical abuse causes physical harm to a child. It may involve hitting, shaking, throwing, poisoning, burning, scalding, drowning or suffocating. Physical harm may also result when a parent or carer feigns the symptoms of or deliberately causes ill-health to a child. This situation is commonly described as 'factitious illness by proxy' or 'Munchausen Syndrome by proxy'.

Emotional abuse

Emotional abuse is the persistent emotional ill-treatment of a child such as to cause severe and persistent adverse effects on that child's emotional development. It may involve conveying to a child that he or she is worthless, unloved or inadequate, or valued only in so far as he or she meets the needs of another person. It may feature age or developmentally inappropriate expectations being imposed on the child. Emotional abuse may cause a child frequently to feel frightened or in danger, or the exploitation or corruption of a child. Some level of emotional abuse is involved in all types of ill-treatment, though it may occur alone.

Sexual abuse

Sexual abuse is forcing or enticing a child or young person to take part in sexual activities, whether or not that child is aware of what is happening. These activities may involve physical contact, including penetrative acts such as rape and buggery, and non-penetrative acts. Sexual abuse also includes non-contact activities, for example, forcing children to watch or participate in the production of pornographic material, getting children to watch sexual activities, or encouraging children to behave in sexually inappropriate ways.

Neglect

Neglect is the persistent failure to meet a child's basic physical and/or psychological needs. It is likely to result in the serious impairment of the child's health and development. It may involve a parent or carer failing to provide:

- adequate food, shelter and clothing
- protection from physical harm or danger
- access to appropriate medical care or treatment
- adequate responsiveness to a child's basic emotional needs.

(Adapted from *Working Together to Safeguard our Children,* Department of Health 1999.)

Signs of abuse

Adults working with children need to understand the physical and behavioural signs that a child is being abused. Early years practitioners are in a good position to observe children and thus notice changes in their well-being. It is important that signs of abuse are acted upon and that judgments are suspended because some behavioural and even physical indicators of abuse have other causes.

Signs of physical abuse

While most young children will have the odd bump or scrape, children who repeatedly have bruising and injuries may be suffering from physical abuse. In some cases, violence against a child can escalate and result in fatal injuries. Some children are given a cover story by their abuser to explain their injuries to others; the child might be threatened with further violence if he or she does not use the story. The fear factor partly explains why children may not reveal that they are being harmed.

Children who have been physically abused are more likely to show aggressive behaviour towards other children, especially those who are younger. This is one way in which the child can feel empowered.

KEY POINTS

Physical indicators of physical abuse

- Unusual-shaped bruises (these might reflect the shape of an object or fingers).
- Bruises and marks on the body not associated with accidental injury, for example, on the chest.
- Burn and scald marks (including small burns from cigarettes).
- Bite marks.
- Fractures or swellings.
- Cuts to the face.
- Black eyes.
- Difficulty in walking, stiffness.

Behavioural indicators of physical abuse

- Showing aggressive behaviour towards others.
- Aggression shown in role-play, for example, hitting a teddy in the face with a pan.
- A child is withdrawn and quiet.
- A child is reluctant to be with a parent or a particular adult in the setting.
- A parent or carer appears to be very aggressive with a child.
- A child does not take part in or is excluded by a parent from activities involving undressing, for example, dressing in costumes for a concert.

What you should do if you have concerns that a child is being physically abused

If a child has a physical injury, it is good practice to ask the child how it happened. You should also mention it to the parent. You should be concerned if the child is reluctant to tell you how the injury occurred or if the parent is defensive. You should also be concerned if the child's and the parent's version of what happened is very different. Usually, children are quite keen to show off their 'war wounds' and tell you about them. In the same way, most parents will, on arrival, mention any injuries that a child has.

Signs of emotional abuse

Emotional abuse accompanies other forms of abuse because they result in children's emotional development and mental health being at risk. Emotional abuse alone can be hard to detect because there are no outwardly physical signs in young children. In older children, we may see self-harm, substance misuse or eating disorders. There are, however, various behavioural indicators of emotional abuse in young children.

KEY POINTS

Behavioural indicators of emotional abuse

- ▶ Attention-seeking behaviours, for example, a child is extremely clingy or deliberately provocative.
- ▶ The child is eager for affection and may seek it inappropriately, for example, by approaching strangers.
- ▶ Telling lies to gain sympathy or attention.
- ▶ Regressive behaviour, for example, baby talk or thumb sucking.
- ▶ Tantrums beyond the age when most children have ceased to have tantrums.
- ▶ Difficultly in socialising with peers.
- ▶ Tearfulness, lack of confidence and poor self-worth.

Children who are 'hungry' for unconditional love and affection are very vulnerable. They may be targeted by paedophiles, who often recognise that the child's need for love may outweigh his or her reluctance to participate. Children who are emotionally abused also lack confidence. This can mean that the child is reluctant to try out new activities for fear of failure or humiliation.

Signs of sexual abuse

Sexual abuse is not always easy to detect because the child may not realise that the actions of the adults are inappropriate. In addition, there may not be any outward physical signs because injuries can be internal or hidden by underwear.

Sexual abuse can be hard to detect because some of the adult perpetrators are extremely clever. They can gradually gain a child's trust (this is called grooming) and over a period include increasingly sexual acts in their relationship with the child. For example, a kiss on the cheek becomes one on the lips. Sexual acts are also sometimes integrated with ordinary play and care activities, for example, bedtime and bathtime, or rough-and-tumble. Some children are told that activities are 'special' and 'secret'. Others may be threatened with violence if they tell another person, or told that something nasty will happen to a family member or person that they care for if they tell.

Physical indicators of sexual abuse

▶ Bruises, scratches and injuries that are not likely to be accidental, for example, bruises to inner thighs.
▶ Difficulty in walking and sitting.
▶ Fear of going to the toilet.
▶ Complaints of pain when passing stools or urine.
▶ Genital or urinary tract infections.
▶ Soiling or dirtying when the child has previously been clean and dry.

Behavioural indicators of sexual abuse

▶ Regression in behaviour, for example, using comforters, rocking or thumb sucking.
▶ Inappropriate sexual behaviour, for example, undressing other children, exposing themselves, sitting on the laps of people they do not know, trying to fondle adults.
▶ Showing sexual behaviour in imaginative play, for example, making dolls 'have sex' or putting a doll to bed and taking its clothes off afterwards.
▶ Knowledge of adult sexual behaviour, for example, knowing the colour of semen.
▶ Unwillingness to be with a particular carer.

Signs of neglect

Neglect causes children to be at risk of accidents and infections, and can prevent them from learning. In severe cases, neglect can result in a child's death. Parents can sometimes neglect their children because they have health problems or are not coping with their parenting role. Sometimes, neglect is the result of ignorance, for example, not understanding that a fruit-only diet will fail to provide sufficient nutrients for a child.

Physical indicators of neglect

▶ Frequent accidental injuries (these are often the result of a lack of supervision or safety equipment).
▶ Children who are underweight and hungry.
▶ Children who are untidy and dirty, including their clothing.
▶ Children who are tired (this can be due to a lack of nutrition as well as inadequate sleeping arrangements).
▶ Children with frequent low-grade infections that go untreated, for example, nits, colds, influenza, coughs and earaches.

Behavioural indicators of neglect

▶ Children may steal food and drink.
▶ Children who take significant responsibility for younger children.
▶ Children who are reluctant to go home at the end of sessions.
▶ Children who mention that they are often left alone.

Looking for changes in behaviour patterns

As well as being aware of signs that a child is being abused, we should look for significant changes in a child's behaviour. This can occur as a result of abuse commencing. A child who previously was settled, happy and confident may quickly become withdrawn or aggressive. In some cases, behavioural changes are a response to other things in a child's life, such as the birth of a sibling or the illness of a family member. Therefore, while changes should be noted and acted upon, it is important not to jump to conclusions. This means that changes to a child's behaviour should be mentioned to parents as a starting point. Most parents will readily provide an explanation. If, however, you continue to have concerns, you should follow the written procedures in your setting.

We should also be aware of changes in children's behaviour towards adults working in the setting. Abuse can happen in care and education settings. This means that you should keep an eye out for children who appear reluctant to be with a particular member of staff.

Look out for children who:

▶ become aggressive
▶ become withdrawn
▶ begin to show sexual knowledge
▶ are more clingy than usual
▶ are reluctant to join their carers or parents
▶ try to avoid being with a particular member of staff or adult in the setting
▶ change their behaviour on particular days, for example, after a weekend with another family member or on days when a certain person is in the setting.

Responding to a child's disclosure of abuse

Sometimes children will seek out the support of adults to prevent abuse from continuing. In other cases, children may unintentionally say something that is significant to us. The term 'disclosures' has been used to describe these types of event; however, this term is now used less frequently in court because the defendant's solicitors can then infer that adults have encouraged or led the child to make a claim. The latest guidance from the Department of Health warns adults working with children to be aware that the way in which we respond to a child who we suspect has been abused can affect the later outcomes.

> *Remember that an allegation of child abuse or neglect may lead to a criminal investigation, so don't do anything that may jeopardise a police investigation such as asking a child leading questions or attempting to investigate the allegations yourself.*
>
> *Safeguarding Children, 2003*

What to do if a child tells you about abuse

There are some simple but essential rules to follow if a child tells you about abuse or says something that is of concern.

Do:

- Reassure the child that you believe what he or she is saying.
- Listen to the child carefully, but do not ask questions as this may jeopardise a police investigation.
- Tell the child that you will do everything you can to protect him or her.
- Tell the child that you will need to talk to other adults in order to help him or her.
- Reassure the child that he or she is not in trouble and that he or she has acted properly.
- Make notes in pen immediately after the conversation has finished and before talking to anyone else. Write down only what the child has told you. Do not speculate or add any comments. Include the date and time, and then sign the notes.

Do not:

- Promise the child that you will be able to keep what he or she has said a secret. This is important because the child can feel let down later and will not trust other adults.
- Question the child or pass any comment other than to reassure the child.
- Make notes while you are with the child or after you have discussed what has been said with another adult.
- Add additional information into the notes later.
- Talk to other people about what has occurred, other than the designated person for dealing with child protection in the setting.

What happens next...

If you have concerns about a child, you should let these be known to the designated person in your setting. This may be the supervisor or another senior member of staff. This person may then seek further advice from Social Services, the NSPCC, or may go on to make a referral. If you are the designated person in your setting, you should follow your local Area Child Protection Committee's guidelines. Once a referral has been received, the social worker will decide on the next course of action, dependent on whether the child is seen as being at risk of significant harm.

The Department of Health has produced a flow chart to show the process that should take place once initial concerns have been expressed (see overleaf).

Requirements of legislation and local guidelines for responding to abuse

The key piece of legislation governing child protection is the Children Act 1989. Under this Act, children's welfare is paramount. The Children Act 1989 attempts to unite different agencies that may care or have involvement with children and their families, so that children do not slip through the net because of a lack of communication.

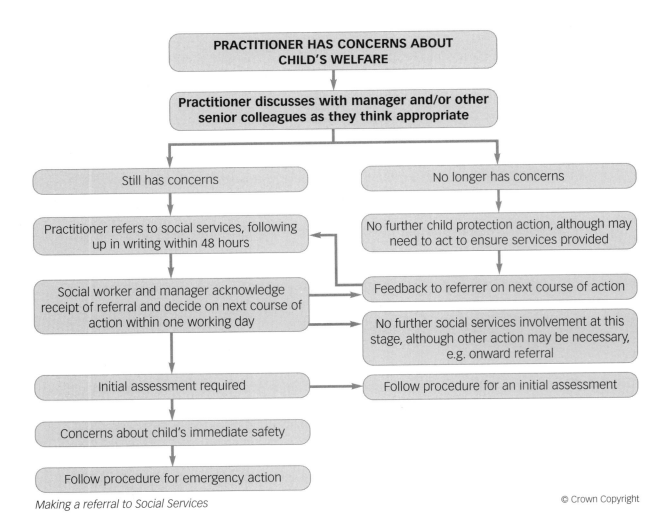

Making a referral to Social Services

© Crown Copyright

Area Child Protection Committee

In 1999, the Department of Health issued a key document entitled 'Working together to safeguard children'. As a result of this work, each local area now has an Area Child Protection Committee (APAC). The committee is composed of senior managers from all agencies that work with children and their families, for example, health professionals, police, social services and education departments. The aim of the committee is to ensure that national policies and procedures relating to child protection are in place. Your pre-school setting should have contacts with the APAC, and the child protection policy in your setting should be based upon their local procedures.

Child protection policy

The Children Act 1989 regulations require that pre-school settings should have a policy in place that outlines how children are to be safeguarded from abuse. The policy also has to outline the procedure to be followed in the event of an allegation of abuse or neglect.

National Standards

In order for pre-schools to be registered, they have to comply with Standard 13 of the National Standards. This standard is wholly about child protection.

Child protection: key questions

- Is there a policy in place that outlines the procedures for reporting suspected abuse?
- Does the policy comply with the procedure designated by the APAC?
- Does the policy include a procedure to be followed if an allegation is made against a member of staff or other adult?
- Is there a member of staff responsible for child protection and liaising with other agencies?
- Are staff aware of the signs that might indicate abuse?
- Is staff training held regularly to update knowledge about child protection?

Procedures for reducing opportunities for abuse in the pre-school

It is essential that we remain aware that members of staff and other adults in the setting might be potential abusers. This sounds rather drastic; however, thinking in this way can help us to establish safeguards that will protect children from abuse and adults from potential allegations. The National Standards provide clear guidance as to the importance of 'suitable people' being with children. This means that new staff need to be police checked and that OFSTED has to be informed of any changes to staff in the setting.

We should also consider our practice with children. It is easy to overreact and withdraw any physical contact between adults and children; however, this is unfair on young children who sometimes need physical reassurance. The key is transparency and respecting children's cues. This means that staff can cuddle children, but this should be done openly rather than hidden from others. It also means that we need to respect children's wishes. This means encouraging a child who wants to slip her hand into ours, but equally encouraging the child to let go when she is ready to leave.

GOOD PRACTICE

Ways of reducing opportunities for abuse

- Make sure that members of staff or volunteers working regularly with children are police checked.
- Maintain a visitors' record book and make sure that visitors wear a badge.
- Do not allow students or visitors to have any unsupervised contact with children in the setting.
- Do not shut doors when alone with children.
- Take cues from the child as to how much physical contact a child wants.
- Encourage children to take as much responsibility and control as they are able for their personal hygiene.
- Respect children's need for dignity and privacy when they are changing or in the toilet.
- Be aware of children's reactions to colleagues.

Professionals who may be involved with children who have been abused

There is a multi-agency approach to child protection. This means that when abuse is suspected, several professionals may become involved.

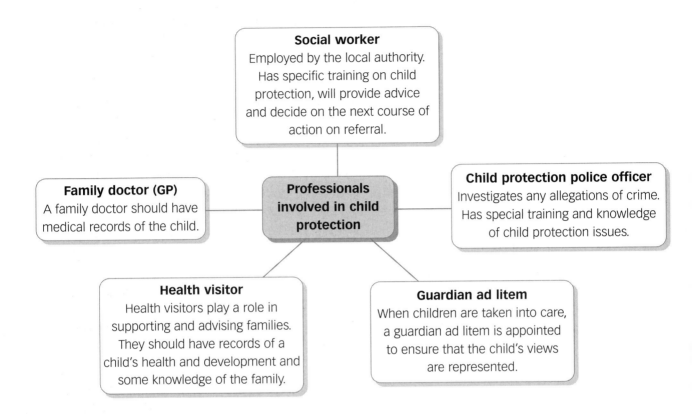

Social worker
Employed by the local authority. Has specific training on child protection, will provide advice and decide on the next course of action on referral.

Child protection police officer
Investigates any allegations of crime. Has special training and knowledge of child protection issues.

Family doctor (GP)
A family doctor should have medical records of the child.

Professionals involved in child protection

Health visitor
Health visitors play a role in supporting and advising families. They should have records of a child's health and development and some knowledge of the family.

Guardian ad litem
When children are taken into care, a guardian ad litem is appointed to ensure that the child's views are represented.

Working with other professionals

Social services or the police will often request information about the child or the family. This information may help with making an assessment of the situation, providing evidence of a criminal assault or creating a child protection plan. You may be asked to go to a child protection conference in which decisions about how best to help the child are made.

Confidentiality

It is important that any information you are privy to during these processes remains confidential. This means that you should not discuss the issues or information that you have been given with anyone other than the authorised persons. Breaching confidentiality can jeopardise children's safety; it may also lead to a prosecution being unsuccessful.

How to respond appropriately to parents and other family members in suspected child abuse situations

It is in the interests of the child for both parents and family members to have good working relationships with us. If trust is breached because parents feel that they are being judged, the parents may decide not to continue bringing the child into the setting. This is not in the child's interest if abuse is taking place.

Nor is it in the pre-school's interest if no abuse is taking place and the parents talk unfavourably about the atmosphere in the setting.

Gaining further information from parents

Where concerns are expressed about a child, it may be appropriate to talk to parents about how the child sustained an injury or the child's behaviour. However, until abuse is confirmed and the perpetrator identified, it is essential not to pre-judge parents because some behavioural and physical signs are not the result of abuse.

When the parent is implicated in the abuse, there can be a conflict between working in partnership with parents and ensuring that the child's welfare is protected. The guidelines from *Safeguarding Children* (2003) suggest that when a referral is made a discussion takes place as to how much information parents should be given. The clear message from the Children Act 1989 is that we should always remember to put the child's welfare first.

Finding support

While helping a child who has been abused is rewarding, many early years practitioners find the process quite stressful. Confidentiality is a key part of child protection and so the normal routes by which we might 'off load' our feelings may not be appropriate. Many people who have been involved with child protection cases find that, for a while, their own feelings towards adults and life in general are altered. This means that it is essential to gain support and consider professional counselling.

Steps we can take to prevent abuse

As well as understanding the signs of abuse, it is important to understand the ways in which we might protect children from abuse. This includes looking at our own practice in the pre-school and considering whether we are empowering

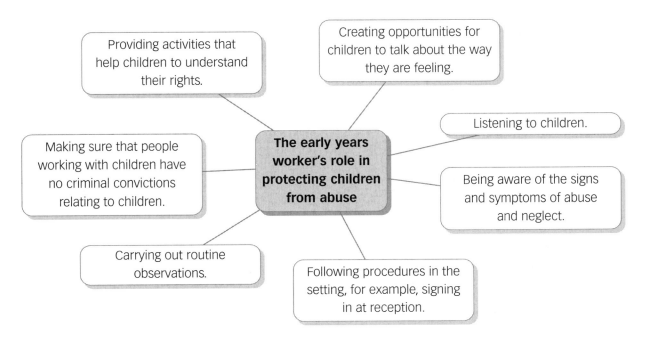

children. Empowering children means encouraging them to take control and become as independent as possible. It means that children are never told to 'do as I tell you' because this teaches children always to obey adults. Unquestioning obedience to authority can put children in danger. We should also avoid using our body language to intimidate children, for example, standing over a child or patting them on the back.

Keeping secrets

One way in which abusers control children is by telling them that they have to keep secrets. This means that we should talk to children about secrets and surprises and teach them that they are allowed to break secrets. This means that it is not good practice to tell children that they have to keep a secret – even if it is a good one.

Ways of working in partnership with parents to promote children's learning and development

It is now a well-established principle that care and education settings need to work alongside parents. This was not always the case; there used to be a 'we know best' attitude in many settings. This was not helpful as it created a 'them and us' approach and prevented a free flow of ideas and information. Today, pre-schools are required to demonstrate their commitment to working with parents as part of the National Standards (Standard 12). This approach is of huge benefit to children in many ways, as the diagram below shows.

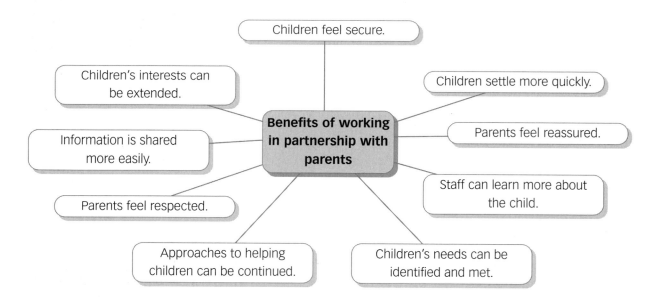

The nature of the parent–child bond

In Core Unit 1 we discussed theories of attachment (see pages 29–35), looking in particular at the importance of children developing in their earliest years a special attachment or 'bond' to their parents. It is thought that this bond is incredibly important in children's emotional and social development. The parent–child bond appears to help children learn to trust others and gives them security and stability.

When Parents make strong attachments

When working with parents, we need to realise that the parent–child bond is not a 'one-way' system. Parents too can have a very strong attachment to their child. This is why in extreme situations parents will readily sacrifice their own lives in order that their child survives. We see this parent–child bond operate routinely when we observe parents with their children. A parent may wait outside in order to double-check that their child is settled, or may painstakingly take their child's coat off and smother the child in kisses before leaving. The nature of the parent–child bond means that we need to be very respectful and avoid situations in which we appear not to value this special relationship.

Parents who find it hard to leave

The parent–child bond means that many parents find it hard to leave their children. They may linger for a while or try to peep through a window. This is perfectly natural behaviour and we can take a lot of pressure off parents by reassuring them that this is so. The need felt by some parents to wait a while or double-check on their children must be accommodated. The danger of not doing so is that parents can convey their anxiety about leaving to the child, who in turn becomes unsettled.

GOOD PRACTICE
Supporting parents who find it hard to leave
- Consider offering to telephone parents.
- Pop outside to tell parents what their child is doing now.
- Make a video to show parents how quickly their child settles down.
- Use modern mobile phone technology to show the child playing happily.

Parents who work

As a society, we send out very discordant messages about whether parents should work when their children are young. Not surprisingly, this causes many parents who work to feel guilty and anxious. This is not helpful because children need relaxed and confident parents. It is essential that pre-school settings act as facilitators for working parents who may sometimes be forced financially to return to work.

GOOD PRACTICE
Supporting parents who work when their children are young
- Make sure that communication systems are in place to allow a good exchange of information.
- Remember that parents who work may be juggling several hats. Be considerate when asking for such things as volunteers, homemade cakes and costumes.
- Be supportive by reassuring parents that their children are safe and secure, and are enjoying their learning.
- Be as flexible as possible, for example, arranging meetings at convenient times, allowing children to be dropped off later.

Parents who are concerned about the strength of their attachments

Some parents who leave their children in day care, particularly in full day care, can worry about whether their child will begin to prefer being with staff members. This can sometimes lead to parents seeing staff members as rivals for their child's affections. In some cases, parents may ask that their child does not have a key worker. It is essential to recognise this fear and show through our interactions with parents that they remain the principal carer. We also need to show parents that while children form an attachment with us, this is of a different nature from the attachment that children have with their parents.

GOOD PRACTICE ✓

Supporting parents with concerns about staff–child attachments

- Make sure that parents understand the benefits to the child of having a key worker.
- Demonstrate to parents the ways in which their child has developed a bond with them.
- Reassure parents that their child will not transfer their affections onto a care worker.
- Do not use expressions that indicate possessiveness about a child, for example, 'Sam's one of my children.'

Talking through our concerns

The SEN Code of Practice makes it clear that parents' concerns about their child's development, behaviour or learning need to be talked through. This is the first step in tackling any problems because parental consent has to be given before other professionals can become involved. The nature of the parent–child bond means that many parents can quickly become defensive in situations in which professionals share their concerns. Again, this is a natural defence mechanism because parents want to protect and nurture their children. We therefore need to consider the way in which we present information to parents. Parents need to hear that we only want the best for their child and that we are not 'judging' him or her. We must also be able to demonstrate that any strategies or plans are of benefit to the child. It is therefore good practice to consider the strengths and the interests of the child. Many parents report that professionals talk to them about their child only in terms of him or her being a 'problem'. Understandably, this is a message that parents do not wish to hear, nor should they have to.

GOOD PRACTICE ✓

Expressing concerns to parents

- Make sure that your interaction remains positive and do not focus on the child being a problem.
- Remember to talk about the child's strengths and interests.
- Listen and take account of parents' views about their child.

How the parent–child bond affects policies in the pre-school

The lessons we learn about parent–child bonds should be reflected in our policies.

Settling-in

Separation is difficult for both children and parents, especially when a child shows separation anxiety. Policies in the pre-school need to reflect this by organising **settling-in** so that it meets the needs of individual children and their families. Some children will need to spend longer getting to know adults in the setting, and some parents may want to spend some time in the setting before they are ready to leave. The key to settling-in is to ensure that the child forms a bond with at least one member of staff before the child is left alone in the setting. This makes the child feel more secure and helps the parents to feel that they are not 'abandoning' their child.

GOOD PRACTICE

Involving parents in settling-in procedures

▶ Make sure that parents understand the purpose of a key worker system.
▶ Encourage parents to visit the setting, but also allow the designated key worker to develop a relationship with the child.
▶ Build up the separation time gradually and in response to the child's reactions.
▶ Reassure parents that it is normal to have strong feelings when leaving their child.
▶ Consider ways of helping parents who are in the same position to support each other.

Special Educational Needs policy

The nature of the parent–child bond is recognised in legislation. The Children Act 1989 states that parents play a significant role in their child's life and that all professionals must respect this. The latest guidelines on working with children who have special needs (SEN Code of Practice) require practitioners to work with parents and to share information with them. This means that if you have any concerns about a child's development, you must talk them through with the child's parents. By regularly giving parents feedback and inviting them to share information about their child, this should be quite straightforward. If regular meetings with parents about their child's progress do not occur, there is a danger that parents can feel that a 'tidal wave' has hit them. Your setting's policy should detail how you share information regularly with parents.

Observations and record-keeping

When we observe a child in the setting, we see only one facet of that child. Children can be very different at home: they may have different interests, show different behaviours and demonstrate different skills. This means that policies on observations and subsequent record-keeping should involve parents. Many settings exchange information with parents at regular intervals about a child's development at home. Comparing notes can be useful and help us to learn more about the child. It is also important to note that parents should have open access to all records about their children. This is a requirement of the Data Protection Act; it also forms part of National Standard 12.

Parents as the prime educators of their children

Traditionally, educators have taken credit for children's learning; it was thought that a child's learning came to an end when the session finished. However, it is now recognised that parents usually play the pivotal role in a child's learning.

In terms of young children, parents provide their children with much of their learning at home. This learning is not likely to be formal or planned, but it is nonetheless influential. Parents give children emotional security, help with their language development and teach them a range of practical skills. The emotional context here is important to appreciate, and it is likely that significant amounts of learning occur because parents act as role models for their children (see social learning theory on pages 43–4). Parents also make great educators because they know their child intimately and have a long-term relationship with him or her. This more recent understanding of the role of parents means that pre-school settings should look for ways of valuing this learning and involving parents.

> **A QUICK THINK!**
>
> *What skills did you learn at home?*
>
> *Can you remember how you learnt them?*

KEY POINTS **Involving parents in their child's learning at the setting: key questions**

> ▶ Are parents involved in assessing their child's progress?
> ▶ Are parents encouraged to share their child's achievements at home?
> ▶ Are children's interests at home developed in the pre-school?
> ▶ How are parents involved in delivering the curriculum?
> ▶ Are parents given suggestions as to how they might extend an activity that was started in the pre-school?
> ▶ Are books and resources available on loan to parents?

Involving parents in their child's learning at pre-school

We have seen that parents play a very influential role in their child's learning. It is important that we recognise this and consider ways of building upon it by inviting parents to become involved. It is important here to stress the word 'invitation'. This is because parents can have demands on their own time and may have a different perspective on how best to help their child. It is essential that parents who decide not to be involved are not seen as being 'disinterested'.

Strategies to involve parents

Open door policy

Years ago, parents simply handed their child over on the threshold; there was a clear divide between settings and home. Parents who wished to become involved or simply talk over their concerns were seen as 'difficult'. Fortunately, this approach has changed and pre-schools have adopted an **'open door' policy**.

This simply means that parents are encouraged to come into the setting at any time and talk to staff or watch their child. An open door policy can be effective only if parents know about it. This means that during the admissions process, parents need to be told that they are welcome in the setting at any time. However, it is worth making sure that parents do understand that while staff will make every effort to talk to them, this might be difficult at busy moments in the routine of the session.

Open days and sessions

Many pre-schools have open days or sessions. These can help parents to see what their child is doing and learning. They can be particularly useful for parents whose children are not yet talking or do not tell them much about what they have been doing. Open sessions work well when members of staff take time to explain to parents about the activities and how they benefit their child.

Open days help parents to see what their child is learning

Planning

Planning works well when parents are involved. Some settings who work closely with parents are able to incorporate parent feedback into their plans. In addition, it is worth making sure that parents know which rhymes, songs and activities will be taking place. Some pre-schools send home their curriculum plans so that parents know what their child is likely to be doing. This can help parents discuss and follow up activities with their child. It is also worth including suggestions for activities that parents might like to do with their child, for example, pointing out postboxes to children when the role-play area is a post office.

Information slips

It is good practice for settings working with babies and toddlers to provide daily information slips. These usually identify how much sleep and food a child has had, as well as other key events in the child's day. Most parents appreciate finding out about what their child has enjoyed doing and any skills he or she is beginning to acquire. Regular feedback to parents is a fantastic way of making contact with parents who are unable to collect their child from the setting (and thus make contact in this way). This approach can be extended into the Foundation Stage.

Date: *12/03/04*

Name of Child: *James Adams*

Preferred Activities:

James enjoyed playing a new game in the sand tray today. He could recognise which container would hold the most sand. James also spent 20 minutes playing in the home corner and phoned all his friends and family!

Comments:

James remembered to get a tissue and attempted to blow his nose independently. We gave him a sticker for this.

An example of an information slip

Home books or slips

The Foundation Stage curriculum identifies that a child's family and home life needs to be recognised. Sometimes young children find it hard to talk about what they have been doing in the absence of any visual cues. The home world can seem very far away when in a different environment. This means that finding out about significant events that have occurred in a child's home life can be hit-and-miss. By providing home books or slips, parents can choose to jot down anything that they think is important for the child, for example, 'Mary's granny came for tea', or 'James washed up his own plate'. It is important that home books or slips are not seen as being compulsory or an attempt to pry into families' lives. To this end, you might consider giving examples of the types of comments that parents might wish to make.

Books, games and resources

Learning does not stop at the end of a session, therefore we may wish to consider whether it is possible for books, games and resources to be lent to parents. Some pre-schools have developed an extensive 'library system' by identifying resources that are plentiful. This is one way in which we can help parents on lower incomes to provide toys for their children.

Workshops and information sessions

Many pre-schools run workshops or information sessions on topics that they feel might be of interest to parents. These can include first aid workshops or sessions on the curriculum, for example, how children's writing develops. These types of session can help parents to understand the approach that the pre-school is taking, as well as provide them with tips on how to support their child at home.

Volunteers and committees

Some parents may have time to volunteer as parent-helpers, committee members or fund-raisers. Involving parents in this way can help the setting both to develop good relationships with parents and to learn more about parents' needs. To make volunteering a successful experience, it is important that parents understand their roles and responsibilities from the outset. You should also make sure that issues of confidentiality are explained and respected.

Involvement in assessment

We have considered how children behave and engage with others differently when at home. This means that we need to involve parents in some of the assessments that we carry out. This can be a good way of jointly focusing on children's needs and planning a tailored learning programme.

THINKING AND RESEARCH

Design a home slip that would be easy for staff members to fill in regularly for children in the Foundation Stage.

Why is it important for parents to know what activities their child has enjoyed?

Respecting family values and child-rearing practices

The stereotypical image of children living with two married parents is no longer realistic. Family structures have changed radically in the past 30 years and while some children do live in the traditional 'nuclear' family, many children do not. Interestingly, social research shows that the majority of householders in this country are single.

In the same way, family values are now very diverse. Some families may be centred on religion, while others may be focused on social activities. It is therefore essential that we avoid making assumptions about families and the way in which they choose to live.

> **A QUICK THINK!**
> *How many people do you know who are not living in a nuclear family?*

Child-rearing

Every parent has his or her own way of bringing up children. This unique approach is linked to the person's childhood, lifestyle, religion and perspective on what children need. Most families do a fantastic job of creating a stable and loving framework in which children can grow. The key to working successfully with parents is to recognise that child-rearing practices do vary and that, unless there is a child protection issue, a parent's right to rear his or her children as he or she sees fit has to be respected.

Differences in child-rearing practices can sometimes mean that a child receives mixed messages about what is acceptable behaviour. It is important to talk to parents about your setting's expectations for behaviour and to look at ways of working together with parents so that children are not confused.

Respecting family values and child-rearing practices

▶ Do not assume that all families will celebrate festivals in the same way, for example, not all families will celebrate a child's birthday.

▶ Check that your resources and activities reflect the diverse nature of families, for example, some children may see their dad only at weekends.

▶ Remember that not all children have both natural parents living with them, so activities such as making Mother's Day cards can create tensions.

CASE STUDY

Molly lives with her natural dad, her stepmother and her half-brother. It is Mother's Day and a staff member is making cards with children. Molly wants to make more than one card, but is told that she can't because she has only one mother.

1 In what ways does this approach show a lack of respect and understanding?

2 What effects might this have on Molly?

3 Explain why 'rationing' activities is limiting to children's development.

Creating an equal relationship between parents and pre-school staff

Working in partnership with parents means understanding that while a parent's role is different from ours, it is just as valuable. Formerly, there was a patronising acceptance that parents did play a part in their children's learning. We now need to see parents as equal and valued partners in their child's learning.

Equal relationships are based upon trust

It is essential that in our dealings with parents we are honest and respectful. If parents feel that they cannot trust us, they will not wish to exchange information with us. This means that we should first talk to parents if we have any concerns about their child. We must also remember the importance of confidentiality. Parents must not feel that we will gossip about them or breach their trust.

THINKING AND RESEARCH

▶ What is your pre-school's policy on confidentiality?
▶ What are the procedures if confidentiality is breached?

Equal relationships are based on valuing parents

Parents need to feel that they are welcome and that the pre-school setting does not have 'favourites'. Parents, like children, can quickly sense if they are welcome by observing body language. Simply smiling and acknowledging parents is a good starting point. It is also worth remembering that while there are differences between parents and staff in their roles and approaches, for example, to child-rearing, that we are united by wanting the best for the child.

Equal relationships are based upon good communication

Effective relationships require good communication skills. This means thinking about all types of communications that are used in the pre-school.

▶ Written communications

These should be legible, clear and accurate, but more importantly they should have a pleasant tone. We must make sure that we do not exclude groups of parents who may not have English as their first language. This means checking whether a translation is appropriate. It is also important to bear in mind that some adults have difficulty in reading. That said, there are some advantages to written communications such as notes and letters. These can be read by parents at their convenience and they also provide opportunity for parents who cannot come into the setting to remain in contact.

▶ Face-to-face contact

Many parents enjoy having some time to talk to members of staff. Face-to-face contact is a quick and easy way to exchange information and offer a response. There are, however, some disadvantages as sometimes parents are in a hurry, and rushed communications can backfire and lead to misunderstandings. In order to communicate well with parents, staff need to listen as well as talk. Active listening skills, which are used in counselling, can be very helpful. It is therefore worthwhile to read up on active listening skills or, better still, attending a basic counselling course.

It is important for some parents to have face-to-face meetings

GOOD
PRACTICE

Good communication with parents

▶ Make sure that parents' confidentiality is maintained.
▶ Consider how parents' views about their children are sought.
▶ Create a welcoming entrance area.
▶ Do not have 'favourites' among parents.
▶ Make sure that sensitive discussions with parents are held in a private area.
▶ Review documents, policies and letters to assess if they are 'user-friendly'.

TEST YOUR
KNOWLEDGE

1 Explain what is meant by the term 'inclusion'.
2 Outline two pieces of anti-discrimination legislation.
3 Explain the importance of providing activities that are appropriate to children's stage of development.
4 Describe three ways in which infection might enter the body.
5 Explain why it is important to talk to parents about children's dietary needs.
6 List four signs that might show that a child is a victim of physical abuse.
7 What are Area Protection Committees?
8 Evaluate the impact of layout on children's safety, learning and behaviour.
9 Analyse how policies in pre-schools can influence practice.
10 Discuss the importance of attachment theories in your pre-school's settling-in policy.

PRACTICE
ASSIGNMENT
TASK

Choose one of the following policies from your pre-school:

▶ Anti-discrimination
▶ Health and safety
▶ Child protection.

Write a brief report that includes:

▶ a description of how the policy was drawn up
▶ an analysis of how the policy is used to inform practice
▶ an evaluation of the effectiveness of the policy.

Further reading and references

British Medical Association (2000) *Complete Family Health*, London: Dorling Kindersley

Health Education Authority (1999) *Birth to Five*, London: Health Education

HMSO (1995) *Manual of Nutrition*, London: HSMO

Issues Series *Looking at Vegetarianism*, Cambridge: Independence Publishers

Red Cross (2003) *First Aid Manual*, London: Dorling Kindersley

Valman, Dr B. (1998) *Children's Medical Guide*, London: Dorling Kindersley

1 Working with Children with Special Educational Needs

Inclusion is the way forward

The term '**inclusion**' is now used frequently when talking about meeting children's needs. The concept of inclusion is to provide the necessary staffing, equipment and support so that all children can play and learn alongside others of the same age. This reflects a significant change to the way education was organised not so long ago. Previously, children who were in any way different from their peers were segregated and seen as a 'problem'; they may have been sent to a 'special school' or educated at home. For many children, this meant that they were unable to achieve their potential, because expectations of children with any disability were low. Such segregation was a reflection on a society that could not cope with diversity. Today's view, enshrined by the 2001 Special Educational Needs Code of Practice, considers that all children are entitled to learn alongside their peers and that the expectation that all children can achieve their potential should be high. This represents a mind shift and for us, as practitioners, it means that we are welcoming more and more children who would previously have been excluded into our settings. It is an exciting and challenging opportunity for practitioners to work with this diversity in their settings.

This unit is divided into three sections:

▶ How to promote the care and education of children with **Special Educational Needs**

▶ Using Individual Education Plans to progress the learning and development of children

▶ Strategies for working with other professionals

How to promote the care and education of children with Special Educational Needs

What are Special Educational Needs?

The term Special Educational Needs (SEN) is in itself quite controversial. Some organisations consider it a redundant term because all children have needs and therefore we should automatically look for ways to meet their needs without labelling them. While this is a powerful argument, and one that should not be dismissed by practitioners, we find ourselves in a difficult position as currently the National Standards, the SEN Code of Practice and other guiding documents use this term. Defining children with SEN is therefore in itself potentially difficult. However, for the purposes of this unit, the term Special Educational Needs will be used to identify children who need extra support in order to access the curriculum alongside other children.

Using appropriate terminology

The language that society develops and uses reflects its attitudes and values. Today, there is a greater understanding of the impact that language can have on people's lives. Much of the language that was previously used to describe disabilities and medical conditions was very negative and largely reflected the medical model of disability. Words such as 'deformed' and 'mental' reflected the fear, hostility and ignorance of earlier societies. Sadly, while attitudes towards disabled people are gradually changing, many phrases and words still remain and continue to cause offence. It is important therefore as a starting point to be sensitive to the language that we use. We should also be aware that language that is today considered appropriate may not always remain so. As practitioners, this means carefully noting changes to language and asking those organisations that represent the people most likely to be affected by the language to guide us.

Terms to avoid	Terms that are preferred
Handicapped person	Disabled person
Invalid	Disabled person
Wheelchair bound	Wheelchair user
Sufferer, victim of, crippled by, afflicted	Person who has …
Spastic	Cerebral palsy
Categories beginning with 'the – 'the deaf', 'the blind'	Deaf people, blind people
Mongoloid, mongol	Person with Down's syndrome
Mental handicap	Learning difficulty
Congenital	Genetically impaired
Disabled toilet	Accessible toilet

Defining disability

- Impairment refers to the loss or abnormality of development of growth, for example, a hearing impairment means that a person has a loss of hearing.
- Disability refers to the restrictions that an impairment causes, for example, a person with a hearing impairment has a disability in hearing.
- Handicap refers to the disadvantage that the person has in relation to others in certain situations. Note that the person is not himself or herself 'handicapped' – he or she is being handicapped by the situation. For example, a person with a hearing impairment is being handicapped when announcements are broadcast in an airport because he or she has a hearing disability. His or her disability does not prevent him or her from reading the signs and getting onto the aircraft, and so he or she is not handicapped all the time.

Understanding models of disability

To work effectively with children and their parents means understanding about the two models of disability:

- the medical model
- the social model.

The medical model

In past years, educational practice was based on the medical model. The key feature of the medical model is that it sees the child who has different needs as being imperfect. The focus is therefore on curing or changing the child to become as 'normal' as possible. Where this was not possible, these children were 'segregated' from other children. The medical model sees such children and their families as helpless, and thus in need of sympathy and charity. This way of thinking is reflected in much of the language that is no longer appropriate (see the 'terms to avoid' on page 214).

The social model

Inclusion reflects the social model of disability whereby children are accepted and valued for who they are. Instead of seeing children who have different needs as a problem, the focus is on changing our practice to accommodate and meet their needs, for example, changing the physical layout of the pre-school. The social model of disability is also about empowerment. Children and their families are seen as equal players in education, and their interests, thoughts

POINT OF INTEREST

Thinking about the child rather than the label

Many practitioners believe that if they 'read up' on a medical condition or impairment, it will help them to work with a child. This is true only in part. The danger of 'reading up' is that it reflects a medical model of disability, i.e. by knowing about the 'problem' it can be sorted. This is a dangerous approach because it neglects the concept that each child is an individual and that we need to start with the child first rather than their needs. In the same way that two children from the same family may have very different personalities, interests and needs, so do two children who have the same medical condition or disability. The key message about working with children is to focus on the person rather than any 'label'.

and views are therefore valuable. The social model of disability has had an impact on the type of organisations that help children and their families, as well as the way in which they work (see end of unit).

The effect of unidentified developmental delay and impairment

The SEN Code of Practice 2001 stresses the importance of identifying as early as possible children who require extra support in their learning. This is because a developmental delay in one area of a child's development can impact on his or her overall development. For example, a child who is not fully hearing may have difficulty in concentrating, socialising and guiding his or her behaviour. Finding out about children's development is therefore important as a way of checking that we are meeting their needs.

Self-esteem

Throughout childhood, children develop both a concept of who they are and expectations of themselves. One of the key dangers of not identifying and supporting children who have additional needs is that they may not realise their own potential. A child who finds it hard to sit still at story time because he or she cannot hear the words of the story may come to believe that he or she is unable to concentrate; a child who cannot remember the letters in his or her name because he or she is not seeing them clearly may come to believe that he or she is not a writer. While these are simplistic examples, they illustrate the importance of making sure that children do not learn about failure because of inadequate support.

Finding out about children's needs

Some children with whom we work will have already had their needs identified. The first port of call will therefore be to talk to the child's parents, who will have developed strategies to meet their child's needs at home and are 'experts' on their child. The parents may have spent hours already in waiting rooms and reading up about their child's disability or medical condition. Tapping into this knowledge is essential because asking parents to advise us will enable us to meet the child's individual needs.

Understanding the effect of children's Special Educational Needs on their learning and development and providing activities that support their learning and development

Areas of need

The SEN Code of Practice 2001 recognises that children may have one or more areas of need. The avoidance of identifying particular 'conditions' or 'disabilities' is deliberate because labelling can lead to children being stereotyped. The Code of Practice lists four areas of need:

- communication and interaction
- cognition and learning
- behaviour and social and emotional development
- sensory and physical development.

Supporting children's communication and interaction

As we saw in Core Unit 1, communication and language is a significant skill that most children are able to learn reasonably easily (see pages 18–23). This is not the case for a few children who may need additional support. The chart below shows some common reasons why this may be an area of need for some children.

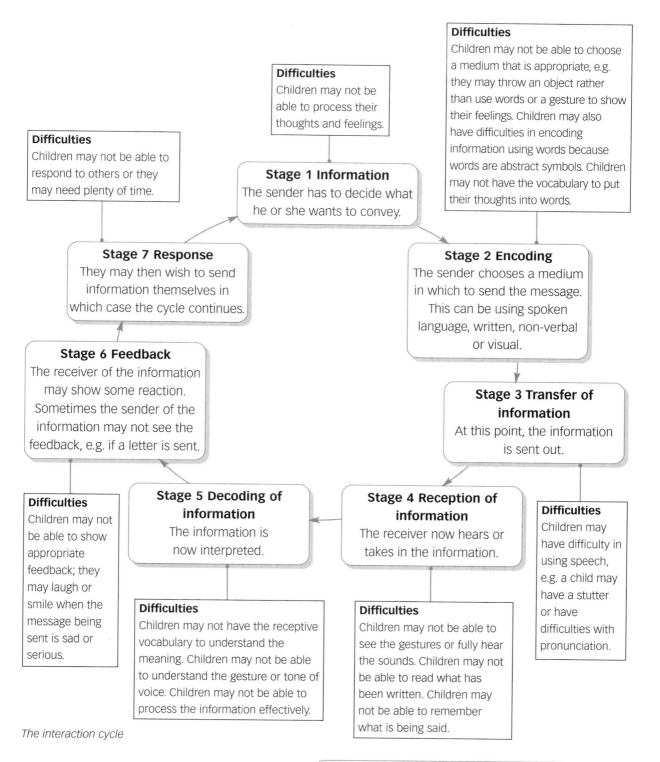

Difficulties
Children may not be able to process their thoughts and feelings.

Difficulties
Children may not be able to choose a medium that is appropriate, e.g. they may throw an object rather than use words or a gesture to show their feelings. Children may also have difficulties in encoding information using words because words are abstract symbols. Children may not have the vocabulary to put their thoughts into words.

Difficulties
Children may not be able to respond to others or they may need plenty of time.

Stage 1 Information
The sender has to decide what he or she wants to convey.

Stage 7 Response
They may then wish to send information themselves in which case the cycle continues.

Stage 2 Encoding
The sender chooses a medium in which to send the message. This can be using spoken language, written, non-verbal or visual.

Stage 6 Feedback
The receiver of the information may show some reaction. Sometimes the sender of the information may not see the feedback, e.g. if a letter is sent.

Stage 3 Transfer of information
At this point, the information is sent out.

Stage 5 Decoding of information
The information is now interpreted.

Stage 4 Reception of information
The receiver now hears or takes in the information.

Difficulties
Children may not be able to show appropriate feedback; they may laugh or smile when the message being sent is sad or serious.

Difficulties
Children may not have the receptive vocabulary to understand the meaning. Children may not be able to understand the gesture or tone of voice. Children may not be able to process the information effectively.

Difficulties
Children may not be able to see the gestures or fully hear the sounds. Children may not be able to read what has been written. Children may not be able to remember what is being said.

Difficulties
Children may have difficulty in using speech, e.g. a child may have a stutter or have difficulties with pronunciation.

The interaction cycle

Language can affect behaviour

The ability to make yourself understood and to interact with others is crucial. Children who have communication and interaction as an area of need can show behaviours that are linked to frustration. They may be more aggressive or attention-seeking than other children of their age. It is important to see these types of behaviour as by-products of children's unmet needs and not to focus on them. Instead, we should concentrate on finding ways of helping these children to communicate their thoughts and wishes, and develop their language skills.

Being a language partner

Children who have communication and interaction as an area of need will often benefit from spending time with a responsive adult. The aim of the adult is both to act as a language partner to help the child develop language and interaction skills, and to 'read' the child effectively. Children who know that they will be understood are far more likely to attempt to interact. Language partners tend to work well because children do not feel under pressure to talk. Children are thus more likely to respond because they are not afraid of saying the wrong thing or not enough.

GOOD PRACTICE ✓

Being a language partner

- Make good eye contact with the child.
- Smile and express genuine pleasure when the child tries to interact.
- Avoid asking the child lots of questions and develop a 'chatty' style.
- Acknowledge the child's communications by answering or responding rather than simply giving praise.

Using visual means of communication

Children whose language skills are still developing often need visual as well as verbal cues. These help children's comprehension and allow them to take in more information. Visual cues are particularly useful for situations in which children may find it hard to concentrate, such as story time. Having a visual cue helps children to understand and focuses their attention.

Puppets

Many children enjoy puppets. Sometimes children who are reluctant to talk will say something to a puppet or cuddly toy. This is because they do not worry about being

Using a puppet can aid communication skills

judged or getting something wrong. Puppets can also be used to model language because we can say something to the puppet and the puppet can then respond.

Picture representations

Picture representations help children to communicate with us by allowing them to point to a picture if they cannot take us directly to the object they want. It is also helpful for us to use picture representations to show children what is going to happen next. Commercial systems of picture representations are available, and speech and language therapists may suggest that you try these.

Sign representation

Some children may need signs to support spoken language. Makaton is a well-known system that is used alongside the spoken word. It is not a language in itself in the same way that British Sign Language is. The decision to use Makaton or another signing system will be made by speech and language therapists in conjunction with the child's parents.

Hearing loss

Some children may have communication and interaction as an area of need because they are not fully hearing. It is important to recognise the signs that children are not hearing as this can be extremely frustrating for them. Hearing loss can affect a child's enjoyment of activities and his or her ability to play with other children.

GOOD PRACTICE

Strategies for supporting children who may not be fully hearing

▶ Always turn to the child so that he or she can see your face clearly.
▶ Make sure that the lighting allows the child to see your face.
▶ Do not cover your mouth with your hands.
▶ Check early on that the child understands the conversation.
▶ Use visual cues such as props and pictures to help the child follow what is happening.
▶ Consider the use of quiet areas for some types of activities.
▶ In group situations, make sure that the child is close by.

Dysfluency

Many children will have some dysfluency (stammering) in their speech when they first begin to put sentences together. For most children, it is simply a phase in which their thoughts travel more quickly than their words. Children may stumble over the initial sounds of words, particularly if they are under pressure to speak quickly. Understanding how to help children relax while speaking is important, because if children feel stressed a vicious cycle can develop in which they stammer more. This can sometimes lead to children not talking in group situations.

Strategies to reduce stammering

▶ Avoid situations in which children compete to talk first, for example, group situations in which children are asked a question and the first to put their hand up can speak.
▶ Avoid situations in which children cannot take their time, for example, circle time in which other children wait their turn.
▶ Reduce the speed at which you talk and make sure that the child feels that you have plenty of time in which to speak.
▶ When speaking, make sure that you are on the same level as the child.

Checklist to help children with communication and interaction

▶ Do children have time with a language partner?
▶ Are visual cues provided to help children?
▶ Are story times organised according to children's language needs?
▶ Are group times 'competitive' in nature?
▶ Are staff aware of the importance of helping children to relax?
▶ Are staff aware that some behavioural responses are the result of frustration?

Supporting children's cognition and learning

Cognition is about the way in which we process and use information, and how we learn to perceive and understand our world. It is linked closely to language, so some children who have communication and interaction as an area of need may also need extra support with cognitive development. There are many components to cognition, which includes attention, concentration and memory. It is not fully understood how we process information and learn, but it is clear that physical development and language play a part in children's early years.

Helping children to concentrate

Concentrating is far more complex than most of us realise. The starting point is to understand that our brains are bombarded by information all the time. For some children, this means that they cannot stay focused because they are easily distracted by new information, for example, seeing another child walk nearby or hearing their name. As our brains mature, they become more efficient at ignoring information that is not required and we find it easier to settle and focus our attention. It is also worth recognising that children find it much easier to process information when it is presented to them in a way that engages their senses and allows them to be active. Using language alone for most children is quite difficult. This is why young children find it very hard to sit still and simply listen passively.

Helping children to concentrate

- ▶ Avoid passive activities – encourage children to be active in their learning.
- ▶ Build on children's interests – when activities have meaning and relevance for them, they are more likely to be able to learn.
- ▶ Use sensory activities that stimulate the brain – such as sand and water play.
- ▶ Remember that children find it hard to concentrate when they are tired.

Encouraging children to make connections

Children find it easier to concentrate and learn when they build on previous knowledge and experiences. This is because it helps them to make connections. It is therefore a good idea to repeat games or activities but with variations. It is also important to encourage children to talk about what they think will happen next and encourage them to remember what they have done before. This helps children to use knowledge they have gained to build new learning. Helping children to find similarities between previous situations can also help them adjust to new situations; for example, saying to children, 'Do you remember how we washed our hands before when they were dirty?'

Understanding that young children often use language to organise information

As we saw in Core Unit 1, language and thought are interconnected (page 26). It is therefore important to encourage children to talk aloud if they wish because this is often a key way in which children acquire information. Sometimes, children talking aloud in situations, for example, circle time, are interpreted as them not being able to listen. The reality is that talking aloud often shows the contrary: the child is thinking and therefore talking about the information they have learnt.

Encourage children to learn about language in a sensory way, for example, drawing letters in the sand

Supporting children's cognitive development

- Make sure that activities are active.
- Look out for sensory activities to help children learn.
- Encourage children's language and do not prevent children from 'thinking aloud'.
- Help children find connections between current and past experiences.
- Make sure that planning reflects individual children's experiences.
- Remember that young children may need to see things rather than imagine them.

Supporting children's behaviour and social and emotional development

There are many reasons why children may find it difficult to show 'appropriate behaviour'. If we are serious about inclusion, it means that our approach to guiding children's behaviour is based on the understanding that most behaviour reflects a child's unmet needs. If we take this approach, it may mean that we need to reflect upon what the child's behaviour is telling us. This approach challenges the traditional ways of managing children's behaviour: instead of focusing on how the child's behaviour is causing us difficulties, we need to think about the how the child can be helped to show alternative behaviours.

Communication
Children who have difficulty in communicating their needs often show more frustrated behaviour than their peers do. Good communication skills enable us to interpret what children are trying to say.

Physical development
Many physical skills give children independence and allow them to join in play with others. Some children who have difficulties with controlling their movements can become frustrated or reliant on adult support.

How behaviour links to overall development

Social and emotional development
Playing co-operatively with other children is linked to skills such as feeling secure and communication, as well as having sufficient experience of playing and being with others. Children who are not able to join with other children in play can show inappropriate behaviour.

Cognitive development
For some children, remembering rules or applying them to different situations is difficult and they may find it hard to show appropriate behaviour without frequent support and reminders. Some children may also find it hard to avoid being distracted and may react impulsively to information, for example, a child notices a door is open and wants to go through it.

Modelling behaviour

We can sometimes help children to show appropriate behaviour by acting as a play partner and modelling behaviour. Children can then learn how to respond to others in a comfortable way. The use of puppets and cuddly toys can also help some children to model behaviour.

Taking a pro-active approach to children's behaviour

Children can sometimes learn habits of behaviour that mean the behaviour is likely to continue. We, too, can become trapped in a cycle of responding to these habits. It is therefore helpful to take a step back and consider why the child is showing the behaviour and what happens when they do. This approach can be quite revealing. Sometimes, children have learnt that they will gain immediate adult attention from a certain act. This attention serves as a reinforcement (see page 42) and the child will go on to repeat the behaviour. If we analyse the child's behaviour, we may sometimes realise that the child's basic need is for adult attention and that he or she has simply learnt to gain it in an inappropriate way. A pro-active approach to such habits of behaviour is therefore to look for ways of giving the child attention, thereby reducing his or her need to seek attention inappropriately.

In the same way that adults can become trapped in responding to a child's cycle of behaviour, so can other children. Sometimes, other children might refuse to play alongside a child or will 'tell tales'. In such situations, we may need gradually to introduce the child into play with others. This might mean asking the child to choose another child to carry out an adult-directed but pleasant activity, such as cooking. Helping children to interact in structured situations can be very helpful.

KEY POINTS

Checklist for a pro-active approach to children's behaviour

▶ What play activities engage and interest the child? Are these being provided?
▶ Are the activities suitable for the child's stage of development?
▶ What level of support does the child need and is this being received?
▶ What situations cause the child to seek adult attention?
▶ Does the child have opportunities to feel in control?
▶ Does the child need adult support to help him of her play with other children?
▶ How are this child's underlying needs being met?

Supporting children's sensory and physical development

Children who have a sensory impairment or whose physical development is atypical will need extra support in order to enjoy experiences and benefit from the learning environment. There is a strong link here to cognition and learning, so sometimes a need in this area will link to children's cognitive development.

Using a multi-sensory approach

All children, regardless of whether they have Special Educational Needs, respond well to sensory materials and experiences. For children who have sensory and physical development as their area of need, a multi-sensory approach is essential. Specialist equipment is often available on loan from toy libraries. It is important not to 'exclude' other children from using such equipment because all children will benefit from playing with it. A multi-sensory approach helps a child to compensate for a particular impairment.

Hand printing is an activity that children of all abilities can enjoy

Helping children who dislike tactile materials

Some children dislike putting their hands in sensory materials such as sand and water. It is important to understand that this is not likely to reflect attention-seeking behaviour, but rather that the hands of some children are over-sensitive. This is referred to as being tactile defensive. Children who find it hard to cope with sensory materials will need support, and the following strategies might be useful.

GOOD PRACTICE ✓

Strategies for supporting children who are tactile defensive
- Do not dismiss children's fears.
- Do not force children's hands into things; this can make them feel panicky.
- Avoid making an 'issue' out of children's reluctance to handle things; some children can then learn to use this as an attention-seeking device.
- Ask parents about materials that the child enjoys at home.
- Choose activities and games that encourage children to touch large-scale things with pressure, for example, bouncing on a trampoline, trampling on wet sand, wearing wellington boots or wringing water out of fabric.

> ▶ Look for materials that are firm for children to explore, for example, dried beans and marbles.
>
> ▶ Encourage firm movements using tools, for example, cutting dough with knives, printing into wet sand with forks, drawing with sticks.
>
> ▶ Consider putting sand or dough into plastic bags so that children can play with it through the plastic.
>
> ▶ Introduce materials that are more tactile, such as cornflour and water, only as children become more confident.
>
> ▶ Model language so that children can learn to express what they are feeling.
>
> ▶ Look for ways of helping children to remain in control; for example, while playing in the sand, allow them to wipe their hands on a towel at any time. The knowledge that they can do this can help children to gain confidence.

Children who show little response to touch

While some children overreact to touch, others show little reaction. These children particularly benefit from daily sensory activities. It is also a good idea to build on their favourite sensory activities by incorporating them into other activities. For example, a child who likes playing with cornflour and water might enjoy mark-making activities in the same tray.

Looking for accessibility

Children who have difficulty with standing or mobility do not necessarily have Special Educational Needs. This is because they are able to learn alongside other children once adaptations or adjustments are made to the physical environment. We should therefore think about the layout of the provision and consider ways in which children might be able to do the same or similar tasks as other children. For example, instead of having to stand at a water tray, water might be provided on a table or other surface that is at a better height. It is important here that all children in the pre-school are invited to play with any new provision because otherwise the child might become isolated. In some cases, we may need advice about specialist equipment or knowledge. A paediatric occupational therapist or physiotherapist working with the child and the child's family usually provides this advice.

Developing co-ordination

The ability to co-ordinate movements is something that it is easy to take for granted. For some children, co-ordination is difficult and we may need to help them by looking at strategies to develop co-ordination or by making activities more accessible for them. As with other areas of need, advice should be taken from parents and other professionals working with the child.

Being ready to improvise

One of the skills in helping children who have one or more areas of need is to think creatively. This requires a 'can do' attitude! For example, a suction cup normally used for holding tea towels may be perfect as a lower coat peg or apron peg for a child who is not able to stand up.

CASE STUDY

Jack was finding it hard to finish a jigsaw puzzle. When he put a piece in, the whole jigsaw puzzle often slipped away from him. His co-ordination was such that he could not put one hand down to act as a stabiliser. The supervisor looked at the difficulty that Jack was having and came up with the idea of putting the jigsaw onto a sheet of rubber matting. This allowed Jack to finish the puzzle without any further adult help.

1 Explain why this adult support was better than helping Jack to finish the puzzle.

2 Why is it important to look for ways of allowing children to be independent?

Using specialist equipment and systems to promote the learning and development of children with SEN

As we have seen when looking at the four areas of need, we may sometimes need to support children by using specialist equipment and systems. This is an area in which we often need to be guided by parents and other professionals. Any piece of equipment chosen, for example, equipment to help a child to stand during activities, must be appropriate for the child's needs. In the same way, if concept boards or a visual signing system is used, it is essential that we seek advice otherwise the investment in terms of time and money may be wasted.

Current legislation

Over the past few years, several pieces of influential legislation have been passed in an attempt to combat the discrimination that disabled children faced in education (see also pages 139–41). The latest pieces of legislation have moved further towards the concept of inclusion. It is important for pre-schools to keep up to date on changing legislation because grants and funding could be removed from settings that fail to comply with the recommendations. Currently, guidance on interpreting the legislation relating specifically to children with SEN is provided by the SEN Code of Practice 2001. The previous Code of Practice is no longer valid.

Children Act 1989

This is a wide-ranging piece of legislation that aims to enshrine children's rights in law. In terms of disability, the Children Act 1989 requires that local authorities compile a register of all children 'in need'. The Act also gives local authorities the responsibility to ensure that these children's needs are met and details the inspection of childcare provisions, which is now undertaken by OFSTED.

Special Education Needs and Disability Act (2001)

This Act is divided into two parts.

▶ The first part of the Act strengthens the rights of parents to send their children into mainstream education. The SEN Code of Practice 2001 (see below) is a product of this legislation.

The second part of the Act extends the 1995 Disability Discrimination Act (see also page 139) and prevents education establishments from denying access to a child because of a disability. This legislation is quite powerful because it means that parents can take a pre-school to court if their child is denied a place because of a disability.

SEN Code of Practice 2001

At the time of writing, this is the latest Code of Practice to be issued for professionals. It is a product of the Special Education Needs and Disability Act (2001). The SEN Code of Practice is essential reading and replaces the guidance in the previous Code of Practice. It explains the duties and responsibilities of pre-schools and outlines the procedures to be adopted in order to identify and work with children who have Special Educational Needs.

Note: This is a DFES publication available free of charge from the order line 0845 6022260 or DFES Publications, PO Box 5050, Sherwood Park, Annesely, Notts, NG15 0DJ (ISBN 184185 537 6)

Fundamental principles of the Code of Practice

The SEN Code of Practice begins by outlining its guiding principles. These are entitled 'Critical Success Factors' and can be found at the front of the Code. It is important to understand that the Code is founded on the key assumption that all

Children with Special Educational Needs should have their needs met
Pre-schools have a responsibility to ensure that children's needs are met. This reflects the social model of disability that values all children.

Children with Special Educational Needs should be offered full access to a broad, balanced and relevant education, including an appropriate curriculum for the Foundation Stage and National Curriculum
This strengthens children's rights to an education: it means that children cannot be discriminated against because of any disability. Pre-schools may therefore have to adjust their traditional ways of working with children or the layout of the provision, so that children with SEN have the same access to learning as other children.

Fundamental principles of the SEN Code of Practice

The Special Educational Needs of children will normally be met in mainstream schools
This again reflects the social model of disability and means that pre-schools should welcome children who previously would have been placed in segregated provision.

Parents have a vital role to play in supporting their children's education
The Code of Practice strengthens parents' involvement in their child's care and education. Pre-schools have a duty to work effectively with parents, which means involving them rather than just informing them.

The views of the child should be sought and taken into account
Previously, children were not consulted about their care and education; we now need to make sure that children's wishes are respected. This links to the concept of empowering children.

practitioners will aim to meet the needs of all children through their daily practice and will, for example, change layouts, differentiate activities or use a variety of resources to this end. Children whose needs can be met by making simple adjustments in this way are not considered to have Special Educational Needs.

CASE STUDY

Fatima has diabetes. She is given an insulin injection before coming to pre-school in the morning. She requires no additional resources or support, although staff make sure that she has her snack on time.

1 Would Fatima be classed as having a Special Educational Need?

Special Educational Needs policy

To ensure that the requirements of the SEN Code of Practice are complied with, every pre-school must have a policy for SEN. This policy should show how children's needs are identified and met. As with the other types of policy that a pre-school may have, there is no single way in which SEN policy should be written. The following information, however, is likely to be included:

- a statement of commitment
- the roles and responsibilities for SEN in the pre-school
- the identification of children with SEN
- involving children
- involving parents in meeting children's needs
- the procedure for meeting children's needs, including Individual Education Plans (IEPs)
- training staff to help meet children's needs.

The role of the SENCO

Under the SEN Code of Practice, every pre-school must have a member of staff who is responsible for co-ordinating support for children with Special Educational Needs. This role is known as the Special Educational Needs Co-ordinator (**SENCO**). The SENCO will have several responsibilities, which include meeting with parents, observing children and supporting colleagues. While a SENCO may advise colleagues about how best to meet a child's needs, he or she will not necessarily work with individual children; rather, the intention is to prevent children from being segregated from others. The Code of Practice therefore suggests that all practitioners should be responsible for meeting children's needs.

Responding to children's needs

The SEN Code of Practice stresses the importance of identifying children who may have particular needs as early as possible. Previously, once a pre-school recognised that a child might have a learning need, specialists were contacted immediately and a 'statement' was eventually drawn up via the local education authority. This practice has now changed; the SEN Code of Practice has introduced a 'graduated response'. The aim of this approach is to encourage early intervention and to avoid labelling children from an early age.

Early Years Action

Early Years Action is the first layer of the graduated response. It is used only after the following conditions have been met:

- the pre-school has thought about ways of differentiating the curriculum for the child
- the pre-school has assessed their practice
- the child continues to give cause for concern.

The aim of this layer of response is to provide 'in house' support that is carefully targeted. This means that the SENCO, practitioner and parents will meet together to share concerns and draw up an Individual Education Plan (or IEP). The SEN Code of Practice suggests that, for most children, this targeted support will be sufficient to meet their needs.

Early Years Action Plus

Early Years Action Plus is the second layer of action. It means that other professionals outside of the pre-school will be contacted to advise and assess the child's needs. It is important here to note that under the SEN Code of Practice parents have to give their consent before outside help is sought. In most circumstances, pre-schools also need to show what steps they have already taken to meet the child's needs. Individual Education Plans will continue to be used, but it is likely that other professionals will also provide help with drawing up and reviewing IEPs. If further help is required that cannot otherwise be funded, a statutory assessment may be requested in order that the child can have a statement (see below).

Statutory assessments (statementing)

Statements are legally binding documents that detail the support to be provided for children by the local education authority. Before a statement can be obtained, a statutory assessment is made of the child's needs. This is a thorough and potentially costly and time-consuming process. The aim of the SEN Code of Practice is to cut the number of statements: it is hoped that, by putting resources into the graduated response system, only children with complex needs will require a statement.

Working in partnership with parents to promote the learning and development of children with Special Educational Needs

The importance of working in partnership with parents

The SEN Code of Practice 2001 strengthens parents' rights and encourages a much closer involvement with them. This approach should pay dividends: before, parents frequently felt very left out of the process and practitioners were often unsympathetic to their feelings or unappreciative of their knowledge of their child. This approach was not in the child's interests because parents' knowledge was unused. For example, for situations in which children were involved with several professionals, it was often only the parents who had a direct overview of what was happening.

> *Parents hold key information and have a critical role to play in their child's education. They have unique strengths, knowledge and experience to contribute to the shared view of a child's needs and the best ways of supporting him or her. It is therefore essential that all professionals (schools, LEAs and other agencies) actively seek to work with parents and value the contribution they make.*
>
> *Paragraph 2.2 SEN Code of Practice 2001*

How to work in partnership with parents

The key to working with parents is to ensure that good relations are established from the start. This is good practice regardless of any particular needs their child may have. It is also important to share immediately with parents any concerns or observations that you have about their child, rather than 'store them up' for later. This is crucial because the Code of Practice states clearly that parents must be involved with the drawing up of Individual Education Plans and that parent's consent has to be given before any professionals are contacted. It also avoids situations whereby a parent whose child has been in the pre-school for a while is suddenly faced with an avalanche of information. This can make parents feel quite defensive, cross and cheated, especially if they have asked after their child and nothing has been said.

The Code of Practice outlines seven key principles that you should adopt when working with parents. These principles are sound ones and should be followed in relation to all children regardless of their individual needs.

1 **Acknowledge and draw on parental knowledge and expertise in relation to the child**
This principle is about recognising that parents really know their children. They may also have contacts with support organisations and other professionals.

2 **Focus on children's strengths as well as areas of additional need**
There is a danger that when children have particular needs, practitioners focus only on these. It is essential to remember the 'whole' child otherwise parents may feel that their child is seen as a 'problem'.

3 **Recognise the personal and emotional investment of parents and be aware of their feelings**
Parents do not see their child in terms of developmental milestones or key learning intentions. Their focus is on the whole child and on nurturing their offspring. This principle reminds us to be sensitive to the emotional tie that exists between parents and their children.

4 **Ensure that parents understand the procedures, are aware of how to access support in preparing their contribution, and are given documents to be discussed well before the meetings**
While some parents may have quite a lot of knowledge as to the procedures of identifying and supporting children's special needs, others

may not. This can put parents at a serious disadvantage and, as a result, they may be unable to participate fully.

5 **Respect the validity of differing perspectives and seek constructive ways of reconciling different viewpoints**

Parents may not always agree about whether their child has particular needs or with the strategies that are being suggested. Confident practitioners are able to understand that views may differ while others may see this as a direct challenge to their expertise. Conflict is not helpful to anyone and rarely meets children's needs. By respecting and actively taking on board parents' views, it should be possible to find positions of compromise.

6 **Respect the differing needs that parents themselves may have, such as a disability or communication and linguistic barriers**

Some parents may have particular needs. If we are not sensitive to these, they may create a barrier to effective communication and information-sharing. This means being ready to take a flexible approach when organising meetings and sharing information for example, some parents may wish to bring a friend or an interpreter to a meeting.

7 **Recognise the need for flexibility in the timing and structure of meetings**

It is easy to pay lip service to involving parents. If parents are to be truly involved, we must ensure that we choose meeting times and places that everyone can attend.

APPLYING THEORY TO YOUR PRACTICE

What do the seven key principles in the Code of Practice mean to you and your team in practice at work?

What adaptations to activities or the environment or working practices might they need to consider?

Using Individual Education Plans to progress the learning and development of children

Individual Education Plans, often called IEPs, are in essence action plans. They are useful because they focus our work and make us consider the child's needs. The use of IEPs is considered by the Code of Practice to be an essential tool when working with children who have Special Educational Needs.

When are Individual Education Plans necessary?

It is a mistake to think that an IEP will be necessary for every child. The key test as to whether a child needs an IEP is whether you need to provide very different or extra support to help that child. The Code of Practice is clear that it is good practice for all children to adapt environments and our practice to meet their needs. IEPs are necessary only when further support is required. This means that a child with a medical condition such as epilepsy is not likely to need an IEP because these types of conditions do not usually affect children's learning and overall development. In the same way, a child who wears a hearing aid may not need an IEP because he or she will be able to participate fully once adjustments are made to activities and the environment.

It is important to think carefully about whether an IEP is necessary. You may otherwise be snowed under by paperwork and fail to use time that should be spent focusing on children effectively. The Code of Practice gives the following guidance (see below).

Children are likely to need an IEP if any of the following apply:

▶ *the child makes little or no progress even when teaching approaches are particularly targeted to improve the child's identified area of weakness*
▶ *the child continues working at levels significantly below those expected for children of a similar age*
▶ *the child experiences persistent emotional and/or behavioural difficulties that are not ameliorated by the behaviour managements and techniques usually employed in the setting*
▶ *the child has sensory or physical problems and continues to make little or no progress despite the provision of personal aids and equipment*
▶ *the child has communication and/or interaction difficulties and requires specific individual interventions in order to access learning.*

Source 4:21 SEN Code of Practice 2001

How to use observations of children with Special Educational Needs to create Individual Education Plans

The starting point when considering drawing up an Individual Education Plan is to observe a child closely. At this point, we should also have communicated our concerns to the child's parents so that any observations we carry out can be shared. By observing children closely, we can focus on areas of need and consider how the child responds in a variety of situations. Ideally, observations in a setting should be ongoing for all children because the Foundation Stage asks that we plan according to children's interests and stages of development.

In order to assess children's needs, it is likely that several observations and assessments will be carried out. As we have seen, children's responses can vary enormously (see pages 59–61). Therefore, basing an IEP on a single observation will be ineffective.

GOOD PRACTICE

Information that might be helpful when identifying children's needs

▶ In what situations does the child need further support?
▶ How does the child respond in these situations?
▶ Does the child have any particular interests?
▶ What are the child's strengths?
▶ Are there any strategies or situations that appear to be helpful?

Observation methods

It is a good idea to use a range of observation methods to find out more about the child (see also pages 59–67). Some pre-schools also find it helpful to use more than one observer because we can sometimes focus on different aspects of a child's development and in this way come to different conclusions. It is also worth talking to parents about what they see of their child at home, which can sometimes reveal a different perspective. In some cases, carrying out a focused observation can provide us with a new approach to try with a child. If this helps the child, it may mean that an IEP is not necessary.

Creating an IEP

If an IEP is considered necessary, the next step is to organise a meeting in which parents and practitioners can discuss how best to help the child. At this meeting, a discussion about the child's needs should take place followed by consideration of those targets that might be recorded as a focus for further work with the child (see below).

People involved in writing the IEP

Once the observations have been carried out, it is important to talk through with parents what has been learnt. This is a key feature of drawing up a successful IEP. It is also important that the child's key worker or a practitioner with responsibility for the child is involved. The idea is that these people should be able to tailor the plan of action to best suit the child. The person who should co-ordinate the creation of the IEP is the Special Educational Needs Co-ordinator (SENCO), although he or she may not necessarily write it.

Information to be recorded

There is no standard format for IEPs, but the following information is usually recorded:

- the child's name and date of birth
- the date of the IEP
- the date and level of support, for example, Early Years Action/Plus
- a brief summary of the child's area of need
- the child's strengths and interests
- the targets the plan is to cover
- how the targets are to be measured
- the teaching methods and strategies to be adopted
- the staff who are to be responsible for the implementation of the plan – this might be more than one named person
- the date the IEP will be reviewed
- signatures of parents and staff.

Writing the IEP

The IEP should not be a lengthy document. It is important to remember that an IEP is a short-term action plan; it is not designed to provide a long-term overview. However, it does help to focus practitioners and parents on short-term targets and priorities that will help the child. Many pre-schools have developed a format so that the information can be fitted onto an A4 sheet of paper. There are also software packages that can be used to write IEPs on computers; however, these need to be carefully evaluated as they may not have been written with the very young child in mind.

The first pieces of information that are recorded on an IEP, such as the child's name, are straightforward. Other pieces of information require more thought, as detailed below.

Areas of need

This section should simply outline the child's current difficulties. The section should be quite short and focused on why the child needs additional or different support. For those children who have many needs, it is important to identify which aspect the IEP will be working on.

Setting targets

As part of the creation of the IEP, some targets are set. These targets allow practitioners and parents to focus their work on developing particular skills in the child. It is important here to note that the targets are not for the child but for the adults working with the child!

Ideally, targets should be small and very achievable. This allows everyone, including the child, to feel a success. Targets are like small stepping stones that will help the child on his or her journey. Each IEP builds on the last; the aim is thus for the child to complete his or her journey little by little. The acronym SMART is used in relation to setting these targets. It is helpful because it reminds us about ensuring that targets are realistic.

S – specific
M – measurable
A – achievable
R – relevant
T – timebound

▶ Specific
As we have seen, targets are small steps. The key is to break down anything we would like the child to achieve into small skills. For example, if we feel that it would be helpful for the child to use a pair of scissors, a first target might be to focus on the child being able to hold the scissors correctly.

▶ Measurable
To help us monitor the effectiveness of the IEP, targets should be measurable. If they are not, how will you be able to check that the child has made progress and is ready for the next target? Thinking about the measurability of a target can help to make the target more focused.

▶ Achievable and Relevant
Targets must be achievable otherwise all involved – the parents, the child and the practitioners – can become despondent and lose motivation. Choosing targets that are relevant is therefore important. Ideally, the targets should concentrate on helping the child rather than the setting. You should consider what targets will best help the child to access the curriculum and meet his or her needs.

Parents may have different views about what is relevant; for example, they may want their child to achieve a skill that will help the child at home.

▶ Timebound

IEPs are short-term action plans. This creates a sense of urgency, which means that they are less likely to be forgotten. The IEP should state when it will be reviewed. Most pre-schools will draw up IEPs every six or eight weeks.

The Code of Practice suggests that IEPs might have three or four targets. This number may be too great if a child attends few sessions, so you may wish to reduce the number of targets.

Teaching methods and strategies

As well as deciding on targets, it is important to record how targets are likely to be achieved. This is an essential part of the IEP because targets alone will not help the child. You will need to consider how best to support the child and how this support will be provided.

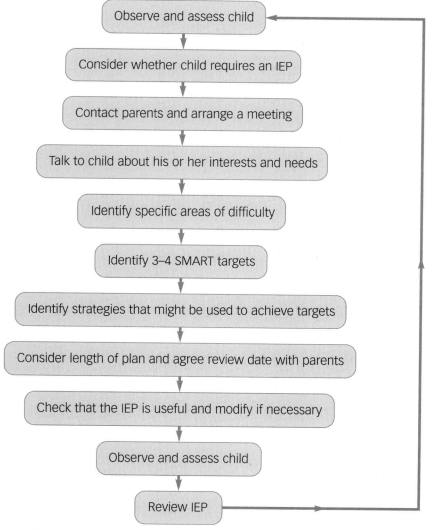

The stages of writing an IEP

Shona is four years old. She was a premature baby, and her physical development is giving her parents and practitioners cause for concern. She sometimes shows signs of frustration during activities and finds it difficult to concentrate. The Special Educational Needs Co-ordinator and Shona's parents have decided to draw up an IEP that will focus on her fine motor skills. This is because they believe these skills to be the underlying reason for Shona's frustrated behaviour and poor concentration. Shona's parents are keen to play a part at home.

1 Explain why Shona's frustrated behaviour may be linked to her physical development.

2 Why will it be important to choose targets that are not just linked to the pre-school?

Name   Shona
Action
Date of Birth   14/4/00
Area/s of concern   Fine motor control
Interests of the child   Shona enjoys helping adults
Review Date   15/3/04
Practitioner responsible for implementation   Margery Dobbs

Targets to be achieved	Achievement criteria	Possible resources/ techniques	Possible strategies	Ideas for support	Outcome
1 To grasp a small object between finger and thumb	1 To pick up 10 small beads using finger and thumb	1 Sorting activities including rice, buttons and threading beads	1 Make sure items are appealing. Make sure that she gains success	Demonstrate movements. Plenty of praise	
2 To strengthen palmar grasp	2 To squeeze dry a small wet sponge	2 Wringing actions, squeezing sponges	2 Put out sensory materials such as dough, sponges and water in trays	Demonstrate movements and make sure that Shona is praised. Look out for opportunities to practise these movements in the routine e.g. wiping tables	

Parents' contribution   Encourage Shona to be more independent at home, e.g. pouring own drinks out of small jug, serving herself with spoons and helping out with household tasks such as wiping tables.

Parent's signature	Date
Practitioner's signature	Date

Storage of IEPs

The parents and the SENCO should sign the finished IEP. It should then be kept in a safe place because it is a confidential document. It is not appropriate for an IEP to be put on display or left in a place where adults who are not directly involved with the child might see it.

Amending an IEP

IEPs should be seen as working documents, therefore the IEP should be checked regularly and, if necessary, amended. For example, it might be that because of a child's absence the timeframe is no longer appropriate. Changes to the IEPs can be penned in and the date of the amendment should be added. It is good practice to let parents know that an IEP is to be slightly amended. If significant changes are required, it is better to draw up a new IEP.

Implementing the IEP in the pre-school

The time and effort that has been put into writing the IEP will be wasted if no further action is taken. Children's IEPs should therefore be considered when

Daily Planner		Monday		
Adult directed activities				
Staff member	**Activity + area**	**Focus**	**Individual needs**	**Comments**
Dianne	Making stretchy dough – messy play area	Experimentation, measuring and noticing changes to texture	Rubber mat for C.K. to stop bowl from slipping	More self-raising flour needed for for tomorrow!
Andraya	Name treasure hunt – outdoor area	Name recognition and searching skills	Put red sticker on L.C.'s card. Encourage to find himself. Repeat	L.C. found his name easily. Repeat tomorrow perhaps without sticker?
Toni	Sandcastles – sand tray	Sizes of buckets and quantities of sand required	J.K. may need thin plastic gloves. Plenty of encouragement	Extend this with flags tomorrow?
Child directed activities				
Gloop – pink	Water tray – shells, pebbles and boats	Role-play area – suitcases, clothes and luggage labels	Writing area – postcards, envelopes and stamping machine	Dough – shells, pot pourri
Jigsaws	Farm animals + small cardboard boxes	Outdoor – large cardboard boxes		

This daily planning sheet shows how children's individual needs will be met

planning activities and staff deployment. It is the role of the SENCO to ensure that the IEP is effective, although this can happen only if all members of the team are aware of its significance. Some settings integrate children's IEPs into their planning by adding extra notes or a column so that it is clear how the activity is to meet the child's needs.

Reviewing IEPs

It is an important part of the process that IEPs are reviewed. Carrying out a review means that we are far more likely to carry out the suggested activities and observe children's progress closely. When a review is due, it is important to observe the child closely once more and consider what progress he or she has made. It is also important to pool together information from colleagues and parents.

Once information has been collected from observations, colleagues and parents, a meeting with parents should be arranged. The discussion should focus on the 'whole' child as well as on those needs identified in the IEP. After the child's progress has been considered, a decision needs to be made as to whether a further IEP is required. The key issues here are whether the child is making progress and whether such progress can be sustained by simply differentiating the curriculum. If the decision is made to draw up a further IEP, the same process is followed as previously. In situations when no IEPs are required, it may be helpful to explain to parents that this does not mean that their child will be left to 'fend' for him or herself. No IEPs may be needed for children showing slower progress than their peers but whose needs can be met by adjusting the setting's activities and daily routine.

The involvement of other professionals, parents and children in IEPs

Involving professionals

Where children's progress remains a cause for concern, it will be important to consider whether other professionals need to be involved. This discussion should take place with parents, and the review meeting might be a good time for such discussion. Remember, parents should be asked for their consent before any professionals are contacted.

The first port of call in many areas might be to contact the Early Years Advisory Team, although in some areas it is possible to gain direct referrals to services such as the Speech and Language Team. In some cases, parents may decide to seek help by contacting their GP or health visitor. The involvement of other professionals outside of the setting means that, in terms of the 'graduated response', children will be accessing Early Years Action Plus.

Involving parents

As we have already seen, it is essential that parents are fully involved in the creation of IEPs. Parents are able to give us a better picture of their child, and they may also have some targets in mind and have developed strategies that might be useful when working with the child. Involving parents can also mean that those skills that are being developed with the child in the setting can be encouraged at home, for example, encouraging a child to put on a coat. During the lifetime of the IEP, it is important to have frequent contacts with parents whenever possible. This enables information to be exchanged about the effectiveness of the strategies and helps everyone to prepare for the review meeting when the IEP is revisited.

Involving children

The Code of Practice makes it clear that even the youngest children should be involved in the IEPs. This is to avoid the idea of the child as a 'passive object'. Very young children can be involved by asking them what they enjoy doing. Understanding and building on children's interests is an extremely effective way of helping them to progress. Once children's interests have been identified through observations or, ideally, by asking the child, teaching strategies should be organised accordingly. For example, a child who particularly enjoys playing with dough and whose target looks at building scissors skills, may be shown how to use scissors to cut into dough.

In addition to thinking about children's interests, it may be possible to ask children directly about what they would like to achieve. Sometimes a child may say that he or she wants to be able to do something by him or herself, or to do something that he or she has seen another child do. When children find it hard to communicate, it can be useful to use a prop such as a teddy and ask the child to show us 'what teddy would like to do'; this sometimes helps children to express what they really would like to do.

CASE STUDY

Helena is three years old. Her speech is slightly delayed as she often lets her twin speak for her. She understands well but she still needs to be encouraged to talk rather than to simply point at objects. Her vocabulary also needs to be built up as she tends still to generalise words, e.g. using 'coat' for all types of clothing or 'dog' for all animals. Her mother finds it hard to give her individual time as she also has two other children. She says that Helena especially enjoys animals and plays a lot at home with a farm set. Helena also enjoys touching and exploring new objects.

1 Think of two possible targets that might be used in drawing up an IEP.

2 Describe two activities that will help Helena to achieve these targets.

3 Explain how the adults in the setting might work with Helena to achieve the targets.

Strategies for working with other professionals

Most children's needs can be met within the pre-school by simply focusing on the child's needs and (in some cases) reflecting on our practice. However, some children will need additional support from other professionals. The idea of collaborative working between different groups of professionals is not new. The

Some children will need additional support from other professionals

Children Act 1989 sent a clear message that this was expected when it stated that children were considered as being 'in need'. Children with 'special needs', an umbrella term that encompasses children with Special Educational Needs, are categorised according to the Act as being 'in need'. In many areas, there currently exist a range of series for children with special needs.

Understanding your local services

The range of services for children and even the titles of these services varies enormously from one local authority to the next. This means that it is essential that you find out about what is available in your area and develop a list of contacts for your pre-school. In the same way, the system for referring children can vary. In some areas, speech and language units will accept direct referrals; in others, referrals may need to come via a family doctor or health visitor.

This section looks at what is likely to be available in most parts of the country; however, it can be thought of as only a general overview. In many cases, we come into contact with professionals via a child's family because the parents may have a long-standing involvement with these services.

Early Years Development and Childcare Partnerships (EYDCP)

EYDCPs can be a useful port of call when seeking advice. They were formed to support the government's National Childcare Strategy, and consist of representatives from different organisations with an interest in working with children or providing childcare places for them. This means that by contacting an EYDCP, you may be put in touch with a helpful contact. Many EYDCPs also employ early years advisers who, again, can be a source of support.

EYDCPs are set up in different ways and therefore the services they provide can vary. Many EYDCPs hold regular local meetings so that providers from across the early years sectors can exchange information. In some areas, these are known as 'cluster meetings'. It is important to try to attend such meetings because they help to foster links with other practitioners and advisory staff. These types of local networks are sometimes asked to comment about training needs in the area.

Special Educational Needs advisory teams

Most local education authorities will have teams that support teachers and others involved with children with Special Educational Needs. In some areas, these teams might be referred to as 'Inclusion Support' or 'SENCO Area Teams'. The differences in titles again reflect the local nature of provision. In some areas, advisory teachers will visit pre-schools to help support SENCOs; in other areas, they will also help with the creation of IEPs. Many SEN advisory teams provide training for pre-school settings, so it can be helpful to check what support is available in your area.

Speech and language teams

Each area will have a Speech and Language Team. This service is usually funded by the health service, although many speech therapists work closely with education departments. Many speech and language teams will allow a direct referral if parents have given consent.

CASE STUDY

Moshe is nearly four years old. His parents and the SENCO are concerned that his speech is not progressing as they had hoped, even though he is receiving more individual support in the pre-school. After a review meeting, it was decided to contact the Speech and Language Team. The pre-school had already built up a good relationship with the team and so it was decided that the SENCO would make the initial contact. Once the team had been contacted, the SENCO phoned Moshe's parents to let them know that he had been referred.

1 Why is it important that information is quickly passed on to parents after a referral?

2 Why is it helpful to develop a directory of local contacts?

Sensory impairment team

Most education services will have a team that supports children with visual or hearing impairments. As with other services, the title of this team may vary from area to area. Most teams will employ specialist staff, who visit the pre-school and family to advise how best to meet the child's needs. This team may be able to advise on layout and equipment when working with children with sensory impairments. Most sensory impairment teams will also have strong links with the speech and language team.

Educational psychologist service

Educational psychologists look at and identify children's learning and development. In cases where a child's needs are complex and a statutory assessment is required, educational psychologists will be involved. As demand on their services is high in most areas, it is unlikely that a referral will be made as a first port of call because usually a member of the SEN team will assess the child first.

Parent partnership services

In order to strengthen parents' rights, the Code of Practice asks that every local education authority has a parent partnership to assist those parents who have a child with Special Educational Needs. The aim of the service is to support parents and provide independent advice. Parents should be told about this service when you first discuss the possibility that their child has Special Educational Needs because many parents find this service very helpful.

Health visitors

Health visitors are qualified nurses with specialist training in health promotion. It can sometimes be very helpful to talk to a child's health visitor, but this must be with parental permission. Health visitors can refer children to other services and have a good knowledge of children's health issues.

Physiotherapy services

Physiotherapists are part of the health service. They may be involved in the care of children who have medical conditions or are recovering from surgery. Physiotherapists will provide advice and guidance to parents – and, if appropriate, to settings – about exercises and movements that might help the child.

Social Services

The Children Act 1989 gave local authorities the duty to provide for 'children in need'. This means that children who have complex or severe needs will be provided with a social worker. The social worker's role is to assess and check that the child's needs and those of his or her family are being met.

Paediatric occupational therapy services

Paediatric occupational therapists work with children to maximise their physical movements with the aim of helping them become as independent as possible. In addition to working with children, they are likely to work directly with the family as well. In early years settings, they may advise on how best to make the layout accessible for the child.

> **A QUICK THINK!**
> Do you know how to contact your local early years advisory team?

Understanding how to work with other professionals

There are many facets to working successfully with other professionals.

Following procedures in the setting

Firstly, it is important that procedures within the pre-school are set up so that everyone knows who is responsible for liaising with which professionals. These procedures should be outlined in the SEN policy and, in general, the SENCO should take the lead. It is also essential that, following meetings with other professionals, information is shared with those responsible for working with the child and, where appropriate, the parents. In some pre-schools, a slot is created in every staff meeting so that staff can be updated; the use of a 'standing item' on the agenda shows a commitment to SEN.

Respecting the contributions of other professionals

When many professionals come together to help a child, each person will have his or her own contribution to make. It is a like a jigsaw, with each person holding a piece of the puzzle. This means it is important to understand the roles and perspectives of other professionals so that an overall picture can be formed. Sometimes, the perspectives of other professionals mean that they have different priorities from us; for example, a professional with a health background will consider a child from the perspective of health, while a practitioner from a pre-school may be more aware of the child's learning and education.

Looking for ways to integrate practice

Many professionals may have limited time to work directly with children; for example, a speech and language therapist may see a child for half an hour once a week. For their work to impact upon the child, professionals may ask pre-schools to integrate exercises or ways of working into the child's day. It is extremely important that this co-operation occurs because it will help the child to make progress and will also meet his or her medical needs.

Being ready to use others' expertise

Other professionals often have considerable expertise and experience that we can find helpful. They may be able to provide us with training or ideas as to how to work best with children.

Explaining our work

Some professionals may find it helpful to understand the work of the pre-school. It can therefore be helpful to invite those professionals working with the child to come into the setting to see the child and the way in which we work. This gives other professionals an insight into our areas of expertise, as well as the constraints under which we work. (Note that professionals can come and observe a child only if the child's parents have given their consent.)

Record-keeping

As part of our work with other professionals, we might be asked to keep records that are additional to those usually kept in the pre-school, for example, a record of a child's exercise programme or certain achievements. It is always useful to discuss with other professionals how they wish the information to be presented and exactly what is required.

Understanding our own role

As practitioners, it is important that we recognise our strengths but also our professional limitations. This means that we should let others know if we have not been trained to carry out certain work, for example, to administer injections. It is also important when presenting our views of the child's needs that this is done accurately and factually. Furthermore, if we are required by other professional to carry out observations, we must be ready to check how they would like them to be completed. This is because our day-to-day work often has a very different focus from that of most other professionals.

GOOD PRACTICE

Good practice when working with other professionals

▶ Make sure that you arrive on time for meetings.
▶ Send apologies or someone in your place if you cannot attend.
▶ Bring any necessary documents with you.
▶ Read any material that you have been sent in advance.
▶ Keep notes of what you are required to do.
▶ Make sure that you brief colleagues and parents afterwards.
▶ Respect the range of approaches and perspectives that others might have.
▶ Be ready to seek clarification about others' roles.
▶ Remember that confidentiality remains important.

CASE STUDY

Manuela has just started in the role of Special Educational Needs Co-ordinator. She attends her first liaison meeting with a speech and language therapist who is keen for one particular child to spend a few minutes of each session practising some blowing movements. Manuela is not sure about how best to organise this activity, but is worried about saying anything in case she looks incompetent. She decides not to say anything and later does not try out any of the exercises.

1 Why is it important to be ready to ask questions?

2 How might Manuela's actions affect the child?

TEST YOUR KNOWLEDGE

1 List two key pieces of legislation relating to children with Special Educational Needs.

2 What does IEP stand for?

3 What is the role of the SENCO in a pre-school?

4 Outline the two-stage approach to identifying and working with children with Special Education Needs.

5 Name two other professionals who might have a role in helping children with identified needs.

6 What is meant by the term 'medical model of disability'?

7 Explain the importance of working from children's interests when drawing up an IEP.

8 Analyse the importance of setting SMART targets on IEPs.

9 Consider how language reflects social attitudes towards disabilities.

10 Evaluate the importance of working with parents when drawing up an IEP.

PRACTICE ASSIGNMENT TASK

Design a leaflet for new members of a pre-school team about the SEN Code of Practice 2001. The leaflet should contain:

▶ an explanation of the term 'inclusion'
▶ an outline of the principles behind the Code of Practice
▶ a description of the role of the SENCO
▶ an evaluation of how the Code of Practice affects the pre-school's everyday practice.

Further reading and references

Tassoni, P. (2003) *Supporting Special Needs: Understanding Inclusion in the Early Years*, Oxford: Heinemann

2 The First Year of Life

Working with babies is extremely interesting, although to do it well is emotionally and physically tiring. The rewards, however, are great. The development of a baby is a joy to watch because the developmental landscape is constantly changing. Working with babies also carries with it a huge responsibility. A baby's first year of life lays down some developmental foundations that will affect the baby for the rest of his or her life.

This unit focuses on babies between six weeks and 12 months of age. It is divided into three sections:

▶ The progress of babies' growth and development

▶ Identifying and meeting the physical needs of babies

▶ Meeting the social, emotional and learning needs of babies

The progress of babies' growth and development

It is essential that adults working with babies have a good understanding of the normal pattern of development. This helps us to meet babies' needs, particularly for toys, equipment and safety. It is also essential so that any developmental delay is investigated and the child's needs met. Early identification is important because delay or difficulties in one area of development can impact on other areas.

The stages and expected milestones of babies' growth and development

Understanding that normative development is only a guide

In Core Unit 1, we looked at the development of children aged 1 to 5 years. The terms 'normative' and 'milestones' were explored (see page 3). When looking at babies' development, we must again remind ourselves that the speed with which a baby reaches milestones is variable. Some babies learn to walk as early as eight months old, while others take double that time.

Physical development

One of the most striking things about babies in their first year of life is the way in which they grow and learn to co-ordinate their bodies. By the end of the first year of life, nearly all babies are mobile and some babies can stand and even walk. Their physical co-ordination is so developed that they can feed themselves and pick up objects that interest them. This is amazing progress given that when babies are born they rely completely on instinctive reflexes for survival.

Sequence of physical development

While babies learn the skills of physical development at different rates, it is striking that all babies follow a sequence or pattern in their development. As we saw in Core Unit 1, this means that babies do not suddenly stand up and walk but first need to be able to lift their head.

Age	Developmental pattern
Newborn  	A newborn baby has many developmental reflexes that are designed to help him or her survive, for example, being able to cry and suck. These gradually disappear as the baby gains voluntary control of his or her body. **Rooting reflex** – moves mouth if face is touched to look for food. **Startle reflex** – throws out hands and legs as if trying to catch something if he or she hears a sudden sound. **Grasp reflex** – fingers automatically tighten around anything put in the palm of hand. The grasp is so tight that baby can be lifted up. **Crawling reflex** – when placed on front, knees are tucked up underneath. This is because of being curled up in the womb.
6 weeks 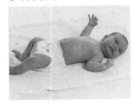	Starting to have more periods of alertness. Looks at carer, stares at bright lights. Is soothed by carer's voice. Follows objects and faces at close range. Arm and leg movements are jerky.
3 months 	Smiles and coos. Kicks legs strongly and moves arms. Movements are less jerky, although still not co-ordinated. Can find hands and bring them to the mouth. Looks at and plays with fingers. Is alert and looks around. Can lift and turn head from side to side when lying on front. Can hold a rattle for a short time, although cannot co-ordinate arms to bring it to mouth.

Age	Developmental pattern
6 months 	Smiles, laughs and makes sounds. Follows adults' movements. Grasps objects. Beginning to roll over. Pulls up legs with hands when on back. May put foot in mouth. Sits up with support, although some babies are starting to sit up for short periods without support. Pushes head, neck and chest off floor when on front.
9 months 	Sits up well without support. Can reach out for toys from sitting. May be crawling or shuffling on bottom. Uses fingers and thumb to pick up objects. Can bang objects together. Babbles and starts to understand words such as 'bye-bye' and 'no'.
12 months 	Most babies are mobile – either crawling, rolling or bottom shuffling. Starts to walk by holding on to furniture; this is often called cruising. May stand alone for a few seconds. Points to objects using index fingers to show adults. Understands name and simple instructions. Drinks from cup; tries to feed using spoon and fingers.

Babies' development

Q: What should I do if I suspect that a baby's development is delayed?

A. It is important to remember that babies do learn skills at very different rates. However, you should talk to the parents if you are concerned. It is likely that they are taking the baby for developmental checks in the baby's first year. If the parents are concerned, they should contact their health visitor who will be able to advise them.

Q: Is it a good idea to use a baby walker to encourage walking?

A. No! Baby walkers are the cause of many serious accidents. Babies have no sense of danger and it is easy for the baby to pull at things or topple over. In addition, baby walkers do not strengthen the spine, which is crucial in learning to crawl and walk. This happens best when babies are placed on the floor on their tummies. Babies who have suddenly experienced the joys of being mobile will find it hard to go back to this position!

Q: How can I encourage a child to learn to crawl?

A. Crawling is an important developmental step. We cannot speed up physical development; however, we can encourage the baby to crawl by allowing the baby to have time on his or her tummy. This helps the baby to raise the head and push up on the arms, and these movements strengthen the spine. However, it is important not to leave babies on their tummies if they are asleep because this is a risk factor in cot death.

Cognitive development

In their first year of life, babies have to take in significant amounts of information because they are trying to learn about their world. This learning is done primarily through the five senses. Gradually, babies build a picture of their world; we can see that their perception develops as their senses begin to work together. Learning about the world takes place primarily through trial and error. This is thought to be one reason why babies repeat their actions. It is as though they are working out how they have impacted on the environment, for example, a baby will drop a rattle; if an adult picks it up, the baby will need to drop it again.

Do babies have memories?

It is now recognised that babies have quite good memories, far better than was previously acknowledged. We now know that a baby can remember a tune that he or she heard while in the womb. Babies can also remember their parents' smells and faces. It would appear that the limitations on a baby's memory are because of the developing retrieval systems.

Object permanence

A key milestone in a baby's intellectual development comes at around eight months of age, when he or she develops object permanence. This concept was described by Piaget (see pages 45–6) and is seen as being quite important. At around eight months old, babies begin to look for an object that they have seen previously but is now hidden. It is as though babies realise that objects and people continue to have an existence even though they cannot see them. This is also the start of separation anxiety (see page 31) because babies are now aware that their parents are around even though they cannot see them.

Language development

In Core Unit 1, we looked at what is meant by language as well as some theories of language development (pages 50–2). In this section, we concentrate on language development in the first year of life.

Language development is intertwined with babies' intellectual development. The first year of life is the start of a language journey for babies. While babies do not actually produce their first words until they are around 13 months old, in their first year of life they learn the prerequisite skills that will enable them to talk. The first year of a baby's life is therefore sometimes referred to as the pre-linguistic stage.

It is interesting to note that babies and children worldwide follow a similar pattern. The first year of a baby's life is spent trying to 'tune in' on the language that he or she hears. The baby will learn communication skills such as making eye contact and responding to people's facial expressions and words. Babies learn the interaction skills of language from being with others, especially key adults in their lives. Without responsive adults, babies will not 'click' and 'tune' into the language that they hear.

Stage	Age	Features	Comments
Cooing	Six weeks	Cooing.	Babies making cooing sounds to show pleasure. These early sounds are different from sounds made later on mainly because the mouth is still developing.
Babbling (phonemic expansion)	6–9 months	Babies blend vowels and consonants together to make tuneful sounds, for example, 'ba', 'ma', 'da'.	Babbling has been described as learning the tune before the words. The baby seems to be practising sounds. Babies increase the number of sounds or phonemes. This is sometimes called phonemic expansion. All babies, even deaf babies, produce a wide range of sounds during this period.
Babbling (phonemic contraction)	9–10 months	Babies babble but the range of sounds is limited.	The range of sounds or phonemes that babies produce becomes more limited and reflects the phonemes used in the language that they hear. In theory, at this stage, it would be possible to distinguish between babies who are in different language environments. At ten months of age, babies can understand 17 or more words.
First words	From 12 months	Babbling and the emergence of first words.	First words often go unidentified by adults as they are mixed in with babbles. Gradually words emerge. Most babies have approximately ten words by 15 months.

The pre-linguistic stage of language development

POINT OF INTEREST

Language – a critical period?

One hypothesis in the study of language is that there is a critical period during which babies and children must learn language. There is considerable evidence to suggest that, while human beings are 'primed' to learn language, this learning must take place in a child's earliest years. Cases in which children have been seriously deprived of human contact reveal that while these children can later learn some words, their ability to crack the grammar, and hence become fluent users of a language, is limited. The lack of stimulation to the areas of the brain used for language is the most likely cause because these parts of the brain simply fail to grow and develop.

Babies who do not hear

It is important that we keep an eye out for babies who are not hearing. This is not always obvious because babies make similar sounds and babble regardless of their hearing. However, key differences are that babies who are not hearing do not develop 'tuneful' babbling and do not reduce the number of sounds they produce, both of which are significant steps in language development. It is important to identify babies who are not hearing so that they can receive the necessary help and support.

KEY POINTS | **Signs that a baby may not be fully hearing**
- Is not distracted by sounds.
- Appears startled when someone approaches him or her.
- Does not turn his or her head in response to sounds.
- Babbling does not evolve.

Factors that influence babies' development

It is important to understand the different factors that can affect babies' development because this can influence the way in which we can meet their needs. Having said this, we also need to observe each child's individual strengths, interests and progress because there is a danger of stereotyping or labelling children.

There are four broad factors that might affect a baby's development:
- pre-conceptual
- antental
- perinatal
- postnatal.

Pre-conceptual care

It is now known that babies' development is influenced even before the mother becomes pregnant; the state of the mother's overall health appears quite crucial. Pre-conceptual care is therefore regarded as important. Women are advised before pregnancy to be aware of their nutrition, alcohol intake and use of drugs, and to be reasonably fit for at least three months before conception. Fathers are also targeted because the quality of sperm can affect the baby's outcomes. A good example of this is smoking: some research findings are that fathers who smoked at the time of conception had children who were more likely to smoke in later life.

Antenatal factors

The term '**antenatal**' describes the time from conception to birth. Many possible influences can affect a child's development during this time; however, this is an area of ongoing research.

Genetics play a part

At the moment of conception, when one sperm fuses with an egg, information that will affect the baby's development comes together. This information is known as DNA (deoxyribonucleic acid) and contains a code that determines the structure and function of the baby's cells. Amazingly, DNA contains information that will influence our physical appearance, our pre-disposition to illness and, according to some scientists, aspects of our temperament.

At the moment of conception, there are occasionally problems with this information that can result in a child being born with a developmental difficulty. One example is Down's syndrome, which is not an inherited condition but is caused by the way in which the parents' DNA is put together. In addition, children may inherit information from one or both parents that will affect their development. Physical features such as our eye colour or hair type are the result of inherited information. Certain diseases or pre-dispositions to illness can also be inherited, for example, epilepsy and conditions such as colour blindness.

The health of the mother

During pregnancy, the woman acts as the baby's life-support machine. This means that the health of the mother is crucial. Fortunately, most women have healthy and non-eventful pregnancies. However, some women are not so lucky and their health affects their developing child.

Lifestyle

Women who smoke may not realise that they limit the amount of oxygen that their developing baby receives. This can result in lighter and sometimes pre-term babies. Furthermore, it is known that the first 12 weeks of gestation are pivotal, although some women may not realise that they are pregnant. Alcohol and drugs, even prescription medication, can affect the baby's later development.

Diet

A woman's diet during pregnancy also plays an important role because women who are poorly nourished will not pass sufficient nutrients to the developing baby. This can result in babies with a low birth weight and who are less responsive. In addition, it is now known that folic acid needs to be present in a woman's diet in the first few weeks of pregnancy because it helps to prevent spina bifida. While folic acid can easily be taken as a dietary supplement or gained by eating additional green vegetables, many women may not know that they are pregnant at the time that this vitamin is required.

Infection and illness

Maternal infections can also affect the developing baby, especially in the first 12 weeks of gestation. Food poisoning and childhood diseases, such as measles and rubella, can have significant effects on the baby's growth and well-being.

Perinatal factors

Perinatal factors are difficulties that occur during the birthing process. Today, because of advances in medicine, especially antenatal care and monitoring during labour, most pregnancies carry a very low risk for both baby and mother. This was not always the case: previously, many women died during childbirth. However, even in the modern world, the risks of childbirth have not been completely eliminated and some babies may be injured during the birthing process.

Anoxia – lack of oxygen

The supply of oxygen to the baby is essential because a lack of oxygen can cause brain damage. During labour, the oxygen supply to the baby might be interrupted for several reasons, including the umbilical cord becoming entangled or the baby being slow to breathe at birth.

Low birth weight

Birth weight is significant because babies who are born light are vulnerable to infection and their internal organs may not be as mature. Common causes of low birth weight in babies include premature delivery, multiple births, poor maternal nutrition and smoking before and during pregnancy.

Premature babies

Some women go into labour early or are induced early because of a serious condition, for example, pre-eclampsia. This means that some babies are born premature. While babies who are born after 37 weeks' gestation are not likely to have any developmental delay (normal gestation is 40 weeks), babies who are born earlier are less physically mature and will therefore continue the maturation process outside of the womb. This is why height and growth charts for babies are plotted according to the gestation week in which the baby was born. In terms of physical and other areas of development, babies who are premature are likely to reach 'milestones' more in line with their expected date of delivery rather than their actual birth date.

Postnatal factors

Postnatal factors (see the diagram opposite) are those that affect the child from the birth onwards. These factors are largely environmental ones; they include where the baby grows up, diet, and the care and love that he or she receives. We also know that some children are genetically predisposed to certain illnesses and that the environment may trigger a condition. A good example of this is asthma: there is a strong genetic link with asthma but it may be triggered in a baby in response to, for example, living in a damp environment.

Recognising the parent–baby bond

In Core Units 1 and 3, we looked at attachment theories and the importance of babies having emotional security (pages 29–33). In terms of our practice with

APPLYING THEORY TO YOUR PRACTICE

One way in which we can help babies feel comfortable is to develop some personal play routine with them. The idea is that every time the baby arrives, the practitioner plays a little game with him or her, depending on his or her age.

Choose one of the following games and play one of them at odd times with a baby you are working with. Aim to play the game on arrival. See how long it takes before the baby appears to recognise the games.

- Peek-a-boo
- Pat-a-cake
- Round and round the garden like a teddy bear
- Peep-po, using a finger puppet

Diet

Nutrition plays a significant role in children's overall health. Children who are well nourished are more likely to resist infections and develop healthy bones and skin. They will also have energy for play and sufficient nutrients for growth. Some research suggests that diet can also play a part in cognitive development.

Accidents

Accidents can leave babies with permanent injuries. Since babies have no sense of danger, it is essential that those working with them are extremely vigilant.

Abuse and neglect

Sadly, some babies are abused in their first year of life. There are various reasons why abuse may occur, including difficulty with the parental role.

Postnatal factors

Infections

Babies are very vulnerable to infections because their immune systems are still developing. Some childhood illnesses, such as measles, whooping cough and mumps, can leave children with permanent disabilities. These illnesses were quite rare when vaccination programmes were effective; however, recent scares have led paediatricians to predict an increase in these illnesses. Babies can also be affected by repeated low-grade infections such as colds and ear infections, which can stunt growth. Repeated ear infections if left untreated can result in hearing loss.

Poverty

Babies who are raised in poverty are less likely to receive good nourishment and may live in unsuitable housing. Poverty therefore increases the likelihood of infections and accidents.

Quality of care

Babies need good care, both physical and emotional, in order to thrive. In some cases, parents may not have the necessary skills or knowledge to provide for their baby's needs. In other cases, parents may not be coping with their parental role, either because of their circumstances or because of depression. Babies also require good-quality care at pre-school. Babies who are unhappy will not feed well and will be less inclined to play, therefore good emotional care is essential in baby units.

babies, this means that we must both respect the parent–baby attachment and encourage babies to develop a strong sense of belonging within the baby unit. It is thought that babies need good-quality care to compensate for the temporary absence of their parents. Ideally, this means that babies need to see familiar faces and have strong and consistent contacts with a key person. It also means that good liaison should take place between that person and the baby's parents. This allows for a free flow of information and helps to reassure parents that their child is being nurtured in their absence.

Identifying and meeting the physical needs of babies

In order to thrive and develop, a baby's physical needs must be met. As practitioners, it is important to recognise how a baby's needs change during the course of his or her first year. It is also essential that we recognise that nurture must be provided alongside physical care. Thus, everyday care routines should be thought of as a way of helping the baby to feel secure. This is why it is suggested that, wherever possible, the same person should be responsible at each session for meeting as many of the baby's needs as possible.

Providing a safe environment for babies

As we have seen in the first part of this unit, a baby's physical development during the first year of life is rapid. In terms of safety, this means that babies have changing needs over the year. The key message to practitioners in relation to keeping babies safe is 'foresight and prevention'. For example, recognising in advance that a baby will soon be able to crawl will mean that potential accidents are avoided.

Preventing falls

A fall can potentially be fatal for a baby if the head is injured. Falls can occur when adults underestimate the strength or speed of babies.

Non-mobile babies

Some accidents occur when babies fall from high surfaces, such as nappy-changing units and sofas, or after being put in a bouncer on a table. The rule is that a baby, even when non-mobile, must not be left unattended for even the shortest moment, and that bouncers should never be put on high surfaces. Some babies have fallen after an adult has turned round literally for a moment. This happens because babies can make sudden and vigorous movements that may cause them to partially roll when lying flat or, in the case of a bouncer, to cause it to slip.

Mobile babies

Mobile babies are at risk of falling down steps and stairways. The key here is to use stair gates and ensure that they are securely fastened. Some falls occur when

Babies need constant supervision – even if they seem to be secure

babies are learning to walk: they may pull themselves into a standing position but the object they are using may not be secure. In other cases, babies may be unsteady on their feet when they first begin to walk and their spatial awareness is not developed; they are in danger of falling and hitting themselves on other objects. These children need good supervision and the layout of the room may need to be adapted.

Using safety harnesses to prevent falls

Safety harnesses need to be used to prevent babies from falling out of high chairs and pushchairs. It is important that the harness fits snugly but can easily be removed in the event of a baby choking. It is therefore a good idea to practice fastening and unfastening harnesses.

Burns and scalds

A baby's skin is extremely sensitive, more so than an adult's is. This means that babies can be scalded or burnt more easily than we can. This has serious implications when bathing babies, heating bottles or feeding them. Temperatures should always be checked beforehand. In the same way, extreme caution is required to ensure that babies cannot access hot drinks, radiators or kitchens.

Poisoning

As part of your setting's health and safety procedures, you should make sure that all dangerous substances are kept out of the reach of babies. It is also important to be aware of the products that are used when nappy-changing because they can be poisonous as well as causing an allergic reaction in some babies.

Choking and suffocation

Babies need to put things into their mouths in order to learn about their world. However, this means that they are in danger of picking up objects that might choke them. It is therefore a good idea for all staff working with babies to have first aid knowledge and to know the procedure if a baby begins to choke.

Food

While they are being weaned, babies are still learning to swallow. This means that a careful eye needs to be kept on babies while they are eating. Staff must stay nearby in case a

First aid knowledge is essential

baby needs to be taken out of the high chair. There are also some foods that should not be given to babies because they are more likely to choke on them, for example, nuts and whole grapes.

Small items

Toys and small items that are otherwise harmless may present a danger of choking. It is therefore essential that toys are checked first to see if they are suitable for babies. In addition, staff must check the floor and other areas regularly for any small items that may have been dropped, for example, bottle tops, buttons or coins. It is also important to check for items that may suffocate a baby, such as plastic bags.

Being aware of ties and ribbons

When putting babies to sleep, it is important to check that there are not any ties or ribbons on the babies' clothes, bedding or toys, because these could become entangled around a baby's neck. In recent years, clothes manufacturers have followed strict guidelines when producing clothes for babies, but homemade items may not be as carefully designed.

Drowning

Babies and toddlers can drown in very small quantities of water. This means that babies should never be left unattended near or in water, even for a brief moment. Be aware when outside, at bathing times or when using water for play.

Being aware of other children

Some accidents occur when older children are being cared for alongside babies. A toddler may pick up a hard toy and hit it against the head of a baby, or may go over to a baby in a bouncer and shake it hard. In the same way, a toddler in a rush to get somewhere may push over a baby who is just beginning to stand. This does not mean that the toddler is at fault, because toddlers also have no sense of danger or responsibility. If babies are alongside toddlers, it is essential that supervision is of a very high standard.

Safety equipment

There are many safety devices that help to prevent accidents (see page 148). For safety devices to be effective, they have to be used consistently and checked regularly to make sure that they are functioning properly. It is also important that safety devices are positioned before the baby actually needs them because babies quickly develop skills. Finally, remember that safety equipment is never a substitute for good supervision.

Babies' hygiene needs

In Core Unit 3, we looked at the importance of good hygiene in providing a safe environment for children. In a baby unit, hygiene plays a significant role because babies' immune systems are still developing and infections can quickly invade and take hold of a baby's body. The procedures outlined on page 156 must be followed and steps to avoid cross-infection need to be introduced.

Avoiding cross-infection

Cross-infection occurs when germs from one person are passed to another person. Avoiding cross-infection is important in any setting, but especially in baby units.

Toys and items

As babies explore the world using their mouth, there is a danger that an object that one baby has played with will go straight into the mouth of another baby. This creates the ideal conditions for germs to be passed from one child to another. Frequent sterilisation of babies' toys and other items is therefore necessary.

Disposing of waste materials

The careful disposal of waste materials is essential to avoid cross-infection. Nappies, wipes and other materials should be handled only with disposable gloves and then carefully thrown away. Bins should be covered at all times, and the nappy-changing and other areas should be thoroughly wiped down.

Physical care

It is advisable for baby units to have labelled, individual items for each baby. Towels, face cloths, toothbrushes and other items such as comforters should be kept separate so that cross-infection is avoided. Some baby units do this by providing lockers or pigeonholes for each child. This makes it easier for staff to find the baby's clothes, nappies and feeding utensils.

Rest and sleep

There are no hard and fast rules about how much sleep babies should have, but most babies need at least 12 hours sleep over a 24-hour period. This sleep is usually taken as one long stretch lasting approximately nine to ten hours, followed by short naps. It is important to respect babies' need for sleep because insufficient sleep can cause them to become fretful and, in the long term, affect their growth and development. Interestingly, babies do not sleep 'on demand' but develop their own routines, which should be talked through with parents. Some babies will therefore have an hour's nap in the morning, while others may have a long nap straight after lunch.

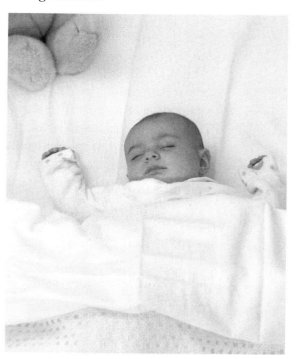

The 'feet to foot' sleeping position is now recommended for babies

Changes to sleep patterns

During the first year of life, the sleep requirements of babies change. Usually, the baby takes less sleep in the form of naps during the day, but may increase the length of his or her sleep at night.

Signs that babies are tired

Babies cannot tell us that they are tired, but there are signs that may indicate that they need to sleep. These include:

- rubbing eyes
- fretfulness, difficult to comfort
- intermittent crying.

Room temperature

Babies cannot control their own temperature. Rooms that are overheated present a risk to babies who cannot throw off a blanket. The recommended room temperature is around 18 degrees Celsius.

Bedding

The use of quilts, duvets and cot bumpers is not recommended for babies under one year old. This is because babies find it hard to regulate their temperature and can become overheated. Instead, it is recommended that babies have light blankets that can be added to if required. In addition, pillows should not be put in with babies in order to prevent the risks of smothering and overheating.

Removing toys and other objects

Before putting a baby down to sleep, you should check the cot carefully and remove any toys or objects that might smother the baby or cause a choking incident.

Checking the temperature of the baby

As we have seen, it is important that babies do not become overheated. The best way to check whether a baby is warm enough is by gently touching his or her neck.

Preventing Sudden Infant Death Syndrome (cot death)

Each year, some babies die unexpectedly in their sleep. This is known as Sudden Infant Death Syndrome (SIDS). Research shows that there are steps that parents and adults working with babies can take to reduce the risk of SIDS. Below are the current guidelines; however, as research is ongoing it is important to keep up to date.

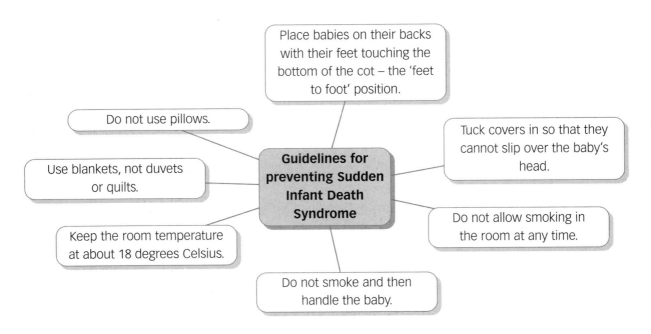

Meeting babies' nutritional needs

Over the course of their first year, babies' nutritional needs change. This is reflected in the amounts and type of foods that they need. Babies begin life completely reliant on milk, taken either from the breast or the bottle, and finish their first year able to feed themselves finger foods.

Types of milk

For the first four or five months, babies require only milk. There are essentially two forms of milk: human and manufactured (formula milk).

Breast milk

The choice whether to bottle-feed or breastfeed depends on the mother. Breastfeeding is considered the best start for babies because the milk is 'designed' for them.

It is possible for a mother to express milk and freeze it so that a baby in group care can continue to have her breast milk. If a mother chooses this option, it is essential to be supportive. Expressing milk and giving it in a bottle is not always completely glitch-free. Sometimes babies can resist taking a bottle or refuse to return to the breast. It can therefore be useful for mothers to seek advice from their health visitor before the baby is left in group care. Bottles and teats, etc. should be sterilised (see below).

Formula milk

Formula milk is given with a bottle, so is often called bottle-feeding. Formula milk is made of cow's milk that has been modified to allow the baby to digest it. Ordinary cow's milk should not be given to a baby until they are at least one year old. There are several brands of formula milk that parents can choose, and it is important to use the brand of milk that they have chosen.

Soya milk

Some babies are allergic to cow's milk and may therefore be given soya milk as a substitute. The decision to feed a baby soya milk is usually made because the baby is showing an allergic reaction. However, this decision should be made only after consulting a doctor. It is also important to ensure that the right brand of milk is given to the right baby.

Sterilising bottles and feeding equipment

Whatever type of milk is chosen, it is essential that bottles and teats are sterilised. Milk provides the ideal breeding ground for bacteria.

Always wash your hands before touching bottles and feeding equipment.

Step-by-step guide to sterilisation

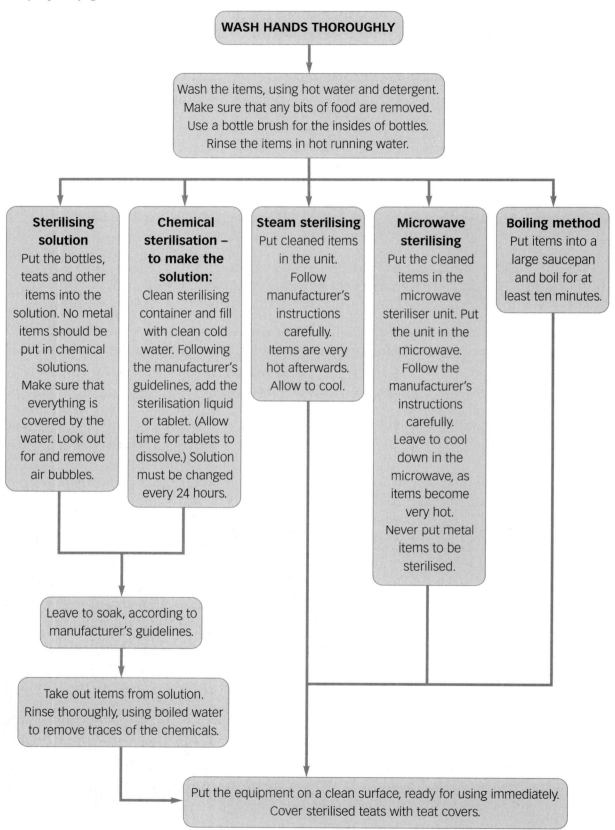

WASH HANDS THOROUGHLY

Wash the items, using hot water and detergent.
Make sure that any bits of food are removed.
Use a bottle brush for the insides of bottles.
Rinse the items in hot running water.

Sterilising solution
Put the bottles, teats and other items into the solution. No metal items should be put in chemical solutions. Make sure that everything is covered by the water. Look out for and remove air bubbles.

Chemical sterilisation – to make the solution:
Clean sterilising container and fill with clean cold water. Following the manufacturer's guidelines, add the sterilisation liquid or tablet. (Allow time for tablets to dissolve.) Solution must be changed every 24 hours.

Steam sterilising
Put cleaned items in the unit. Follow manufacturer's instructions carefully. Items are very hot afterwards. Allow to cool.

Microwave sterilising
Put the cleaned items in the microwave steriliser unit. Put the unit in the microwave. Follow the manufacturer's instructions carefully. Leave to cool down in the microwave, as items become very hot. Never put metal items to be sterilised.

Boiling method
Put items into a large saucepan and boil for at least ten minutes.

Leave to soak, according to manufacturer's guidelines.

Take out items from solution. Rinse thoroughly, using boiled water to remove traces of the chemicals.

Put the equipment on a clean surface, ready for using immediately.
Cover sterilised teats with teat covers.

Making up a bottle feed

Most parents who choose formula milk for their babies will use powdered milk because it is cost effective. However, it is possible to buy ready-mixed milk, which can be useful for journeys or if time is limited.

Bottle feeds should be made according to the manufacturer's instructions. It is important to follow these carefully and not adapt the formula milk in any way. Putting too much powder in a bottle can cause babies to gain too much weight, while insufficient powder can mean that babies lose weight or become distressed.

Feeds are usually made in batches for the day and then refrigerated. Any unused bottles must be thrown away after 24 hours. It is important to ask parents about how much feed needs to be made up because they will have a good idea of how much and when their baby feeds.

How to feed a baby

Feeding is a pleasurable time for babies. It is also an important emotional time in which the baby feels secure and can build an attachment to the person feeding him or her. It is therefore good practice for the baby's key worker to feed the baby so that a good relationship can develop. It is important to adopt the 'natural' position of a mother suckling a child at the breast. This gives the baby support, but also allows him or her to look directly into the face of the key worker.

The amount of milk taken at each feed needs to be recorded to enable us to check that the baby has had sufficient amounts over the course of a day. Most babies are now fed 'on demand', which means that their own pattern for feeds is respected. As babies self-regulate and learn to take only as much as they are hungry for, it is important not to force a baby to finish a bottle. The ultimate test

When feeding a baby, it is important to adopt the 'natural' position

as to whether a baby is gaining enough nutrition is to check his or her weight and consider how settled the baby seems.

Bottle-feeding a baby: a step-by-step guide

▶ Wash your hands.
▶ Warm the bottle by using a bottle warmer or by standing it in a jug of hot water.
▶ Change the baby's nappy if required.
▶ Collect tissues and bibs, etc. so that everything is to hand.
▶ Make sure that the bottle is at the correct temperature.
▶ Check the flow of the milk.
▶ Angle the bottle so the teat is completely covered with milk.
▶ Talk to the baby as he or she is feeding.
▶ Allow the baby to take breaks and suckle gently.
▶ Wind young babies by sitting them up and gently rubbing their backs.
▶ Do not force the baby to take more than he or she wants.
▶ Throw away any unused feed.

Weaning

Weaning is the process by which babies move from taking only milk to eating proper foods. This is an essential process because milk alone will not provide the nutrients required by the growing baby after six months. It is therefore important that, by six months, babies are used to additional food.

When to begin weaning

Weaning usually begins when the baby is four to five months old. It is not recommended that babies are given any other food before this time without medical supervision. This is to prevent digestive difficulties and allergies.

There are a few signs that babies are ready to wean. These include the baby seeming much hungrier or becoming unsettled. In addition, the baby may begin to wake during the night when previously he or she slept through. The baby's weight may also stop increasing, or the baby may even begin to lose weight. The decision as to when weaning should start lies with the parents or, in the case of babies who are weaned before four months, with a health visitor.

Introducing babies to weaning

Babies have to learn to take food from a spoon. For some babies, this comes easily, while other babies need to be

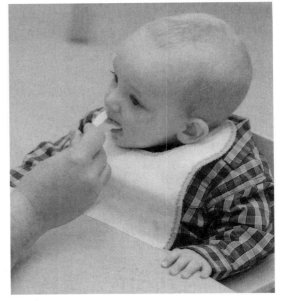

Starting to wean

coaxed. The first spoonfuls are usually baby rice mixed with a little of the baby's usual milk. Baby rice is usually recommended because it is unlikely to cause an allergic reaction.

The best time to introduce the first spoonful is when the baby is not tired and is not too hungry. Put a bib on the baby and have some tissues to hand. Feed the baby some of their usual bottle and then put a little mixture onto a spoon, just touching the baby's lips. The baby will hopefully suck the food from the spoon. If the baby becomes distressed or repeatedly spits the food out, it is important to remain calm and simply try again another day.

4 to 6 months: introducing puréed foods

Once a baby has grown used to taking from a spoon, it is important to build up a range of foods that he or she can eat. Foods should be introduced one at a time so that any allergic reaction is detected. Foods should be fairly liquid in form so that the baby can swallow them easily. Most foods are therefore puréed and either water or the baby's usual milk added, to make a smooth consistency. The amount of food should be built up gradually so that by around six months the baby is having three meals a day. During this time, the amount of milk the baby takes will gradually lessen, although it is recommended that the baby should continue to have between 500 ml and 600 ml of milk a day.

When preparing foods, you should not add any sugar or salt. This may make the food seem bland to you, but it will still be tasty for the baby. Salt must be avoided because it can affect the baby's kidneys, while sugar can lead to dental decay and cause babies to become overweight.

If commercial foods are chosen by parents, it will be important to check that they are suitable for the age of the child and not past their best-before or use-by date. It is also essential to read the manufacturer's instructions about storing jars.

Foods that might be introduced	Foods to avoid
Meat (puréed)	Honey
Poultry	Sugar and salt
Lentils	Eggs
Vegetables	Fatty food
Fruits (not citrus fruits)	Nuts and seeds
Full-fat natural yoghurt	Cow's milk
Fromage frais	Fish and shellfish
	Wheat-based foods, e.g. pasta, bread
	Spices, e.g. curry, chillies

Introducing puréed foods

Water

Babies will become thirsty once they begin to take solid foods. This means that cool boiled water should be offered as well as bottled milk. If babies do not drink sufficiently, there is a danger that they will become constipated. A record should therefore be kept of the amount of drink as well as food that a baby consumes. After six months, you do not have to give water that has been boiled to a baby. Never use bottled mineral water with babies unless a medical practitioner has been consulted because they contain high levels of minerals such as salt.

Should babies be given juice and other drinks?

Over the past few years, dentists have been concerned about the number of babies and young children with serious dental decay. While cooled boiled water is considered the best drink for babies, there are also many baby juices and drinks on sale. To prevent dental decay and gum disease, dentists advise that these drinks be given in cups. Using bottles and beakers means that babies and toddlers are likely to have repeated sips and their gums will therefore be repeatedly exposed to the natural sugars and acids in these drinks. The current advice is to use these drinks sparingly and to encourage babies to become used to drinking water, which is a healthy habit.

6 to 9 months: introducing lumpy foods

The next step in the weaning process is to provide babies with foods that are both more varied and more textured. Instead of puréeing food so that it is smooth, foods can now be mashed or minced. This encourages the baby to learn to chew a little, which helps the tongue and jaw to develop and is important for later speech.

The baby should now be starting his or her feed with solid food and finishing with milk. It is still important for the baby to have sufficient milk during the day, and the recommended amount is 500–600 ml. While full-fat cow's milk can be used in cooking, it cannot be used for a baby's main drink, and formula milk should still be used. It is also recommended that babies should have two or three servings of starchy foods, such as rice and potatoes, every day. Unless the baby is known to have an allergy, wheat-based foods such as pasta and bread can also be introduced into the diet. When introducing new foods, it is still important to watch out for allergic reactions, the symptoms of which might include diarrhoea or skin conditions.

At this stage, feeding becomes a little messy because babies want to play a more active part in the process. They may try to grab the spoon or the food. This is to be encouraged, so provide an extra spoon for the baby and cover him or her as well as you!

Foods that might be introduced	Foods to avoid
Fish and shellfish	Sugar and salt
Well-cooked eggs	Raw eggs, such as boiled eggs with runny yolks
Wheat-based foods	Honey
Citrus fruits	Nuts and seeds
	Ordinary cow's milk as a main drink

Introducing lumpy foods

9 to 12 months: introducing finger foods

This is the final phase of weaning. Babies should be starting to feed themselves because their hand–eye co-ordination is sufficiently developed to allow for this, and they are used to chewing and swallowing. The baby should also be eating a good range of foods that provide him or her with a balanced diet. Foods can be cut into small pieces that the baby can pick up, for example, small pieces of toast with cheese or chopped banana. Milk should continue to play a vital role in the baby's diet, and he or she should have at least 350 ml of milk a day. If a baby is reluctant to drink this much milk, the amount of other dairy products in the diet should be increased.

Introducing finger foods

Foods to avoid

Salt
Additional sugar
Uncooked eggs
Nuts, seeds and honey
Cow's milk for drinking (until babies are one year old)

The safe preparation of food

It is essential that high standards of hygiene are in place when providing food for babies. Most settings continue to sterilise feeding equipment beyond the recommended six months in order to avoid any possible cross-infection. It is also important to throw away all unused foods after they have been served to babies.

GOOD PRACTICE ✔ **The safe preparation of food for babies**

- Use separate spoons, bowls and other feeding equipment for each baby.
- Use separate face cloths and towels to clean each baby afterwards.
- Throw away all unused food that has been served.
- Store foods correctly.
- Make sure that formula milk powder and jars of baby food are not past their use-by or best-before date.

Keeping babies safe

Babies should never be left unattended with food or drink because there is a danger that they might choke. Ideally, all staff should know what to do if a baby begins to choke. It is also important to keep an eye on a toddler who may wish to 'share' his or her food with a baby.

Working in partnership with parents

During the weaning process, it is essential that information is exchanged with parents and their views are sought as to the type of foods to be provided for their baby. This is because food plays an essential part in many religions and many parents have strong feelings about what their child should be fed. It is also important to tell parents when new foods are introduced in the setting and to ask parents to inform the setting when new foods are introduced at home so that any reactions can be noted and tracked. (The need for a good dialogue to exist between parents and staff is identified in the National Standards Annex A.)

GOOD PRACTICE

Information that should be noted and exchanged with parents

▶ Quantity of milk consumed during the session.
▶ Amount of food and drink consumed.
▶ Baby's preferences, e.g. dislikes and likes.
▶ Any reactions to foods.

CASE STUDY

Roseanne is a new member of staff. She has been asked to warm two bottles because two babies will be having their feeds soon. She takes the first two bottles that she can see from the fridge. She does not think that it matters which bottle she takes because the babies are roughly the same age. She knows that one baby's parents have asked for their baby to have soya milk, but she thinks that they are just being 'picky'.

1 What are the possible consequences of Roseanne's actions?

2 What systems could be put in place to prevent staff from giving the wrong foods to babies?

3 Why is it important for staff to respect the wishes of parents?

Meeting babies' personal hygiene needs

As well as babies relying on us to meet their nutritional needs, we must also meet their personal hygiene needs. Keeping babies' skin clean can prevent the risk of infection and help to maintain their physical comfort.

Nappy-changing

Nappy-changing plays a key part in caring for babies' skin. It is important to change nappies regularly to prevent nappy rash and possible infections. A separate nappy-changing area is recommended to prevent the spread of infection, although the National Standards do not necessarily insist on this being a separate room.

Change a nappy: a step-by-step guide

1 Get the entire equipment ready *before* taking the nappy off.

2 Wash your hands and put on gloves.

3 Remove the baby's clothes from the lower part of the body and undo the nappy.

4 Using tissues or cotton wool, wipe the faeces off the baby's bottom and place the dirty nappy and tissues into a nappy sack.

5 Using wet cotton wool or baby wipes, wash the baby's bottom from front to back. Throw each piece of tissue away after one wipe. Do not pull a boy's foreskin back during washing.

6 Dry the baby's bottom with tissues or cotton wool.

7 Apply a barrier cream.

8 Put a clean nappy on and dress the baby.

9 Clean the mat, remove and dispose of the gloves, and wash your hands. Don't forget to talk to the baby during nappy-changing. Babies also like a chance to kick their legs while the nappy is removed.

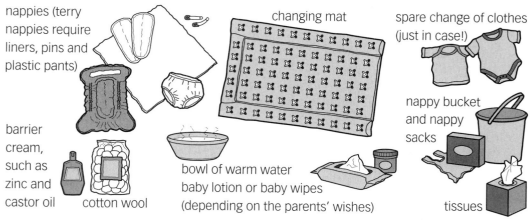

nappies (terry nappies require liners, pins and plastic pants)

barrier cream, such as zinc and castor oil   cotton wool

changing mat

bowl of warm water baby lotion or baby wipes (depending on the parents' wishes)

spare change of clothes (just in case!)

nappy bucket and nappy sacks

tissues

Nappy-changing equipment

Preventing nappy rash

Although nappy rash is quite common in babies, it is distressing for them and every step must be taken to prevent it. One of the best ways of preventing nappy rash is to change nappies frequently and put the baby on a towel without a nappy for a short time each day. It is also essential that a baby's skin is completely dried after bathing and nappy changes. Putting a nappy onto a damp bottom will increase the likelihood of nappy rash.

Although there are several causes of nappy rash, it is usually aggravated by ammonia in a baby's urine that has an acidic effect on the skin, or by bacteria in the baby's stools. Other causes include:

- sensitive skin
- poorly fitting nappies
- allergic reaction to detergent, bubble bath or other skin products
- baby wipes that contain alcohol
- dietary changes.

Upon the first signs of redness, blisters or soreness, it is essential to take the following measures:

- change the baby's nappy more frequently
- allow more air to the baby's skin, for example, allow time without the nappy on after each nappy change
- some parents may ask you to use a barrier cream.

If the nappy rash does not improve, it is important that medical advice is sought promptly.

Noting changes to stools

It is important to note any changes in the baby's stools or the frequency of urination. Stools that are particularly hard may indicate constipation while a baby whose nappy is dry may not be taking in enough fluids. Diarrhoea should also be noted because this can be caused by a food intolerance or an infection. It is important to talk to parents about any changes that you see because they may wish to seek medical advice.

Washing and bathing

During the course of a session, it is likely that babies will need, as a minimum, their faces and hands washed. It is important to discuss with parents which skin care products, if any, should be used. You should also ask parents whether they have any preferences about how skin care should be carried out, for example, some parents may prefer that their child's hands are washed under running water, while other parents may prefer to use baby oil.

Drying babies' skin

Babies' skin is more sensitive than adults' skin. This means that after washing and drying a baby's hands and face, care must be taken to dry the skin properly in order to prevent it from becoming chapped. This is best done by gently patting the skin rather than rubbing it. Some babies' skin can be dry and parents may therefore ask that we use lotions or oils.

Bathing

While most parents will choose to bath their babies at home, it may be necessary from time to time to bath a baby in the setting. Keeping babies warm and safe during bathing is a priority. This means that everything should be in place and the baby bath should be filled with warm water prior to the baby being undressed.

Care of teeth

Many babies will have their first teeth at around six months old. Once a baby's teeth have appeared, it is important that they are cleaned. This needs to be done gently because gums can become sore and irritated. A soft brush should

Prepare all the equipment and fill the baby bath with warm water

1. Put the baby on a flat surface, undress him/her and take off the nappy. Clean the nappy area.

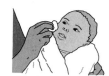

2. Wrap the baby gently but securely in a towel, so that the arms are tucked in. Wash the face with moist cotton wool.

3. Hold the baby over the bath and wash the head and hair.

4. Take off the towel. Holding the baby securely under the head and round the arm, lift him/her into the water.

5. Use your spare hand to wash the baby.

6. Lift the baby out of the bath supporting under the bottom, and quickly wrap him/her in a warm towel.

A step-by-step guide to bathing a baby

be used along with toothpaste designed for babies; adult toothpaste is not recommended. Brushing teeth should take place after meals and each child should have his or her own brush.

Teething

When teeth are coming through, the gums can become sore and swollen. Parents often report an association with teething and nappy rash. Signs that babies are teething include:

- the desire to chew on items
- irritability
- stronger smelling urine
- red patch on cheeks.

To help babies cope with the sensation, it can be helpful for them to chew on something soft, such as a specially designed teething ring. Products to rub onto gums should not be used unless parents have given their permission.

Working with parents to meet babies' physical needs

In order to meet babies' individual needs, it is important to work closely with parents. Parents will be able to tell us about their baby's preferences, routines and particular needs. It is essential that these are carefully recorded and that members of staff are aware of this information.

Using a key worker

It is good practice for babies to have a key worker and for this person to do as much of the baby's personal care as possible. This allows the baby to feel secure and cuts the risks of the baby being given the wrong food or care products. The other key advantage is that one person can note any changes in the baby's sleep, feeding patterns and stools, and relay this information to parents. It also helps parents to know who is responsible for their baby's day-to-day care, and with whom they might share information or concerns.

Exchanging information

There are many different ways of exchanging information, but most settings use daily slips. These allow parents in a hurry to read the information later and provide a good record of any changes. Annex A of the National Standards suggests that daily information should include:

- details of how the baby has spent his or her time
- discussion about feeding, sleeping or settling concerns
- feeding routines and requirements
- sleeping and nappy-changing routines
- developmental milestones.

THINKING AND RESEARCH

Devise a format for presenting information about a baby's day. Make sure that the format includes the information suggested by the National Standards in Annex A.

Meeting the social, emotional and learning needs of babies

Caring for babies is about more than simply meeting their physical needs. In the first year of life, the baby's brain requires stimulation in order to develop. This means that we must think about providing babies with activities, communication and experiences that will help with their emotional, intellectual and physical development.

What do babies need to learn?

The first year of life is crucial in terms of a child's overall development. We have seen in Core Unit 1 that babies should be breaking into language, and learning about relationships and how to control their body (see pages 2–23). This learning does not happen by accident: babies need to be provided with the optimum conditions for their development. The key way in which babies' development can be secured is through a responsive adult. This necessity is highlighted in the latest guidance for practitioners working with babies, Birth to Three Matters.

Birth to Three Matters

In recognition of the importance of babies' and toddlers' development in their early years, a framework to help practitioners has been developed. The framework is called *Birth to Three Matters* and it is essential reading for practitioners working with young children. The framework is divided into four sections, with each section subdivided into aspects (see the table below).

Using the framework

The *Birth to Three Matters* framework can be used to help plan the daily routine of the setting and those experiences to be offered within the setting. By reading the cards that come with the pack, you can check that your provision is meeting babies' overall needs. Most EYCDPs are now offering courses to help settings plan according to this framework.

Ways of providing playful experiences

Babies have to learn how to play. They do this initially by playing with adults. Simple repetitive games such as peek-a-boo are often the first games that babies learn to enjoy. From this type of game, the baby learns to take turns and about socialisation. Playfulness is also learnt from being with adults. Babies sense whether we are enjoying the game and they learn how to be playful.

Repetition is important

One characteristic of babies' play is the importance of repetition. Playing a simple game of knocking down beakers repeatedly allows the baby to learn to

Section	Summary	Aspects
A strong child	This section is about children learning to become confident and establish secure relationships.	Me, myself and I Being acknowledged and affirmed Developing self-assurance A sense of belonging
A skilful communicator	This section is about helping children to learn about communication and use language.	Being together Finding a voice Listening and responding Making meaning
A competent learner	This section is about helping children to explore and understand their environment.	Making connections Being imaginative Being creative Representing
A healthy child	This section is about meeting children's physical and emotional needs.	Emotional well-being Growing and developing Keeping safe Healthy choices

A summary of the Birth to Three Matters framework

predict and anticipate what is going to happen. This understanding contributes enormously to their enjoyment of the game. In terms of development, the repetition also allows babies to develop physical co-ordination. This means that adults need to be ready to play a simple game several times over, taking the cue from the baby when to stop.

Showing a baby how to play

Sometimes babies need to watch us play with an item. This allows a baby to both see its possibilities and learn how to play with it. For example, pushing a button down so that the baby learns that a noise is made might encourage him or her to have a go. Again, as with many other areas of child development, a balance has to be struck between allowing babies to explore for themselves and providing sufficient adult interaction.

Encouraging babies to take turns

Some games help babies learn to take turns. Putting out your hand and saying 'thank you' can encourage a baby to put a toy in it. The game here is to give the object back to the baby so that he or she learns that it is returned. Quickly, this movement can become a game in itself, which a baby may repeat again and again.

Adults are great playthings

It is often said that the best toy for a baby is an adult. There is a lot of truth in this because adults can adapt their responses to meet a baby's needs. An adult can rock a baby or take the baby over to the window to point something out. An adult can build a pile of beakers for the baby to knock down or simply play peek-a-boo. No toy designed so far has been able to do all of this! It is essential to remember the role of adults in play when thinking about how best to stimulate babies. Toys and equipment do have a part to play, but being near to and playing with an adult matters far more to a baby.

The best toy for a baby is an adult

Sensory play

Babies learn about the world by using their senses, so we should plan sensory activities for babies. As with any activity involving babies, supervision is essential. In addition, most sensory play is, by nature, quite messy. The best way of managing the mess is to keep rooms warm and to take clothes off!

Play with water

Babies love to play with water, especially as they get older. It is important, however, to remember that children can drown even in small quantities of water, therefore supervision is essential. In warm weather, it should be possible to provide a paddling pool and to allow babies to sit and crawl in the water. Nappies should be kept on; if possible, use aqua nappies.

When playing with water, toys that encourage scooping and pouring are especially popular, for example, buckets, jugs and funnels. Water play can also be done as an indoor activity using baby baths or washing-up bowls. Again, even with small quantities of water, supervision is essential.

Play with gloop (cornflour and water)

A mixture of cornflour and water provides a runny and sometimes solid texture for babies to feel and play with. It can be put on trays in high chairs for babies who need support, or in a tray or container on the floor for babies who are mobile. These types of activities stimulate babies' hands and senses, and develop physical movements. Gloop is very messy, but if left to dry it hoovers up easily. Older babies may enjoy using spoons when playing with gloop.

Play with cooked pasta

Cook pasta such as spaghetti in coloured water and leave it to cool, then give babies helpings of cold pasta for them to eat and play with; they enjoy the sensory feel and taste of the pasta. Babies can play with the pasta while sitting on the floor on a plastic sheet, or in a high chair.

Note: Food materials have traditionally been used as play materials for babies and young children. However, you should check with parents beforehand that they do not have any objections.

POINT OF INTEREST

Treasure basket play

Treasure basket play encourages babies to explore and learn about different objects. It is based upon the idea that babies are naturally curious and that modern, purposely designed toys are limiting. Objects that are 'real' can have far more value because the baby is able to explore them in a range of ways. Treasure basket play was advocated by Elinor Goldschmied in 1994, and in some ways links back to a more traditional way of baby-rearing in which the objects that babies were given by their parents were those that came to hand!

How treasure basket play works

A group of natural objects are placed in a basket and given to the baby for him or her to explore. Objects might be chosen because of their texture, smell or shape, for example, feathers, shells, fir cones. The adult's role is to remain nearby, but not to guide the baby. The idea is that this encourages the baby to play in his or her own way and gain his or her own sense of achievement and satisfaction. Treasure basket play should offer endless possibilities because new objects can be included each day for the baby to explore alongside existing ones.

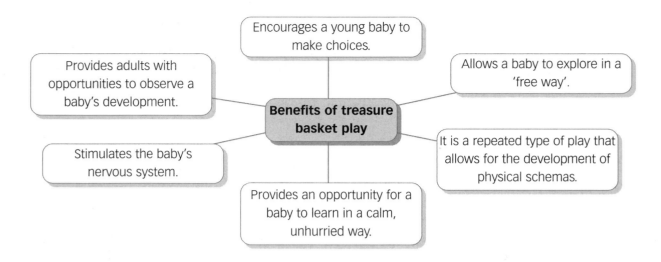

Provides adults with opportunities to observe a baby's development.

Encourages a young baby to make choices.

Allows a baby to explore in a 'free way'.

Benefits of treasure basket play

Stimulates the baby's nervous system.

It is a repeated type of play that allows for the development of physical schemas.

Provides an opportunity for a baby to learn in a calm, unhurried way.

Using everyday routines to enhance babies' development

Some settings make the mistake of trying to plan formal activities for babies and neglect to look at the possible learning that can take place during everyday routines. The physical needs of a baby are important because they keep the baby healthy and provide opportunities for adults to engage with him or her.

Nappy-changing

Talk to the baby. Count the poppers on his or her clothes while they are being undone and fastened. Play games with the baby's toes such as 'this little piggy'. Pick up the baby so that he or she can enjoy being up high and also so that the baby can see his or her environment.

Hand and face washing

After meals and at other times, a baby's face and hands may need washing. This can provide an opportunity for a baby to enjoy the sensory feel of water and discover about feeling clean. During face wiping, you can play the game peek-a-boo to encourage the baby to wipe his or her face. Alternatively, take a baby to a bowl of water or mixer tap to wash his or her hands so that he or she can feel the running water and soap.

Feeding

Feeding is an especially sensory experience that should be extremely pleasurable for babies. Encourage babies to touch their food and to attempt to feed themselves; this is an important self-help skill. Talk to the baby about the food and count as he or she takes mouthfuls. Do not rush mealtimes because they provide a huge learning opportunity.

Choosing objects

Babies will explore primarily with their mouths and hands. This means that objects must be chosen that cannot be swallowed and can be washed afterwards. Treasure basket play (see page 275) in its purest form incorporates only objects that are made from natural materials, for example, a comb made from horn or a box made from wood.

Selecting appropriate equipment and materials

It is important to have a range of developmentally appropriate toys and equipment for children. Not surprisingly, babies can have quite different play preferences, even at the same developmental age. A good selection of toys and equipment is therefore important.

Safety

Safety is paramount when choosing any toy or piece of equipment for a baby. This means checking the manufacturer's instructions carefully and that toys and equipment carry a safety mark.

Developmentally appropriate toys and equipment

The type of toys and equipment that children enjoy during their first year changes, especially when babies become mobile and better co-ordinated. This means that careful observation is required when selecting toys. Babies can become frustrated if the toy they have chosen does not 'work' or respond.

Natural objects
Feathers
Fruit and vegetables, e.g. lemon, orange, potato
Shells
Sponges
Wooden blocks
Fir cones
Large stones

Metal objects
Spoons, ladles
Keys
Key-rings

Materials that can be used for treasure basket play

Wooden objects
Honey spoon
Wooden spoons
Eggcups
Clothes-pegs
Brushes, e.g. make-up brush, paint brush

Leather, textiles and fabrics
Purses
Scarves
Rubber ball
Beanbag
Teddy bear
Cardboard
Boxes

Creating spaces

It is important to think about where babies will play with toys and equipment. Non-mobile babies are sometimes in danger of having their toys taken by mobile babies, because babies do not yet understand possession or turn-taking. This may mean looking at the layout of the room and considering ways of creating 'safe havens' for non-mobile babies. It is also worth thinking about how much physical space can be made available for mobile babies to use equipment, for example, brick trolleys, and how they can be used safely. This type of equipment is extremely important to provide because it helps to develop babies' locomotive skills.

Choosing toys and equipment for babies

There is now a huge selection of toys available for babies and toddlers. The key is to choose toys based upon the interests and stage of development of the child. The chart below outlines some of the most popular types of toys and equipment and their potential developmental value. The chart also includes ideas as to how adults may enhance the learning experience of the child. Note that the ages given are an approximate guide only.

Toys and equipment	Suitable for	Role of adult	Skills developed
Mobiles	All babies and toddlers	Make sure that they are out of reach.	Helps babies become aware of colours and shapes, and stimulates vision.
Baby gym	Babies who are not mobile	Play with the baby and make objects move.	Encourages physical movements. Helps teach baby about cause and effect.
Bouncing chairs	Babies who are not able to sit unsupported	Do not leave baby unattended or on high surfaces. Talk to baby.	Allows baby to be propped up and see what is going on.
Rattles and shakers	Babies and toddlers, but of interest to the younger baby	Make rattles move and pass to baby.	Helps baby become aware of sounds. Encourages fine motor movements.
Stacking beakers	Babies from around 4 months	Stack beakers up and encourage baby to knock them down. Model imaginative play for older babies.	Encourages baby to learn about cause and effect. Helps older baby to develop cognitive skills and hand–eye co-ordination.
Simple picture and fabric books	Babies from 3 months or even earlier	Sit baby on lap and point to pictures. Choose some books that have familiar objects. Look for wipeable or fabric books for very young babies since they will put then in their mouths.	Stimulates an early interest in books. Helps babies with language.

Toys and equipment	Suitable for	Role of adult	Skills developed
Activity quilts	Babies from 3 months	Make sure that all items are securely fastened. Show baby how to make the items work.	Develops sensory awareness and discovery.
Pop-up toys	Babies from 3 months	Show baby how the toys work. Encourage baby to make movements.	Builds strength in hands and encourages babies to learn about cause and effect.
Posting boxes	Babies from 6 months	Put bricks in. Encourage baby to find them. Older babies will learn to do this themselves. Choose very simple posting boxes.	Helps babies to learn about object permanence. Encourages hand–eye co-ordination and visual discrimination.
Bathtime toys	Babies from 6 months	Put in washing-up bowls for babies to play with. Make sure that all water play is supervised. Show babies what they can do.	Helps with hand–eye co-ordination. Babies find out about the properties of water and different objects.
Mirrors	Babies from 6 weeks	Point to baby's reflection. Encourage babies to look at themselves.	Helps babies learn that they have a separate identity.
Balls	Babies from 6 months	Sit on the floor with the baby between your legs. Roll the ball back and forth. Look out for balls that have a bell in them or are transparent with a floating figure inside. Encourage the baby to roll the ball. Note that older babies may throw the ball, so choose soft, light balls for them.	Encourages babies' visual skills and stimulates their interest in the world. Helps with children's physical development.
Push-and-pull toys	Babies who are sitting or are mobile	Show the baby how to make the toy move. Encourage the baby to move the toy. Help the baby if the toy falls over. Note that older babies who are walking may swing these toys and this can be dangerous for other children.	Encourages physical movements and co-ordination. Helps babies to find out about surfaces, wheels and speed.
Large wheeled toys, e.g. brick trolley	Babies who are walking or are stable on their feet	Observe babies carefully and supervise. Some toys move more quickly than the baby's feet! Choose toys that are stable.	Develops locomotive skills, spatial awareness and balance. Encourages babies to transport objects.

How to communicate with babies

One of the key roles of an adult is to interact and communicate with a baby. This is essential because in a baby's first year of life he or she will learn the skills of language and begin to break its code. Adults must therefore spend time talking, responding and playing with babies. However, it is important to understand that babies do not learn language in a vacuum. They pick up words and skills because of the emotional relationship they have with their carer.

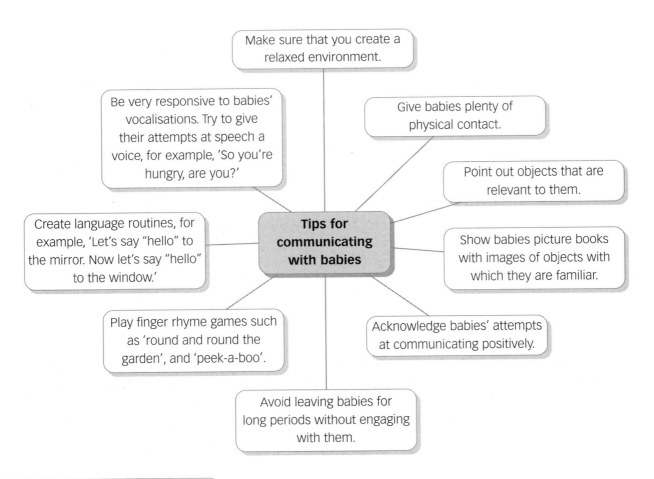

Make sure that you create a relaxed environment.

Be very responsive to babies' vocalisations. Try to give their attempts at speech a voice, for example, 'So you're hungry, are you?'

Give babies plenty of physical contact.

Point out objects that are relevant to them.

Create language routines, for example, 'Let's say "hello" to the mirror. Now let's say "hello" to the window.'

Tips for communicating with babies

Show babies picture books with images of objects with which they are familiar.

Play finger rhyme games such as 'round and round the garden', and 'peek-a-boo'.

Acknowledge babies' attempts at communicating positively.

Avoid leaving babies for long periods without engaging with them.

Linguists looking at the ways in which adults engage with babies have found that we naturally use a different pattern of speech with babies. This has been dubbed 'parentese'. When parentese is used, we actually help the baby to break the language code. Our facial expressions become more exaggerated, we emphasise the key words in sentences and use a lot of repetition. Interestingly, our voices also change: intonation is stronger and pitch is higher. It is much easier to 'switch' into parentese when you are holding a baby. When you are in close contact in this way, the baby can see your face more easily and this helps him or her to gain emotional security and learn language skills.

Older babies will try practising the language code before they have completely cracked it. They will start to put pauses in their babbling and raise their voices as though waiting for a response. These early attempts at speech have been called 'learning the tune before the words'. It is vital that we acknowledge babies' early attempts at communication with a smile and a comment. This helps babies learn that conversation is a two-way process in which they play a vital role.

As well as using parentese, babies need us to point out and name objects that are relevant to them, for example, saying, 'Look there. There's your HAT. It's a big HAT for a little boy isn't it?' By showing the baby the object that you are talking about and stressing the word slightly, he or she can begin to work out what the word means. Later, at around nine months of age, babies begin to point things out to us. We will also find that when babies speak their first words, these usually relate to things that they can see rather than abstract words. However, an exception to this rule is often the word 'no'!

How to work in partnership with parents to meet babies' social, emotional and learning needs

Babies develop at such a rapid rate that it is important to have good relationships with parents. This will allow us to consider with parents the changing interests and skills of their baby. For example, during a holiday, a baby may begin to show an interest in rolling a ball; finding this out from parents allows us to further develop this new interest and skill. In addition to finding out about babies' interests, it is important to know about the ways in which parents engage with their child at home. They may have favourite rhymes and songs or a favourite book that they enjoy with their baby. Incorporating those activities and preferences into our routines is extremely important because it gives the baby continuity. This in turn helps the baby to settle and learn.

GOOD PRACTICE

Working in partnership with parents

▶ Encourage parents to tell you about what their child has enjoyed at home.
▶ Report back regularly to parents about what their baby has enjoyed doing.
▶ Observe the baby and notice any new or emerging skills.
▶ Provide opportunities to plan activities with parents.

THINKING AND RESEARCH

Tariq is five months old and has just rolled over for the first time.

1 Why is it important to share this information with his parents?

2 Think of two ways to encourage Tariq's movement.

3 Why will mastering this movement provide Tariq with new opportunities?

Creating an overall routine for babies

The routine that we create for individual babies should reflect their overall needs. To create a routine we first need to talk to parents about their baby's physical needs and preferences. It also means taking into account babies' developmental needs in general and considering how best to provide a stimulating environment for them. Each baby in the setting should therefore have a tailored plan that is holistic in approach. Babies' everyday physical care needs should be seen as a possible source of stimulation and interaction.

THINKING AND RESEARCH

Record the care routine of a baby in your work or placement setting. Consider how the care routine:

▶ meets this child's physical care needs
▶ ensures his or her safety
▶ contributes towards his or her growth and development
▶ meets the child's emotional needs
▶ provides sensory stimulation.

Using the Birth to Three Matters framework, consider how this care routine links to the four sections – a strong child, a skilful communicator, a competent learner, a healthy child.

TEST YOUR KNOWLEDGE

1 Explain the importance of sharing information with babies.

2 Describe three toys that can be offered to a six-month-old baby.

3 Outline the stages of weaning.

4 List three pieces of safety equipment for use with mobile babies.

5 Explain why it is important to follow the latest guidelines when putting babies to sleep.

6 List three foods that would be unsuitable for a nine-month-old baby.

7 Describe ways in which nappy rash might be prevented.

8 Analyse the importance of working closely with parents.

9 Consider the role of the adult in promoting a baby's language development.

10 Evaluate the role of the key worker in promoting a baby's development.

PRACTICE ASSIGNMENT TASK

Produce a series of information sheets about promoting babies' development for a new member of the pre-school team. The information sheets should include:

▶ a description of babies' physical development in the first year
▶ a description of the type of activities and toys that might be used to promote development
▶ an analysis of the importance of working closely with parents
▶ an evaluation of the role of the key worker in promoting a baby's development.

Further reading and references

Books

Manolson, A. (1995) *You Make the Difference in Helping Your Child to Learn*, Toronto: The Hanen Centre

Featherstone, S. & Beswick, C. (2003) *Little Baby Books Series*, Lutterworth: Featherstone Education Ltd.

Lindon, J., Kelman, K. & Sharp, A. (2001) *Play and Learning for the Under-Threes*, London: Nursery World/TSL Education

Videos

Goldshmied, E. (1986) *Infants at Work: Babies of Six to Nine Months Exploring Everyday Objects*, London: National Children's Bureau

Goldschmied, E. & Hughes, A. (1992) *Heuristic Play with Objects: Children Of Twelve to Twenty Months Exploring Everyday Objects*, London: National Children's Bureau

③ Community Development

Pre-schools have long had a tradition of meeting the play needs of children in the local community. Today, many pre-schools are in the process of adapting the way in which they work in order to meet the changing needs of the community, employment legislation and the recent introduction of the National Daycare standards.

This unit explores the place of pre-schools in the local community and the impact of recent legislation and other developments on practice. It is divided into four sections:

▶ The function of pre-school settings as a community development activity

▶ The role of the parent management committee/support group

▶ The contribution of an effective adult team to community development

▶ The contribution of activities to involve parents in pre-school settings

The function of pre-school settings as a community development activity

Meeting the needs of families of young children in the community

The starting point for any pre-school wishing to be an integral part of the community is to ensure that its provision meets the needs of families with young children. Family life and working patterns have changed enormously over the past few years. This means that the needs of parents have also changed, with many parents working during the day or taking up training opportunities. For pre-schools to continue to play an important part in the life of the community, they must adapt to the changing needs of parents. They must therefore find out from parents about their needs. To do this effectively, it is worth carrying out some market research to see whether we are meeting parents' needs or whether changes or extensions to provisions are required.

Research methods

There is a range of research methods that can be used to gather information. Each has its own advantages and drawbacks. Ideally, to gain the best overall picture, it is worth using more than one method of research.

Questionnaires

Questionnaires are easy and cheap to produce. They can be sent out in the post, handed out directly to parents, or left with others in the community who come into contact with parents. The main disadvantage of questionnaires is that a vast percentage of them will not be returned and you may gain information only from people who have quite strong views or who are already very committed to the service you provide.

There are broadly two types of questions that can be used: open questions or closed questions.

▶ Open questions
Open questions ask people to expand on how they feel or what they think, for example, 'How could we improve the service we are offering?' Open questions are useful because they have the potential to generate more information. The main difficulty is that many people tend not to write very much or to ignore them.

▶ Closed questions
Closed questions ask people to give a definite yes/no answer, for example, 'Do you think that the pre-school should be opened in the school holidays?' Because closed questions ask for clear-cut answers, they are easy to process and collate, and people find it easy to respond. The danger of relying completely on closed questions is that, in the design of the questionnaire, we may not be asking the right questions!

Most questionnaires use a mix of open and closed questions, and encourage people to provide more information in a further comments section. It is useful to try out a questionnaire on a sample group to see if you are getting the type of information that you want. It is also important that you think about who needs to fill in the questionnaire, for example, prospective parents as well as existing parents, and consider how the questionnaire can be distributed to them.

> **A QUICK THINK!**
>
> *Do you like filling in questionnaires?*
>
> *What factors would encourage you to complete a questionnaire?*

GOOD PRACTICE ✓ **Designing questionnaires**
- Avoid putting too many questions onto a sheet.
- Trial a few questionnaires.
- Use a mixture of open and closed questions.
- Make sure that questionnaires are translated when necessary.
- Remember that the return rate on questionnaires can be small.

Face-to-face interviews

Face-to-face interviews are an effective way of focusing a conversation with someone in order to gain specific information. It is often helpful to prepare some questions ahead so that the information you receive can be channelled. The key advantage of face-to-face interviews is that they allow the researcher to get more depth because he or she can ask extra questions or clarify points. However, it is important to avoid situations in which interviewees feel that there is a 'right' answer or that they will be letting the 'pre-school' down if they say anything that might appear negative.

Informal consultation

Informal consultation means talking to people and simply listening to their views and ideas. It is a good way of getting a feel for the issues that are affecting the community. It is also a good way of communicating with people who may not be comfortable filling in questionnaires or do not want to participate in a face-to-face interview.

Remember to listen to people's views and ideas

Focus groups

Focus groups are used to ask questions of a small group of people – usually around six to eight people. Typically, structured questions are prepared and a facilitator is brought in to listen to the responses. Focus groups are a good way of listening to several different viewpoints, although it is important that the facilitator is able to guide the group and make sure that everyone's opinions are heard.

Collating information

Once sufficient information has been gathered, it is important that it is collated and analysed. In some cases, we may decide that the needs of families are being met by the provision's current arrangements. There may also be times when the provision needs to draw up plans to extend or change the type of activities on offer.

The Busy Bees pre-school's committee was concerned that the numbers of children were beginning to fall. This was partly because the local school had changed to one single admission date in the year; however, the committee wondered whether their current provision was sufficient to meet the needs of parents. Over the past few months, several prospective parents had been in contact to see if the pre-school offered places all day. The committee decided to find out more information. It was decided to begin the research with a questionnaire for existing parents, and to contact parents who attended a parent-and-toddler group. Some of these parents agreed to be part of a focus group.

The committee soon began to discover that demand in the area had changed. Parents' comments showed that while the work of the pre-school was valued, some parents could not use its services because they needed longer periods of childcare to fit in with their working hours. Over the next two years, the pre-school gradually extended its session hours and improved its building by bidding for grants. The numbers of children attending the pre-school increased and the pre-school began to take part in family learning projects.

1 Why is it important to look regularly at the activities of the pre-school?

2 Explain why prospective parents should be approached for information?

3 List ways in which a pre-school might meet the needs of its local community.

Creating and maintaining partnerships with parents

Today, parents must be seen as equals. We have seen the benefits to the child of working collaboratively with parents. However, there is a further reason of which we should be aware. In simple business terms, failure to respect the wishes and needs of parents will result in the economic failure of a pre-school. This is because childcare provision is increasingly available for parents, so they have a wider range from which to choose. Parents therefore need to feel comfortable with your setting and feel that the setting is responsive to their needs. This means that everyone in the pre-school setting needs to understand the importance of valuing and respecting a range of family values and practices.

Sharing information with parents

One way in which we create and maintain a partnership with parents is by sharing information with them. We have looked at the importance of sharing information with parents about their child. In terms of community development, we must also consider sharing information about our provision. Sharing information should be a two-way process, with parents being able to contribute their thoughts and ideas.

Sharing development plans

A good community pre-school does not see its provision as static. It should always be considering how to adapt to the changing needs of the community. There are also significant community initiatives available that pre-schools might consider. This means that it is good practice both to seek the views of parents and to share ideas for development. There are various ways of doing this, which are detailed below.

Noticeboards

Noticeboards are one way of keeping parents informed about what is happening. They are a cheap way of sharing information, but they also have many limitations. Firstly, some parents will not be leaving or collecting their child, so may not see this information.

GOOD PRACTICE ✓

Noticeboards

▶ Make sure that information on noticeboards is up to date.

▶ Take down any information that is no longer relevant.

▶ Avoid cluttering up noticeboards.

▶ Look for ways of drawing the eye to noticeboards, for example, using arrows or coloured paper.

▶ Make sure that information is easy to read at a glance.

▶ Consider whether translations need to be provided.

▶ Remember that not all parents will read the information.

Newsletters

Regular newsletters or bulletins are a good way of informing parents about possible future developments in the pre-school and of celebrating recent achievements. Recent advances in information technology mean that newsletters are easy to produce and can include photographs. Newsletters can also include contributions from outside agencies and can be an effective way of providing community information.

Websites

Increasingly, many organisations use web pages as a way of providing information. It is important, however, to remember that not all parents have access to a computer or will be interested in this approach.

An example of a pre-school brochure

When creating websites, it is important to remember that people outside of the community can view them, therefore the use of photographs of children should be very carefully considered.

The importance of the pre-school setting as an integral part of the community

Pre-schools have an important role to play within the community. They have the potential to act as a resource for parents by not only providing early years care and education but also by helping families to see themselves as part of the community. Pre-schools encourage this active participation by helping parents to gain skills, confidence and knowledge.

In order for pre-schools to become a key part of community provision, it is essential that local liaison takes place and that the pre-school encourages involvement from other local organisations. This requires time and effort, therefore liaison may be a designated role for one or more members of the management committee.

Examples of local links

Local businesses

Local businesses provide services for the community, so it is important to develop a good relationship with them. Ideally, we should aim to provide a mutually supportive relationship. For example, a local printer may help us with the cost of printing a newsletter in return for some advertising space on a noticeboard. It is also important to try to support local businesses by using their services, for example, buying fruit from the local store.

Colleges of further and higher education

Many colleges of further and higher education are keen to foster community links. Nationally, there are many examples of pre-schools working closely with colleges of further and higher education to promote adult learning. In some areas, pre-schools provide childcare places, which allow parents to learn a new skill or gain vocational training. In some areas, the relationship between college and pre-school means that parents work as volunteers in the pre-school and are assessed for a vocational qualification by a member of the pre-school under the guidance of the college.

Schools

The Foundation Stage curriculum promotes the sharing of information between the primary school and the pre-school. A good partnership with the local school can help children to make the transition between the pre-school and the reception class more easily. It also means that ideas and, in some areas, resources can be exchanged.

Local health services

Good contacts with local health services are important if pre-schools are to play a part in the community. The pre-school can help to provide health information for doctors' surgeries, dentists and other health professionals. Good contacts with local health services also enable us to gain information and training about health issues that affect the setting.

Religious organisations

In some areas, religious organisations play a central part in families' lives. It is therefore important to have a good relationship and understanding of the work of religious organisations in the community. Respecting their role in the community is essential if we want to play an integral part in the whole community.

Libraries

In many areas, the role of the library service is adapting to the needs of the community. In some areas, libraries are providing a range of educational services as well as resources. A good relationship with the local library is therefore mutually beneficial. Libraries can provide pre-schools with resources, while pre-schools can help parents to be more aware of the range of services that the library provides.

Local regeneration partnerships

In some areas of the country, funding is available to improve facilities and prospects for the local community. Ideally, pre-schools in these areas should take an active role and develop a good relationship with these partnerships.

Gaining feedback

We should be keen to get feedback about the services we provide on a regular basis and be ready to receive comments and suggestions. Feedback should be seen as a way of ensuring that our provision meets the needs of those we serve. There are several ways of gaining feedback, which are described below.

Suggestions box

Some parents find it hard to pass on suggestions and comments verbally. They may be afraid that their comments will be seen as critical. This is why it can be good practice to have a suggestions box in the pre-school. Some pre-schools find that the suggestions box is hardly used, but its very presence sends out a powerful signal to parents. It shows that we are keen to work in partnership with them and want to meet their needs.

Feedback sheets

Feedback sheets can help us to monitor the effectiveness of the provision. It is important that parents can fill them in anonymously if they wish. This encourages feedback that is more realistic because parents may not wish to 'upset' staff.

Being responsive to comments

It is important that every comment made is valued, even when the comment is a criticism. This is essential because sometimes a single comment may reflect the 'hidden' views of others who are less forthcoming. Being ready to consider all comments can help us to improve and adapt our provision and, in the long term, help the pre-school to remain effective.

Advertising pre-school facilities

In order for the pre-school to remain viable and take its place in the community, there needs to be sufficient children in attendance. This means that parents new to the area or with their first child need to know about the work of the provision. It is also important that existing parents learn about any new service that we intend to provide, such as lunchtime clubs or parent-and-toddler groups. We might advertise new services in different ways, including noticeboards and newsletters. Ideally, it is worth considering using several advertising methods to increase the potential coverage. Some further ways in which to advertise the work of the setting are detailed below.

Word of mouth

Word of mouth is a good way of passing on information. Ideally, we need to let our community partners and contacts know about what we are doing so that they can let any potential parents know about what is on offer. It is also important to remember that existing parents can also pass on information in this way.

Parents who talk about the work of the pre-school are more likely to recommend it to others. Since personal recommendation is powerful, this is an effective way of distributing information and advertising the work of the pre-school. However, word of mouth can be a 'double-edged sword': if parents tell others that they are unhappy with the service, this can be extremely damaging.

Leaflets and other written information

Leaflets and other written information can help parents to find out about the pre-school's services. It is important that the information is well written and attractively produced. It may also be necessary to translate the information so that it is more accessible. Producing leaflets can be expensive; therefore, it is important to have a good distribution network for them. This is one reason why it is important to have good contacts with other organisations within the community.

Children's Information Service

As part of the National Childcare strategy, each local authority has set up a Children's Information Service. The aim of this service is to provide parents with up-to-date information about childcare facilities in their area. It is essential to check that the pre-school's details are up to date and that sufficient information has been provided to help prospective parents make an informed decision.

Local newspapers

Local newspapers are sometimes overlooked as a way of marketing a pre-school's activities. While taking out advertisements can be expensive, providing a story about the pre-school is free. It can therefore be worthwhile to send in press releases that might interest the newspaper.

Parental involvement in community development

It is important to remember that many parents will have good contacts within the local community. For example, it is likely that some parents may work with our community partners. Encouraging parents who have existing links in the community to help the pre-school develop is thus a possibility. In some cases, parents may be ready to distribute leaflets or have ideas about how to develop the pre-school's involvement in the community.

The role of the parent management committee/support group

Traditionally, pre-schools were formed by groups of parents who wanted to provide play and socialisation opportunities for their children. The development of committees allowed for the long-term running of these groups and the involvement of parents in the care and education of their children. Today, the role of the pre-school committee is still important, although the responsibilities of committees have grown. A key feature of community pre-schools is the direct involvement of parents in the pre-school's running and management. Today this remains the case, but the way in which parents may be involved depends very much on the legal status that the pre-school has adopted.

The traditional way in which most pre-schools operated, and to a large extent still operate, is as an 'unincorporated associate' that is regulated by the Charity Commission. Under the terms of the constitution adopted by most pre-schools, the pre-school has to have an elected committee that is responsible for its running and management. As most constitutions stipulate that 60% of the committee must be parents, it is usually known as a **parent management committee**.

In recent times, some pre-schools have chosen to change their legal status and to operate as limited companies. One of the main advantages of this change is that it limits the liability to those running the group should the pre-school run into financial difficulties. The change in legal status has meant that support groups have taken the place of committees, although legally the power of running the pre-school rests with the named directors. This has meant that some support groups act more in an advisory capacity.

> **A QUICK THINK!**
> *Find out the legal status of your pre-school.*

What do committees do?

Pre-school committees are elected by the playgroup members, i.e. parents, to manage the playgroup on their behalf. This means that parents can have a direct influence on the nature of the care and education that their children receive; an influence that gives pre-schools their distinctive character. Since committees actually run the pre-school, they take on the administrative and financial workload that goes with running any business or organisation. Committees are also employers and will therefore have legal duties and responsibilities towards their employees. In addition, committees are bound by the rules and procedures of their own constitution, which would have been drawn up when the pre-school was created. The constitution forms a legal document and is a framework as to how the committee should conduct their affairs, for example, how many people there should be on the committee, etc.

Areas for which a committee is responsible include:

- finance
- administration
- pre-school policies
- staff employment
- premises and equipment.

Roles and responsibilities

The responsibility of running a service is reflected in the roles of its committee members. It is important for any management structure to have clear roles because this avoids duplication of work and communication difficulties. In the case of a committee that is managing a pre-school, it is important that committee members carry out their duties because the committee will have legal requirements to fulfil, for example, complying with health and safety legislation.

Composition of a committee

The exact composition of a committee will reflect its needs and purposes. However, there are three essential posts:

- the Chair
- the Treasurer
- the Secretary.

In addition to these three posts, most pre-school committees create other posts to help spread the workload, for example, fund-raising officer, press officer and minutes secretary.

The Chair

The Chair's role is to conduct the meetings of the pre-school committee and act as a spokesperson and representative for the pre-school. This means that the Chair will usually take the lead when dealing with staffing issues, will attend meetings on the pre-school's behalf, and will act as a spokesperson as and when required. The Chair should also ensure that the decisions of the committee and the way in which it is run are in accordance with its constitution.

The Treasurer

The finances of the pre-school are the overall responsibility of the committee, but the Treasurer has the task of bookkeeping, setting budgets and paying bills. The Treasurer is also responsible for preparing the annual accounts, which are shown to committee members each year at the Annual General Meeting (AGM).

The Secretary

The Secretary is responsible for much of the background administrative work that ensures the smooth running of the committee. This includes preparing agendas for meetings, writing up the minutes and dealing with correspondence that comes to the pre-school.

Meetings of the committee

To ensure the smooth running of the group, the committee will need to meet regularly throughout the year. Many committees find that they need to meet every six or eight weeks, although this will depend on forthcoming events and issues that affect the running of the pre-school.

What happens at the committee meeting?

At least two weeks before the meeting, the Secretary should draw up an agenda and send it out in advance with copies of the minutes from the previous meeting. This enables committee members to recall what was decided at the previous meeting and check that they agree with the record. Members of the committee who cannot attend the meeting should send in their apologies to the Secretary.

When the meeting is held, it is traditional for the Chair to welcome everyone and then proceed to the agenda. As a standing item, minutes from the previous meeting are read and have to be agreed by the committee. It is then usual for time to be allocated for any matters arising from the previous meeting. This allows everyone to be updated on what has happened since, which may include finding out if tasks previously allocated have been completed. It is also common for the Treasurer and the Supervisor to make a report at each meeting because this means that the committee can be updated as to the day-to-day running of the pre-school. Once any other standing items have been considered, items on the agenda are then looked at individually. Finally, items not on the agenda are considered. Meetings should end with committee members agreeing the time, date and venue of the next meeting. Minutes are written up later and sent out to all committee members, including those not in attendance.

In addition to the committee meeting, there are two other types of meeting that might be called:

▶ Annual General Meeting
  The Annual General Meeting is extremely important. It is a requirement under most pre-school's constitutions and is a key way in which parents can hold the committee to account over their management of the pre-school. During the Annual General Meeting, the committee gives a report of its activities during the year, and the Treasurer presents the accounts and a summary of the pre-school's financial position. The Annual General Meeting is also the time when elections are held for membership of the committee.

▶ Special General Meetings
  Special General Meetings are held when members (including parents) need to come together to discuss a specific concern or issue. This usually happens only when the committee feels that they cannot take a decision without the approval of parents. Most constitutions also have provisions to allow parents who are not on the committee to call a meeting.

Minutes of the meeting

It is important to keep a record of what happens during any meeting. This record is known as 'minutes'. Keeping minutes is normally the responsibility of the Secretary, but sometimes a Minutes Secretary is appointed to help spread the workload.

Being a good committee member

Committee members have significant responsibilities and these cannot be taken lightly. For the committee to work well, it is important that the workload is shared and that everyone completes tasks for which they are responsible.
It is also important for committee members to be professional in their outlook, to attend meetings punctually and to understand the need for confidentiality. Pre-school committees must also be aware of the needs of the staff they employ. Supervisors and members of staff will need to be responsible for the day-to-day running of the group and committee members will need to be supportive of their work.

Ways in which activities and decisions can be communicated to parents

It is essential that parent management committees have a good system of communicating with parents. Lack of clarity or poor communication can lead to parents feeling excluded, which in turn may prevent parents from passing on comments or volunteering their services. There are many ways in which committees can communicate their activities to parents, and these are described below.

Publishing the agenda and minutes of meetings

The most common way in which committees communicate their activities to others is by publishing agendas and minutes of meetings. These are often displayed on noticeboards. For this method to be effective, it is important that the agenda is displayed ahead of the scheduled meeting and that parents' comments are invited. It is also important that the minutes of meetings are displayed promptly afterwards.

Articles in newsletters

As we have already seen on page 289, a newsletter can be an effective means of communication for the pre-school. Regular contributions in the newsletter that inform parents about committee meetings and decisions are helpful.

Open meetings

Ideally, all committee meetings should be open, whereby parents who want to come and observe the workings of the committee can attend. In addition, it is important to hold some meetings in which parents can contribute. Some pre-schools find that attendance at, for example, an Annual General Meeting, can be boosted if the meeting is tagged onto a social event.

CASE STUDY

The editor of the Summerfields Pre-school newsletter felt that not enough was known about the work that the committee undertook. She thought it might be helpful to run a series of articles about each of the committee members and the role they played in running the pre-school. She included some personal background about each member and, with his or her permission, a photograph. The feedback from parents was very positive and quite a few parents felt that it placed a 'human' angle on the work of the committee. The committee members also found that the articles were helpful because quite a few parents later went up to speak with them at a social occasion.

1 Why is it important for parents to know who is on the committee?

2 Why might parents find it easier to contact a person about whom they have read?

Personal outcomes for committee/group members

While committee and group members volunteer their services for the good of the pre-school, it is also important that they gain some personal satisfaction and

Develop new skills
Many committee and group members find that they develop new skills as a result of their work, for example, acquiring new computer skills or learning to take minutes.

Make new friendships
Many committees and groups develop a social function alongside their work. This can result in new friendships and social contacts. For families new to an area, this can help them to settle into the community.

The benefits of being a committee member

Access to training and qualifications
In order for some members to fulfil their roles effectively, it might be necessary for them to undertake training. Attending training alongside the staff team can help committee and group members to understand curriculum development and update their knowledge about current practice. In this way, policies will reflect current practice in the pre-school. In some cases, a committee might consider contributing to the cost of a qualification that cannot be funded by outside agencies such as the EYDCP.

Develop expertise
Most committee and group members find that their knowledge about childcare and education develops, as well as gaining expertise in their role. For example, a Treasurer might discover more about audits while a member of the curriculum committee might discover more about childcare regulations.

benefit from their work. Creating situations in which everyone gains from their hard work is essential because it can otherwise be hard to recruit new volunteers. It is useful to explain the benefits of becoming a committee or group member to potential parents. This is especially so because parents will not necessarily continue their work on the committee once their child has moved out of the pre-school. This usually means that there are regular vacancies on the committee.

> **A QUICK THINK!**
>
> *What are the benefits to you of being on the committee?*
>
> *What are the benefits to your setting?*

The contribution of an effective adult team to community development

The composition of the adult team in a community pre-school

In a pre-school setting the adult team would include everyone who has an association making the pre-school function – including parents. For the purpose of this section, the composition of the adult team is seen to be the committee/support group. The size of the adult team will often vary and will often reflect the scale of the pre-school's work. To co-ordinate and manage the day-to-day running of the pre-school, specific members of the team will have particular roles such as the treasurer or health and safety officer.

Roles and responsibilities within the team

The allocation of roles and responsibilities within a team can vary between different pre-schools and is largely dependent on the management structure. In deciding upon the roles and responsibilities within the team, the following should be considered:

- the requirements of the National Standards
- professional qualifications within the adult team
- the interests of team members
- the experience of team members
- the time available.

Compliance with legislation

Compliance with legislation should be the starting point when allocating roles and responsibilities. This means that a member of the adult team will take the lead on, for example, health and safety to fulfil the pre-school's obligations under the 1974 Health and Safety Act; another member may take responsibility for child protection, etc.

Professional qualifications of the adult team

Some roles have to be linked to professional qualifications. For example, a supervisor must have a recognised Level 3 qualification.

Interests of team members

Ideally, allocation of roles and responsibilities should reflect the interests of the team members. Enthusiasm is a great motivator and a person who is interested in the issues surrounding their responsibilities is likely to have a greater impact.

Experience of team members

For some roles and responsibilities, a level of experience is required. Ideally, a mentoring system should be in place to ensure that less experienced members of the team have access to knowledge and some guided experience. Thus, when a vacancy in the adult team becomes available, roles and responsibilities can be transferred smoothly.

Time available

No one performs well when given tasks that he or she does not have the time to complete. Therefore, when roles and responsibilities are allocated, the amount of time required to fulfil tasks must be considered. It may not be possible for a member of the team to take on several large areas of responsibility.

How to ensure that members of the adult team are able to fulfil their responsibilities

Training

Members of the adult team might require training in order to fulfil their duties. A system of professional developments should therefore be in place to help identify the requirements of individual team members, and those of the setting. A record of training should be kept, and this should be cross-referenced to show the training that individual team members have had and the training input into different roles and responsibilities. This prevents situations in which legislation or curriculum practice changes but no one has attended professional updates.

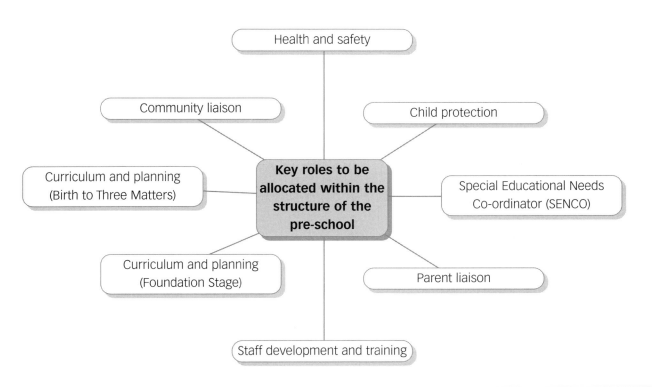

It is important that there is excellent communication between the committee/group and the staff when allocating responsibilities.

The committee is usually responsible for the overall policies of the pre-school, but these policies are put into effect by the staff. Therefore, there may be a committee member with responsibility for health and safety, including organising insurance, but in the pre-school setting, a team member is responsible for putting the policy into practice. This system can work well only when there is good interaction and communication between the people involved.

Recording roles and responsibilities

To avoid situations in which people are unsure about the extent of their responsibilities, it is important to write clear job descriptions. In terms of paid staff, these are essential. Each job description should clearly define what is expected of the person in that role. In addition, the description should be reviewed regularly to check that the tasks are still relevant and achievable. Where roles are divided between committee members and the adult team, it is also important that links are shown in the **job descriptions** so that it is clear where the boundaries of responsibilities lie.

Job description – playgroup assistant

Post: Playgroup Assistant

Responsible to: Playgroup Supervisor

Responsible for: Helping to ensure that a safe, secure and stimulating environment is provided in the playgroup.
To take responsibility for the curriculum area Mathematical Development.

Hours of work: 8.30am–1.00pm

Main duties

1. To ensure that the aims and objectives of the Busy Bees playgroup are met and policies and procedures are followed.

2. To work in accordance with the Children Act 1989 and the National Daycare standards.

3. To provide stimulating activities for children based on the Foundation Stage curriculum.

4. To provide support to other members of the team and to be responsible for the mathematical development.

5. To share responsibility for creating a stimulating, hygienic and safe environment for children.

6. To liase with parents and other professionals as appropriate.

7. To attend monthly staff meetings and other meetings requested by the supervisor.

8. To attend training when identified by the supervisor.

A job description

Reviewing and monitoring responsibilities

It is useful if some system of reporting and monitoring the work of the adult team is created. This should be a way of liaising with committee members and ensuring that problems in fulfilling a responsibility are identified. Most organisations build this system into their staff development and appraisal function.

Staff appraisal and development

People in paid or unpaid work tend to gain more satisfaction from their work if their contribution is recognised. However, **staff appraisal** and development systems are sometimes given a bad press because many business organisations use it as a way of rewarding or disciplining staff. This creates a negative framework from the outset. However, this does not have to be the way in which staff appraisals are used. Organisations who use staff appraisals to value the work of their staff and who genuinely want their staff to enjoy their work are able to create a good forum for communication.

A good staff appraisal process should allow team members to talk about those aspects of their work that they enjoy and would like to develop further, as well as any difficulties they are having. This allows training and further experiences to be planned in order that the team member can gain more satisfaction from

Staff-appraisal Form
Name:
Position held:
What areas of your work do you enjoy?
What do you feel are your professional strengths?
Are there are any areas of your work that you do not enjoy? If, so why?
Have you identified any areas of training from which you would benefit?
What are your professional goals?
How can we help you to move towards these goals?

A staff-appraisal form

his or her work. If a positive appraisal system is organised in the pre-school, it is important that it is not available only to paid members of staff. The benefits of regularly giving team members an opportunity to talk about their role and responsibilities are enormous, and can often iron out small difficulties before they turn into crises!

Effective communication between members of the adult team

Good levels of communication are essential for teams to function effectively. In community pre-schools, there is an added dimension of communication between the pre-school committee and the adult team. Breakdowns in communication can have operational implications; for example, a child may be given food that creates an allergic reaction or a child may be collected by a person who is not the named adult. Breakdowns in communication can also create discord within the team. For these reasons, it is essential to create good communication systems.

Briefings

Briefings are short, focused meetings that can be held informally. Many pre-school settings find it helpful to have a five-minute meeting before the start of a session so that all members of the team can come together. The type of information that might be exchanged during a briefing could include information about training courses or the needs of children, and details of changes to activities or in the deployment of staff. It is also helpful if a further short meeting is held at the end of the session so that information about children and the success of activities can be exchanged.

The advantage of holding regular briefings is that any difficulties can be discussed and often quickly resolved. Furthermore, it is an opportunity to remember odd details that might otherwise be forgotten, for example, the need to order some new stock.

It is important that briefing meetings do not become long sessions because otherwise adults may be reluctant to attend them. The supervisor therefore needs to ensure that briefings end on time. Any matters requiring longer discussion should be noted for the next staff meeting.

Staff meetings

In addition to regular briefings, it is important to have staff meetings. Ideally, these should occur each week because otherwise it is likely that there will be too much information to be exchanged. In settings where staff are reluctant to attend staff meetings, this is usually because the meetings carry on beyond the original schedule. Keeping a meeting to schedule is the responsibility of the supervisor; to achieve this, it is a good idea to run the meeting formally with an agenda. It is also a good idea for the adult team to invite the Chair or a member of the committee to attend because this helps the flow of communication. In the same way, the committee should ideally have a representative from the staff board so that both teams can work together.

Recording information

Recording information can be another helpful way of passing on information. Noticeboards and weekly newsheets can be particularly helpful in keeping part-time staff updated. Where supervisors are job-sharing, it is also a good idea for a diary or log to be kept, which allows daily information to be passed on.

Reviewing systems of communication

When there has been a breakdown in communication, it is important not to focus on what happened but to consider how the communication system can be better organised. Most breakdowns in communications are actually 'system' problems. Communication breakdowns therefore require that we look at additional or easier ways of passing on information.

CASE STUDY

Wendy went to the stock cupboard expecting to find some tissue paper there, which she had asked to be ordered a few weeks ago. However, no tissue paper had been ordered. Wendy realised that the activity she had planned would therefore not be possible. This was not the first time that resources were not available, although there was a member of staff responsible for ordering new stock. Wendy told the supervisor what had happened and the activity was changed.

The supervisor decided that there was a need to rethink the process of ordering stock. She asked the person responsible for the stock to give it some thought, and put the issue on the agenda for the next staff meeting. The supervisor also asked everyone in advance of the meeting to think about the ordering system and how to make it more effective. At the staff meeting, it was decided that a 'shopping list' should be put on the staff noticeboard in the kitchen. This was an immediate improvement because previously staff just mentioned what they needed in passing.

1 Why did the supervisor choose to discuss this issue at a staff meeting rather than a briefing meeting?

2 Why was this issue a 'systems' problem?

3 Why is it helpful for all members of staff to be involved in discussions about improvements to communication systems?

Building trust and supportive relationships between members of the adult team

As well as ensuring that good systems are in place for passing on information, it is important that teams work well together. This requires members of the adult team to develop trusting and supportive relationships.

In many ways, it is the supervisor and the Chair of the committee who set the tone in a community-run pre-school. The quality of their relationship is often paramount to the success of the pre-school. Sadly, there are many examples of pre-schools that have run into difficulties because of a poor relationship between the committee and the staff team. In order for relationships to be harmonious in teams, it is important that team members can demonstrate the following attributes:

- respect
- understanding roles
- valuing difference
- listening skills
- valuing and appreciating others
- putting children first
- the ability to move forward and learn.

Respect

The starting point for developing good relationships with others is to show respect. In some organisations where there is a hierarchy, equal respect is not shown to members of the team. This can lead to 'them and us' attitudes or create situations in which a less experienced member of the team does not feel valued. Respect for others is shown through the language that we use and the accompanying body language.

Understanding roles

It is important that each team member understands both his or her own responsibilities and the roles of others. The pre-school staff team will therefore need to understand both the responsibilities of the committee and the limitations they face. In the same way, committee members should know what the adult team do and the difficulties they face. Understanding everyone's role, and the responsibilities, limitations and difficulties attached to each role can help team members to appreciate other people's perspectives.

Valuing difference

As well as understanding the part that others play in the pre-school, it is important that everyone accepts that there will be differences in approaches and ideas. Sometimes, differences in ideas can seem threatening; however, if used positively they can actually lead to improvements.

Listening

For good communication, respect for others and effective relationships, team members must be ready to listen to other people. Listening should be about trying to understand something from another person's perspective. Problems often arise in teams because someone has reacted first rather than asked questions.

Valuing and appreciating others

It is important that team members get into the habit of valuing and appreciating the work of others. Interestingly, while team members may be quick to value and praise children, they may not necessarily think to say anything appreciative to colleagues. Thoughts such as 'you handled that situation well' may go unsaid. Teams that can recognise each other's work continually strengthen so that when a potential conflict or problem does occur it has less impact because the team members feel secure. In terms of the community pre-school, this also means that the committee team needs to find ways of valuing and appreciating the work of the adult team and vice versa.

Putting children first

It is important that everyone in the pre-school remembers why they are there. This is sometimes forgotten when there are tensions in the team. It can therefore be a useful strategy for supervisors and Chairs of committees to remind everyone that they all share the same overall purpose and values. During conflicts or crises, this can help people to put things back into perspective.

The ability to move forward and learn

It is important that members of the team are able to adopt a 'move forward and learn' attitude. The supervisor and the Chair need to set the example of how to do this in their work. Thus, when a problem occurs, they should focus on how to solve the immediate difficulty and look forward as to how it can be prevented in the future.

What happens if there is a problem?

Communication problems can quickly escalate once trust has been lost between team members. This means that it is important to deal with difficulties as and when they occur, and why holding regular briefing meetings can be helpful. The starting point should always be to clarify what someone has meant by his or her words or actions. Many misunderstandings grow because of a failure to clarify the situation immediately; quite often, the person has not realised that his or her actions or words are a problem. Furthermore, it is always important to reflect on whether the underlying cause is the absence of an efficient procedure.

CASE STUDY

Rani has just finished preparing the children's snacks. She spent quite a lot of time the night before shopping for the fruit. She comes into the hall and is told by another member of staff that the committee had, as a special treat, organised some tropical fruit to be brought in for the children. Rani feels that this is just another example of how no one notices her work. She is fuming and goes to tell the supervisor how fed up she feels.

1 Explain how you would deal with the immediate situation.

2 How would you prevent this situation from re-occurring?

3 What improvements could be made to the way that the team is functioning?

Building an effective partnership between parents and the adult team

For community pre-schools to function effectively, it is important that relationships are good between the adult team and the parents. Parents must feel sufficiently valued and interested in order to play an active part in providing for the pre-school. Failure to create this relationship can mean that posts are not filled on the committee; in turn, this can lead to the pre-school closing because decisions cannot be made. (See page 288 for ways to build effective partnerships with parents.)

The contribution of activities to involve parents in pre-school settings

Today, a number of initiatives aim to support local communities. Community involvement in areas such as education, combating crime and improving the environment are now seen as fundamental to community development. Interestingly, community pre-schools, which have traditionally been run by members of the community for the benefit of the community, are now being encouraged to extend their work. Projects such as family learning, in which parents and grandparents learn skills alongside their children, are becoming enormously successful. This section looks at ways in which parents can become involved in the pre-school.

The value of parental involvement in the activities of the pre-school

Community pre-schools can be special places because of the contribution of parents; ideally, everyone should gain from their involvement.

Benefits to parents

Firstly, the parents themselves should benefit because they are able to shape and influence provision. Many parents also find that through their involvement in the pre-school, they learn more about education and gain confidence in their ability to play an active role in their child's education. Parents may also gain specific skills and knowledge that are often transferable to other roles.

Benefits to children

Children themselves benefit immensely from parental involvement. They feel more secure if they are with people from the local community and gain by having access to a local facility. Many friendships begun with other children in the pre-school continue into school and beyond.

Benefits to the pre-school

Put simply, the pre-school cannot run effectively without sufficient parental involvement. The idea of a community pre-school is that it should be a resource for the community, and that it is also a part of that community. Parental input and vision is used to shape the pre-school, this ensures the long-term existence of the resource for the community.

The range of activities with which parents may be involved

There are huge opportunities to involve parents in the pre-school. The key to their involvement is to make sure that there are different levels of involvement available to suit the needs and preferences of parents.

Committee membership/group membership

Committee and support group membership give parents a huge role in shaping the work of the pre-school. For parents to become interested in joining the committee, it is essential that its work is visible.

Expertise and services

While some parents may wish to play an active role, others may be happy to offer their expertise or services occasionally. Again, it is important to make sure that parents with limited time can contribute, although they may be able to donate only an hour or two of their time on specific occasions.

Parent helpers

Some parents may wish to take work in the pre-school setting from time to time. Some pre-schools offer a rota system, while others are happy to accept help as and when it comes. Regular parent helpers should be encouraged, and it is important that they are given tasks and work that is of interest to them. Some parent helpers have carried on to train and then become leaders! However, it is important to remember that parent helpers cannot have unsupervised access to children unless they have been checked with the Criminal Records Bureau.

Fund-raising and social events

Most pre-schools organise fund-raising activities. Parents who are not able to come to the pre-school regularly may enjoy helping out at these occasions. Sometimes, fund-raising is linked to social events such as quiz nights or outings.

Family learning

While pre-schools provide care and education for children, some also look to provide learning opportunities for parents; some are able to offer learning activities for the whole family. Drop-in sessions and workshops on, for example, IT, numeracy and literacy, benefit parents who have not previously had the opportunity to develop new skills.

Factors that may affect parental involvement

It is important to realise that not all parents will play an active part in the pre-school. This does not necessarily indicate that they are not interested in the work of the pre-school or their child. There are many reasons why parents may not become involved. Understanding these reasons can help us to break down some of the barriers that might prevent their involvement.

Time

Some parents have very limited time. They may work full-time and have other priorities and commitments that mean they are unable to commit to regular involvement. Using newsletters and making sure that these parents know what is happening at the pre-school will be particularly important. You may also need to make sure that these parents know they are welcome in the pre-school at any time.

Previous experiences

Some parents may have had poor experiences of education or organised group activities. They may feel awkward in such situations, or have lost confidence in the education system. Some parents may also have difficulties in reading and writing, and be afraid that other people will find out. These examples underline the importance for pre-schools to be welcoming and treat parents as equal partners. It is also important that once parents' interests and confidence are gained, their experiences in the pre-school are positive ones.

Interest

While time and previous experiences are key factors, parents need to be interested in being involved in the pre-school. This highlights the importance of finding out about parents' needs. For example, if we are planning learning activities for adults, these must be of interest to them. Ideally, we need to think about ways in which parents with different needs and interests can participate in the pre-school. For example, dads traditionally have limited involvement, but some pre-schools have attracted dads to learn alongside their children by putting on IT workshops.

Timing and venue

For some activities such as committee meetings, social events and workshops, it is important to consider the timing and the venue. Some parents may have limited access to transport or have difficulty in finding a person to mind their child during the evening. This means finding out about parents' needs and preferences, and possibly varying the times or venues of events so that a greater range of parents can be involved.

Perception

Some parents may not become involved in the activities of the pre-school because they have a perception that they will not 'fit in'. For example, a single parent may feel that all the other committee members are in a relationship, or a parent living on a restricted income may feel that other parents have more money. Care therefore needs to be taken to avoid 'cliques' developing in the pre-school. By making sure that all parents are made to feel welcome and comfortable, we can avoid this situation from occurring.

Ensuring that opportunities for involvement are accessible to all families in the community

We have seen that there are many reasons why parents may not become involved in the pre-school. Pre-schools that wish to play an active part in the community must therefore work hard to break down potential barriers. The checklist below looks at some of the barriers that need to be overcome so that all parents can feel welcome.

KEY POINTS

Opportunities for parental involvement: a checklist

▶ Are newsletters and other written documents available in other languages?
▶ Are meetings and activities held at convenient times?
▶ Are meetings and activities always held at the same times?

- Are parents able to bring their children to meetings and social events?
- Are arrangements in place to help parents with alternative childcare needs, for example, a crèche?
- Are venues chosen that are easy for parents to reach?
- Is there a scheme in place so that parents can share transport?
- When arranging social events, are the costs taken into consideration?
- Is it clear to parents that regular involvement is not necessary?
- Are introductions made when a new parent attends?
- Are new parents befriended?
- Are some activities 'drop in' in nature?

CASE STUDY

Mark has two young children who attend the pre-school. He is a widower and is adjusting to the loss of his wife. He works full-time and has moved into the area so that his mother can help with some of the childcare arrangements. Whenever he collects his children at the end of the session, Mark feels quite awkward because mostly he is the only father collecting children. He has seen notices about social events and an IT club, but does not feel that they are aimed at him, although he rarely goes out.

1 Explain the benefits to Mark and his children of his becoming involved in the activities of the pre-school.

2 Identify the reasons why Mark may not feel that he can become involved.

3 Suggest ways in which the pre-school could help Mark to become involved.

TEST YOUR KNOWLEDGE

1 Give examples of services that a community pre-school may offer.

2 Outline ways of gaining information from parents about their needs.

3 Give advantages and disadvantages of using questionnaires to assess community needs.

4 List ways in which the pre-school committee might provide information for parents.

5 Give two ways in which a pre-school might advertise its services.

6 Describe the role of the committee in community pre-schools.

7 Explain the factors that might affect parents' participation in pre-school activities.

8 Analyse ways in which a pre-school may reflect the needs of the local community.

9 Evaluate how a community pre-school may help children and their families.

10 Consider the importance of effective communication in running a community pre-school.

PRACTICE ASSIGNMENT TASK

Produce a leaflet for parents about the activities of a community pre-school.

The leaflet should contain the following information:

▶ an outline of the aims of the pre-school
▶ an analysis of its current provision
▶ an evaluation of how the provision might be expanded.

Future reading and references

The Pre-School Learning Alliance is an excellent source of information about the role of the pre-school in community development. You can contact them at:

Pre-School Learning Alliance
69 Kings Cross Road
London
WC1X 9LL
www.pre-school.org.uk

Pre-school Learning Alliance publications available from www.pre-school.org.uk:

Adults Learning in Pre-schools
Parental Stake in Pre-school Education
The Parent Pack: Looking at Learning Together
Expand Your Pre-School

Glossary

Allergic: a physical reaction to a substance.

Antenatal: the period in a pregnancy from conception until birth.

Anti-discriminatory: ways of working which include and value all children and their families regardless of their ethnic or cultural backgrounds.

Areas of learning: sections within the Foundation Stage curriculum containing learning outcomes.

Behaviour: responses and reactions to people and situations, in particular socially appropriate or inappropriate responses displayed by children.

Critical period: the theory that some aspects of child development are time sensitive and have to take place within given periods.

Behaviourist: theories that suggest patterns of learning and behaviour are repeated because of associations with positive or negative experiences.

Bi-lingual: a person who speaks two languages.

Confidential: information that should not be passed onto others without consent.

Conserve: one of Piaget's tests of children's logic, based on whether children recognise changes in the appearances of objects.

Constructivist: theories that suggest that children are active in their learning and draw conclusions based on what they have seen, done and heard.

Curriculum: a programme of activities or learning intentions.

Discrimination: a term used to describe situations in which a person, or group of people, are not treated as fairly as others based on judgements of gender, sexual orientation, lifestyle, religion or culture.

Early Learning Goal: targets given in the Foundation Stage curriculum for children to reach by the end of their reception year.

Feedback: information gained from others which can be used to improve practices or performance.

Fine manipulative: hand movements that involve the thumb and fingers e.g. drawing or picking up objects.

Fine motor: movements that involve the hand and wrist.

Gross motor: movements that involve the use of a whole limb such as walking or throwing.

Hand–eye co-ordination: movements that involve using vision to direct the hands.

Inclusion: an approach to working which allows all children to participate in the activities of a setting regardless of disability, gender, religion or culture.

Individual Education Plan (IEP): a plan drawn up by a setting, in conjunction with parents, to target support for children who have some area of difficulty in learning.

Individual Learning Plan (ILP): a plan of activities tailored to help childrens' learning and development.

Job description: a document showing what is expected of a person employed in a particular post.

Longitudinal: a term used in conjunction with assessment to suggest monitoring over a period of time.

Metacognitive skills: the ability to retrieve and use existing memories and information in order to make sense of new information or situations.

Milestone: skills that are looked for as children develop, which are usually linked to age.

Multi-lingual: a person who speaks more than one language.

National Standards: a set of standards against which early years settings are inspected.

Normative development: a term used to suggest which skills the majority of children will have at any given age.

Nativist: a biological approach to psychology which highlights the instinctive or inherited facets of behaviours and learning.

Object permanence: the realisation that objects and people, when out of sight, continue to exist.

OFSTED: the organisation which inspects early years settings and schools.

Open-door policy: an approach to working with parents which encourages parents to feel that they can come into the setting and talk at any time.

Parent management committee: an elected committee, under the terms of a pre-school's constitution, that is legally responsible for the management of the pre-school.

Perinatal: around the time of birth.

Physical development: the gaining of control over bodily movements.

Play leader: job title for the staff member of a pre-school responsible for managing the day-to-day provision of care, usually employed by the parent management committee.

Postnatal: the period following the birth of a baby.

Pre-linguistic phase: the stage in language development that precedes a baby's first recognised spoken words. This phase includes babbling, gestures and understanding the meaning of a few key words.

Procedure: a set way of carrying out actions e.g. fire drills or responding to an emergency.

Reflective practice: a way of working whereby practitioners think about their own effectiveness in order to improve the quality of their work.

Role model: a person who a child watches and consequently learns behaviour and attitudes from.

Role play: (also known as pretend or imaginative play) is where children pretend to be something or someone other than themselves e.g. the part of an animal, other children or an adult.

Routine: regular events and timings of a session or day.

SEN: acronym for Special Educational Needs.

SEN Code of Practice 2001: government guidelines on which early years settings and schools base their decisions and practice of Special Educational Needs.

Scaffolding: a term used to describe how adults support childrens' learning by sensitively intervening, questioning or planning appropriate activities.

Separation anxiety: a child's fear of being separated his or her main carer.

SENCO: acronym for Special Educational Needs Co-ordinator. The person in a setting who co-ordinates and oversees the setting's Special Educational Needs policy.

Settling in: the process by which early years practitioners help babies and children to be at ease in the pre-school or school setting.

Small world play: pretend play in which children use figures of people or animals and create an environment for them.

Social learning theory: the theory that suggests that children learn by watching the actions and reactions of others.

Social referencing: the way in which babies and young children look at the reactions of adults in new situations in order to understand how they should react.

Stranger Danger: baby's and young children's reluctance to leave their parent or carer to stay with an unfamiliar person.

Special Educational Needs: a generic term used to identify children who may need additional support in order to facilitate their learning.

Staff appraisal: a system of identifying areas for individual staff development.

Statements: a term used for the process by which children with identified special educational needs receive a statutory assessment of their needs.

Stepping Stones: a term used in the Foundation Stage curriculum indicating skills that children will master on the way to reach the Early Learning Goals.

Supervisor (see Play Leader).

Support group: a group of parents who advise and support the direction of a pre-school in situations where the pre-school is run as a limited company.

Weaning: the process of encouraging a baby to take food in addition to milk.

Zone of Proximal Development: a term used by Vygotsky to explain the relationship between a child's possible learning and his or current abilities.

Index